WAGE AND SALARY ADMINISTRATION: A GUIDE TO JOB EVALUATION

Lawrence S. Aft

Reston Publishing Company, Inc.
A Prentice-Hall Company
Reston, Virginia

69340

Library of Congress Cataloging in Publication Data

Aft, Lawrence S.
  Wage and salary administration.

     1. Job evaluation.   2. Job evaluation—Case studies.
3. Job analysis.   4. Job analysis—Case studies.
I. Title.
HF5549.5.J62A35   1985   658.3'06   84-27533
ISBN 0-8359-8528-8

copyright 1985 by Reston Publishing Company, Inc.
A Prentice-Hall Company
Reston, Virginia 22090

*All rights reserved. No part of this book may be
reproduced, in any way or by any means, without
permission in writing from the publisher.*

10   9   8   7   6   5   4   3   2   1

Printed in the United States of America

HF 5549.5
.J62A35
1985

1/30/91

CONTENTS

CHAPTER FIVE——PRICING THE JOB, 123

CHAPTER SIX——PERFORMANCE APPRAISAL, 157

HF5549.5
.J62A35
1985

1/30/91

CONTENTS

CHAPTER FIVE——PRICING THE JOB, 123

CHAPTER SIX——PERFORMANCE APPRAISAL, 157

CHAPTER SEVEN——INCENTIVE PAY (PERFORMANCE RELATED PAY), 215

INDEX, 261

PREFACE

This book has been written to fill the need for an introductory text in wage and salary administration. Emphasizing the procedures involved in job evaluation, while providing an overview of the other key wage and salary functions, the book is written for the individual who must actually perform the analysis tasks. Being practitioner-oriented, the text provides a no nonsense procedure for analyzing, describing, and evaluating the work performed by people, as well as the procedures for evaluating and compensating the performance of individuals on the job.

The text is designed to fill the needs of the practitioner in industry and business, as well as the student in a technical or business education program. For the practitioner faced with having to evaluate jobs, appraise performance, or set up an incentive pay system the book explains the basic "nuts and bolts" procedure to make the system work. For the student, the text is suitable either as an overview of the compensation field or as the basis for an in-depth applications oriented job evaluation course.

In addition to a description of the procedures used in typical wage and salary programs, the text includes numerous industrial examples of job descriptions, job evaluations, and performance appraisal forms. The sections of incentive systems include many examples of the application of both individual and group incentive plans. Additionally, at the end of the incentives chapter many practice problems are provided to allow the reader to gain a mastery of the different procedures used to determine incentive wages.

Case studies are a key part of this book. There are actually two different types of cases provided. First, there is the continuing saga of Mountain View College. Introduced in the second chapter, Mountain View College provides an on-going situation to explain and tie together all the aspects of job evaluation. The jobs that are analyzed in Chapter Two are described in the standard format at the end of Chapter Three. These are evaluated after Chapter Four, and the pay level is determined in Chapter Five. If the reader desires, these jobs can also be evaluated using the examples of appraisal forms presented in Chapter Six.

The second type of case study appears at the end of many of the chapters. These cases provide an opportunity for additional discussion of some of the key points presented in the text. In some instances they illustrate potential difficulties that may confront the individual involved in the wage and salary administration process. Discussion of the problems should show the proper way to handle these difficulties if they should occur in real life.

The preface would not be complete without a public word of thanks to some of the people who helped make the book possible. First of all are the many people who participated in the review process. These constructive critics include the following people: Roger C. Crowe of State Technical Institute at Knoxville, H.W. Lacquement of Greenville Technical College, Neal W. Slack of Cumberland County College, Don Tritschler at Southern Technical Institute, and Michael S. Bowman in Indianapolis. My research was made much easier due to the help of Dory Stamps at the Southern Technical Institute Library. She is fantastic at tracking down obscure information with a minimum number of hints from me as to where it might be located. Gerrie Kriner helped with the clerical work and made my job easier. Reston editors Dan Bassett and Jim Stephan were most supportive of the work initially. The rest of the Reston editorial staff was also very cooperative and easy to work with. Brad Young at Southern Technical Institute was an invaluable proofreader and sounding board as the text was written. Finally, a large amount of appreciation again goes to my wife Susan and our children Steven and Dana for putting up with me while I prepared this material. Without their patience and understanding it would have been a much more difficult task.

Chapter One

INTRODUCTION TO WAGE AND SALARY ADMINISTRATION

INTRODUCTION

Describing the work people perform, specifying the skill required to perform the work, measuring how well the work is performed, determining the relative worth of the work performed, and developing a fair method of paying for the work performed is the function of a wage and salary administration program. These tasks, often placed under the umbrella of compensation administration, are a necessary and important part of any organization's managerial or administrative activities.

The overall objective of any compensation management program is to pay salaries adequate to attract and retain the kinds of employees needed to run the business. Pay is based upon responsibilities, competitive levels of compensation, and performance. There are many factors that must be considered when developing this information. These factors will be discussed in this chapter and examined in depth throughout this book.

The following is a summary of some of the common factors influencing the compensation administration program within a company: skill, effort, responsibility, and working conditions of the job; the supply, motivation, and performance of the employees; the productivity, profitability, costs, and type of industry; the cost of living, area wages, legislation, traditions; and the relationship between the union and management in collective bargaining.

An effectively administered wage and salary administration program is obviously an important function of management. It is necessary for a business to continually be successful in its operations. In addition to the fact that such a function is "good management practice," there is a second reason for having a compensation administration program, and specifically a job evaluation program; that is the legal requirement to do so.

REASONS FOR HAVING WAGE AND SALARY JOB EVALUATION PROGRAMS— MANAGERIAL

If employees are to make an enterprise successful, the relationship between the managers and the employees should be at least a satisfactory one. Part of making it a satisfactory relationship is management fulfilling its responsibilities regarding wage and salary administration and job evaluation.

One of the major responsibilities of management is to motivate employees to optimum job performance. No variable is a more important determinant of an organization's internal relationship than the assumptions management makes concerning employee motivation.

One generally accepted way of motivating most people is through the use of money. According to James A. Lee of Ohio University, there are many myths currently in vogue relating to worker motivation. One of the more popular myths is that money no longer motivates (Lee:465). However, most people will work harder, or more productively, if they perceive that they are being fairly compensated for the effort they expend. This is not to neglect the non-financial or intrinsic rewards found in many jobs, but the obvious rewards, such as money, have always been effective motivators, especially for typical production jobs.

A second responsibility management has is to control employee costs. One of the largest costs many companies face is that of compensating its employees . . . wages and salaries . . . which must be controlled . . . if an enterprise is to be successful in its field.

A third function of wage and salary administration is to develop procedures for effective selection of, efficient utilization of, and rational promotion of the company's employees. Managers, after hiring employees, must have the tools available to help all employees meet their potential. Bright, energetic individuals are identified and become well known to the chain of authority through the normal course of daily communication and association, even in large organizations. But, unless a manager knows that he will be measured and then rewarded in accordance with how well he promotes the growth of his people he is likely to pay lip service to employee growth, while continuing to do those things that companies ordinarily reward managers for doing. For organizations and their workers to continue to grow, it is essential that compensation and evaluation programs be developed to support that growth.

Besides the fact that sound management practice necessitates implementation of a wage and salary/job evaluation program, there are legal reasons for maintaining such a function.

REASONS FOR HAVING WAGE AND SALARY JOB EVALUATION PROGRAMS—LEGAL

Most basic management decisions involving employment relations must be made with regard for some law. Every business enterprise in the United States is subject to Federal and state regulations and sometimes municipal ordinances as well. During the 20th century numerous laws regarding compensation and working conditions have been enacted by the governments of this country. Although the major determinants of compensation and benefit levels are economic, there are also a number of constraints that prevent an organization from responding to shifts in these factors. The first, and most severe constraints are legal. There are major Federal Laws restricting the amount, type, and administration of both salaries and benefits. While not a complete listing, the following section will describe many of the Federal Laws that affect compensation administration. Following the descriptions of the most important laws is a more complete listing and summary of laws in this area.

Davis Bacon Act: The first Federal Law passed relating to wage payments was the *Davis Bacon Act* of 1931. This law, often referred to as the prevailing wage law, required all Federal contractors receiving more than $2000 per year in Federal payments to pay workers the prevailing wage rate for the given geographic area. This is often viewed as a pro-labor union law in that the prevailing wage is usually interpreted as the "union wage" for the jobs in question. The Davis Bacon Act is significant in that it was the first law that dealt with the compensation issue. It has recently been amended to include fringe benefits in the prevailing wage package. In 1934 the *Copeland Act* was passed to prevent abuse of the minimum wage provisions of the Act.

Walsh Healy Act: In 1936 Congress passed the *Walsh Healy Act,* also known as the *Public Contracts Act.* Walsh Healy established, for Federal contracts exceeding $10,000, a 40 hour week and extra compensation, mainly time and a half, for work exceeding 8 hours in a day or 40 hours in a work week. The Walsh Healy Act also permits the Secretary of Labor to establish minimum wages for Federal contractors, regardless of the industry Fair Labor Standards Act.

The private sector has not been immune to laws governing compensation. Congress enacted the *Fair Labor Standards Act,* or the *Wage and Hour Act,* in 1938. There are several major provisions to this law, which applies to any organization involved in interstate commerce. First, it established a 40 hour work week for all covered employees. Second, it established a national minimum wage. At the time the law was passed this was $.25 per hour. By 1983 it had increased to $3.35 per hour.

However, not all workers are covered by minimum wage provisions. Some employees are exempt, and the distinction is made by personnel managers between exempt and non-exempt employees. Exempt employees include executives, administrative and professional employees, outside salespersons, fishermen, seasonal employees of amusement or recreational organizations, some farm workers, and casual babysitters and companions. Third, the Fair Labor Standards Act restricted child labor. Children under 18 years of age are prohibited from holding certain types of jobs. It must be noted that many states have enacted more restrictive child labor laws than those found in the Fair Labor Standards Act.

Fourth, the Walsh Healy Act provides that work in excess of 40 hours a week be paid at a rate of at least one and a half times the base hourly rate. In all businesses except hospitals, these 40 hours must be in one seven-day period. (Hospitals use a 14-day period and 80-hour minimum.) The exempt employees, as noted above, are also exempt from overtime provisions.

The fifth major requirement of the Fair Labor Standards Act is the record keeping requirements. Great quantities of compensation data must be reported to the Wage and Hour Division of the Department of Labor. Some of the information reported includes employee information, total hours worked on a daily and weekly basis, regular payrate, overtime wages paid, deductions, and total wages paid.

Equal Pay Act: A most important law was passed by Congress in 1963. Congress' purpose in enacting the *Equal Pay Act* was to rectify what was perceived to be a serious problem of employment discrimination in private industry——the fact that the wage structure of many segments of American industry has been based on an ancient but outmoded belief that a man, because of his role in society, should be paid more than a woman, even though the duties are the same. This law makes it illegal for an employer to pay a woman less than a man if she is doing the same work under the same conditions as a man.* A very important part of a wage and salary administration program is the definition of the work content and working conditions for the jobs within the organization. This is a necessary way of complying with the Act.

The Equal Pay Act also establishes four specific exceptions to the equal pay for equal work provisions.

1. Seniority systems, where pay depends on length of service.
2. Merit system, where pay depends on performance appraisal results. However, any system based on criteria such as supervisory ratings raises problems because subjective human judgments are involved.
3. Systems basing pay on quantity or quality of production.
4. Systems which differentiate pay on any factors except sex.

Title VII—1964 Civil Rights Act: The *Civil Rights Act* of 1964 includes in Title VII a number of provisions regarding compensation policies. Specifically, it forbids discrimination in hiring, terms or conditions of employment, union membership and representation, [and] specifically forbids any employer from failing or refusing to hire or from discharging or otherwise discriminating against any individual with respect to compensation, terms, conditions, or privileges of employment, or otherwise adversely affecting his status as an employee due to race, color, religion, sex, or national origin.

Title VII of the Civil Rights Act also established the Equal Employment Opportunity Commission (EEOC) to administer the provisions of Title VII. The EEOC currently has power to pursue court actions in cases of alleged discrimination. Employers do have the right to insist that a prospective applicant meet job qualifications, but the qualifications must we well defined and relate directly to success in job performance. This is the key area for involvement for a wage and salary administration program. Areas such as preparing job descriptions, performing job evaluations, appraising performance, and setting pay rates have to be done in such a manner as to comply with these legal provisions.

---

*Not to be confused with comparable worth, an entirely different concept.

Executive Order 11246: *Executive Order 11246,* as an adjunct to these equal employment opportunity and compensation laws, established the Office of Federal Contract Compliance Programs which issued a requirement that contractors develop written affirmative action plans containing goals and timetables to correct deficiencies in equal employment opportunity. A defensible system regarding affirmative action must be developed by an organization's wage and salary administration function.

Non-Discrimination Laws: Almost indistinguishable from the compensation legislation, especially in its intent, are the non-discrimination laws. Title VII of the Civil Rights Act mentioned non-discrimination in compensation based on a variety of factors. In 1967 the *Age Discrimination in Employment Act* was passed. This specifically forbade discrimination against employees 40 to 65 years of age. This was amended in 1970 to include people up to 70 years of age. The law relates to discrimination in matters such as hiring, discharge, leave, compensation, promotions, transfers, and all other factors affecting employment. This pointed out the requirement for a system, free of bias because of race, sex, or age, for measuring the worth of a job. A well run wage and salary program can provide this for an organization. In 1984 the U.S. Supreme Court, in a case involving the Memphis Fire Department, ruled that employers may not be forced to scrap seniority plans that favor white males when "hard times" hit. The court indicated that special preference for past injustices is available only to individuals who can prove they were victimized by the bias.

Other Compensation Laws: While most of the compensation legislation can be viewed as non-discrimination legislation, there is one other classification of legislation that has direct impact on wage and salary administration. These laws began with the passage of the *Social Security Act* in 1935, which has been amended many times since. This class of law provides for unemployment benefits, disability, and retirement benefits. Medicare and Medicaid benefits are also included as social security benefits.

Unemployment Insurance: The unemployment insurance programs are administered and run by each state. The plans, which vary from state to state, provide for a partial income replacement, for a limited period of time, when a worker is laid off or otherwise loses a job through no fault of his or her own. Employers contribute a percentage amount of wages paid to each state's funds.

Workers' Compensation: Workers' Compensation programs provide immediate money for medical care and support to workers who are injured on the job, and provide for medical care and support to workers' dependents if the worker is killed. Each state has its own plan which it administers, either by itself or through designated insurance carriers.

There are additional laws and regulations relating to employment and compensation. All of the laws that apply to an organization must be included as guides to an effective compensation administration program. Organizations must design compensation systems that reward performance and at the same time provide acceptable levels of security for all their employees. Figure 1–1 enumerates some of the additional laws relating to employment and compensation practices.

FIGURE 1–1   Statutes Governing Employment and Compensation

Year	Name	Summary
1908	Federal Employee's Compensation Act	Eliminated uncertainties about compensation when workers are injured on the job. Provided prompt payment when workers are injured on the job.
1923	Classification Act	Attempted to achieve uniform alignment of jobs within the Federal sector regarding wages and salaries.
1931	Davis Bacon Act	Required construction contractors to pay prevailing wages.
1934	Copeland Act	Prevented abuse of Davis Bacon wage floors.
1935	Social Security Act	Provided unemployment, disability, and retirement benefits for protected workers.
1935	National Labor Relations Act	Permitted employees to bargain collectively concerning wages, benefits, and working conditions.
1936	Walsh Healy Act	Established minimum wages and maximum weekly working hours for Federal contractors.
1938	Fair Labor Standards Act	Established minimum wages and maximum weekly working hours for all employees involved in interstate commerce. Restricted the use of child labor.

FIGURE 1–1. Statutes Governing Employment and Compensation *(continued)*

Year	Name	Summary
1947	Taft Hartley Act	Amended the National Labor Relations Act, restricting to some degree the rights granted labor unions under the National Labor Relations Act.
1955	Landrum Griffin Act	The Labor Management Reporting Act limited and regulated the activities of labor unions.
1963	Equal Pay Act	Required equal pay for equal work, regardless of sex. Forbade different pay levels based solely on sexual differences if the same work is performed under the same conditions.
1964	Title VII Civil Rights Act	Forbade discrimination in all employment matters based on race, sex, etc. Also established EEOC to enforce employment legislation.
1965	Executive Order 11246	Banned discrimination based on race, sex, religion, and national origin for all Federal contracts exceeding $10,000.
1965	McNamara O'Hara Service Contract Act	Extended Davis Bacon provisions to the services sector of government contracting.
1967	Age Discrimination Act	Forbade discrimination in employment practices for workers aged 40 to 65.
1968	Consumer Credit Protection Act	Limited the amount of employee wages subject to garnishment.
1970	Occupational Safety and Health Act	Established minimum safety standards (and hence, job safety requirements) for industry.
1973	Health Maintenance Organization Act	Required organizations with 25 or more employees to offer an HMO for employees if available.
1973	Rehabilitation Act	Prohibited discrimination against the handicapped.
1974	Employee Retirement Income Security Act	Established fiscal guidelines to guarantee fiduciary responsibility for pension programs.
1975	Age Discrimination in Employment Act Amendments	Extended age of discrimination from 65 to 70.

FIGURE 1–1 Statutes Governing Employment and Compensation (*continued*)

Year	Name	Summary
1978	Pregnancy Discrimination Act	Forbade discrimination against pregnant workers.
1983	Social Security Reform Act	Changed the funding and benefits provisions of the Social Security System.

<u>Tax Laws:</u> Besides the legal requirements there is a second constraint governing the operation of compensation programs. Tax programs, while not forbidding any payment practices, make certain methods of payment far more costly to the employee and the organization than others. Tax laws, although constantly changing, have two implications for compensation. First there is the direct withholding of a portion of each employee's wages. Second, there are the regulations governing how much of what type of benefits are taxable. The deferral of income, payment of pensions, and stock plans are examples of this. On the Federal level, the Internal Revenue Code governs, while each state has its own tax laws as well.

WAGE AND SALARY DEPARTMENT FUNCTIONS

In order to comply with the many laws that govern compensation administration, the following functions are usually performed by wage and salary administration departments. While the listing and description that follows is by no means a detailed guide, it does present the outline for a successful program.

First is the analysis of all company jobs. This involves the preparation of job descriptions and job specifications. Job descriptions describe the content of specific jobs, while job specifications describe the requirements of the individual necessary to fill the job as described.

Second is evaluation and classification of the jobs within the company. Using job descriptions that have been prepared, the jobs are compared, either qualitatively or quantitatively, and the relative worth of each job in the organization is established.

Third is the relative worth of each job in the organization as converted into a dollar amount. Pricing the jobs or determining the hourly, weekly, or monthly pay rate is an important task. The equal pay for equal work provisions of the law must be followed, while at the same time making jobs attractive to the local labor market and competitive within the market and also economically feasible for the organization.

Fourth is the evaluation of the performance of each individual, regardless of the job evaluation. Only by regularly evaluating employees is it possible to reward employees for exceptional contributions or for extra effort put forth in maintaining the highest quantity and quality of production.

Fifth is the motivation of employees which is most important. Achieving maximum productivity is essential. Many compensation administration or wage and salary or job evaluation programs use financial motivation, such as incentives, for achieving this.

SUMMARY

"The function of wage and salary administration has become a permanent part of the industrial engineering field because of its activities in setting work standards for job performance, and time standards for piece rates and other wage incentive plans. To accomplish the latter, the industrial engineer makes a job analysis of each step in the manufacturing process, along with very closely detailed specifications. All elements involved in performing an operation are described sequentially." (Zollitsch and Langsner :55) Specifically, the compensation administration program has a number of objectives it tries to attain.

1. Maintain control of all matters relating to compensation.
2. Inform all company personnel of wage and salary policies and procedures.
3. Eliminate pay inequities regarding equal pay for equal work.
4. Establish complete job descriptions and specifications in order to attract and maintain a qualified work force.
5. Evaluate the relative worth of jobs within the organization.
6. Appraise the performance of the individuals within the organization in order to determine which employees deserve merit raises and which employees require additional training, motivation, or disciplinary action.
7. Comply with applicable Federal, State, and Local Laws governing the labor factor of production.

When all of these functions are performed, the wage and salary administration will [hopefully] help the organization prosper. The remaining chapters of this book will examine and explain in detail the functions of wage and salary administration, especially as they relate to job evaluation and wage payment. The reader should remember that these functions are performed first because they represent sound management practice, and second, because they are generally mandated by statute.

Review Questions

1. What are the major functions of a wage and salary administration program?
2. What is the overall objective of a wage and salary or job evaluation program?
3. What factors are pay based on?
4. What factors influence the compensation administration program within a given company?
5. Why is an effectively administered wage and salary program an important function of management?
6. What are the management responsibilities regarding the wage and salary administration program?
7. What is one of the most popular management myths in vogue today?
8. Summarize the Davis Bacon Act.
9. Summarize the Walsh Healy Act.
10. Summarize the Fair Labor Standards Act.
11. Summarize the Equal Pay Act.
12. Why is the 1964 Civil Rights Act (Title VII) important in Wage and Salary Administration?
13. What is the EEOC?
14. What did Executive Order 11246 do?
15. What is affirmative action?
16. Describe the function of unemployment insurance.
17. Describe the function of workers' compensation legislation.
18. Summarize the job evaluation-related functions of a wage and salary administration department.

References

Beachem, Samuel T., "Managing Compensation and Performance Appraisal Under the Age Act," *Management Review*, January, 1979.

Britton, Donald E., "Common Practices in Wage and Salary Administration," *Personnel Administration*, January-February, 1974.

Chamberlain, N.W., Cullen, D.E., and Lewin, D., *The Labor Sector*, McGraw-Hill, New York, 1980.

Henderson, R., *Compensation Administration*, Reston Publishing Company, Inc., Reston, Virginia, 1985.

Lee, James A., "Myths in Management Theory," *Proceedings*, 1982 Fall Industrial Engineering Conference, I.I.E, Norcross, Georgia, 1982.

Miller, Paul F., "Salary Administration—Science or Art," *Personnel Administrator*, November-December, 1969.

Myers, A.H., and Twomey, D.P., *Labor Law and Legislation*, Southwestern Publishing Company, Cincinnati, 1975.

Patton, Thomas H., *Pay*, Free Press, New York, 1977.

Schneier, Dena B., "The Impact of EEO Legislation on Performance Appraisals," *Personnel*, July-August, 1978.

Smith, Lee, "The EEOC's Bold Foray into Job Evaluation," *Fortune*, September 11, 1978.

Wallace, Marc J., and Fay, Charles H., *Compensation Theory and Practice*, Kent Publishing, Boston, 1983.

Wolfe, Arthur V., "A Managerial Approach to Compensation," *Personnel Journal*, April, 1975.

Zollitsch, H.G., and Langsner, A., *Wage and Salary Administration*, Southwestern Publishing Company, Cincinnati, 1970.

"Oh sure, I thought it would be easy at first too."

Chapter Two

JOB ANALYSIS

INTRODUCTION

There are, as Chapter One indicated, two major reasons for having a wage and salary administration program. The first reason is sound management practice, either motivated by sincere beliefs or by the requirements of a union contract. The second reason is legal, primarily revolving around the equal pay for equal work doctrine.

Many of the activities of the wage and salary function revolve around the task of job analysis. Job analysis has been a part of management practice for many years. It was an integral part of Taylor's scientific management. It has remained, in various forms, part of the management literature since receiving renewed interest after the passage of the equal employment opportunity legislation.

Job analysis is the process of carefully observing a job and recording all pertinent information so that management may make effective use of the information. Specifically, as it relates to wage and salary administration, there are four major uses of the information provided by job analysis.

First of these uses is the preparation of job descriptions and employee specifications. The second use is the development of the organization's job evaluation system. The third use of job analysis data involves the job payment, job classification, or pricing structure for jobs. Finally, the information gathered through job analysis can be used in individual performance appraisal. While the succeeding chapters will deal with each of these uses in depth, the following paragraphs will serve to introduce the activities.

The job description not only defines job duties for the current job holder, but, when it has been carefully developed in conjunction with others throughout an organization, forms the basis for comparing the job in question with others in the organization, thus serving as a standard in the pressing issue of equal pay for equal work. The employee specification delineates the requirements of the individual required to perform the job.

The job evaluation system uses job descriptions to determine the relative worth, to the organization, of the job. This worth will be translated into dollars to pay the person who performs the job. A variety of procedures, some subjective, some quantitative, and some a mixture, have traditionally been used to evaluate jobs. Some of the simpler systems involve only a ranking of the jobs, while the more sophisticated involve evaluating the jobs based on the amount that certain key factors are contained in the specific jobs.

Job pricing involves a classification of similar jobs in the same pay range. Job classification is the process of categorizing positions according to the type of work performed, the type of skill required, or other job-related factors. Determining which jobs fall into which classes is often done with a job specification. This involves the use of the job description in conjunction with the job evaluation system. The result is a grouping of jobs with the same relative worth to the company. These jobs are then assigned pay or wage rates based on such factors as the organization's ability to pay and prevailing wage rates for the same types of jobs. This comparison of ability to pay and worth of the job depends upon the results of a wage survey. In order for this to be useful, the correct information must be gathered during the job analysis.

Another use of job analysis data is in performance appraisal. This is the evaluation of the individual's performance on the job; that is, how well the worker meets and/or exceeds the minimum and/or expected requirements of the job. Proper statement of these expectations is essential for successful performance appraisal.

Almost the entire function of wage and salary administration depends on a correct and current job analysis. The next section will look at the requirements of job analysis in more depth.

JOB ANALYSIS—EXPLANATION

Job analysis identifies the work content of each job in an organization. Specifically it addresses not only the work done, but also the knowledge and skills necessary for an individual to perform the job. (Henderson:149) Not only must it state that the position requires the preparation of typed reports, but it also must state that the person filling the job must know how to collate the specific type of report and prepare the actual copy using a word processing system. Job analysis must now be performed because of legislative mandate. Organizations no longer have a choice. Job analysis may be called for in a collective bargaining agreement. Job analysis provides management information it must have in order to perform effectively.

Change is always occurring in organizations. If organizations are to be able to cope effectively with change, they need a constant flow of valid and reliable information on the content and requirements of their jobs. As John Zalusky of the AFL-CIO stated, "Few of the changes in job content that make the job worth more or less take place in a formal way. . . . Most take place through creeping change." (Zalusky:18)

The types of management information that job analysis can provide falls into two major categories: maintenance and administrative functions. Maintenance functions include organizational development, manpower planning, career planning, counseling, and training.

Organizational development is maintaining the proper positions with the proper requirements for the organization to function and attain its objectives. For example, in the 1960s relatively few organizations had much demand for computer people. Those few individuals filling data processing or systems analysis slots usually just slid into the roles as an outgrowth of other activities. In the 1980s nearly every organization had a large demand for computer systems experts. Job analysis, by collecting job information, should pick up these trends and help the organization develop to meet the future.

Closely tied to this is the maintenance function of manpower planning. An organization must know how many workers with which specific skills will be required. Knowing after the fact that the organization is short 50 systems analysts or 3 industrial engineers is useful, but not nearly as useful as predicting that fact ahead of time. Job analysis, by coping with change, can help predict future needs.

Knowing the needs of the future helps managers to counsel their employees regarding career development. Managers should want the organization to succeed, and one effective way for that to happen is for the employees to grow with the company. In order to perform this task, managers need the kinds of predictive information job analysis can provide.

Training, especially the development of training programs, is also an important function in maintaining the health of the organization. Once trends in organizational development have been ascertained, positive steps must be taken to assure that qualified people will be available to fill these new organizational roles. Training can take many forms, including in-house courses for both new and experienced workers, professional short course attendance, or coordination with educational institutions to develop appropriate degree, diploma, or certificate programs. If the job analysis has been done properly, then the organization is literally in position to guarantee jobs for new graduates.

The administrative management functions include recruitment, selection, orientation, appraisal, job evaluation, complying with legal requirements, and training. The appraisal and job evaluation tasks, as well as the legal requirements, are covered elsewhere in this book.

Recruitment involves attracting the best people for the jobs that are available. Job analysis, primarily through the vehicle of the job description and employee specification, states the requirements of the open position. When properly stated, this information can be matched against the individuals available in the labor market. There is a much better chance for a good fit when the requirements are known. Job analysis provides a management document which allows the manager to organize his/her area most productively, with respect to work performed, expected performance standards, qualifications, career paths, and so forth.

Similarly, the orientation of new employees is made easier when complete job analysis information is available. Most new employees want to know what is expected of them in order to successfully perform their job. They also generally have an interest in what should be expected of them in order to advance in the organization. Job analysis can provide these "rules of the game."

Job-related training, in order to be successful, requires knowledge of the performance criteria. All training courses need to know what the worker is expected to be able to perform and how well that skill must be performed. How well the machine tool operator must be able to use the tool to remove metal has to be known before any training can be developed. Many training courses are unsuccessful because the specific objectives are not understood by all parties involved before the training began.

JOB ANALYSIS—PROCEDURE

As has been stated, job analysis is the process of identifying all the important information about a job. In order to do this successfully, certain conditions must be present. First of all, management should assist the analyst by publicizing the purpose and expectations of the analysis. This implies that top management understands and supports the job analysis program. These programs can have significant impact on an organization, especially regarding time,* cost, worker attitudes, and even organizational structure. Without top management support the program is likely doomed to failure.

Once top management has indicated its support, line management must also be brought in on the team. The immediate supervisors of the workers are the people who must live with the system when it is completed. If they don't completely support it from the start, the job analysis program will have little likelihood for success. Along with securing support from supervisors, it is also necessary to have the full cooperation of the employees whose jobs are to be analyzed as well as their union.

After all the support for the program has been generated, the information must be collected. The specific information to be collected fits certain major categories.

General Identification Information: This is the factual information about the job. It includes the correct titles, departments where the job is found, pay range, and the relative position of the job within the hierarchy of the organization. It also names the analyst and the date compiled, and has space for the appropriate approvals.

This general type of information may be available on the formal organization chart. However, since organizations are constantly evolving, it is easy for organization charts to become outdated.

Summary: This is a brief statement about the nature and purpose of the job. Although a more detailed summary will be included later in the job analysis, a preliminary summary or abstract provides useful information. It not only provides easy and quick reference information about jobs, it also identifies those jobs which require additional details.

Work Description: This information provides a complete listing of all the activities, both major or significant, and minor, that are

---

* Zollitsch and Langsner point out that the average time required to perform one job analysis can take up to eight hours, with four hours per job being a reasonable estimate of the time to expect to spend on each analysis. (Zollitsch and Langsner:279).

performed or should be performed on a given job. It is also useful for the work description to include approximate amounts of time spent on each of the major tasks of the job. This is valuable for the recruitment and training uses of job analysis.

Equipment: All tools, equipment, and special materials needed for the job must be included in the job analysis. This information is necessary for the specification of special skills required for performance of the job. This also has a significant impact on the recruitment and training process.

Work Environment: The conditions under which the work is performed is very important information. Special environmental conditions regarding temperature, humidity, noise, illumination, smell, vibration, and so on can have a significant effect on the work and how it is performed. This can have a major impact on the job evaluation and job pricing policy. A production job located adjacent to a blast furnace would logically be worth more, in terms of pay, than would the very same job performed in an air conditioned, environmentally controlled, clean room.

Standards: These are the minimum performance expectations for a job. An individual must meet these minimums in order to successfully complete the job. Employee performance must be evaluated compared with some set of expectations in order to determine "how well" the employee is performing the job. These must be established as part of the job analysis.

Requirements: Job requirements refer to the abilities the individual must have in order to perform the job. This portion of job analysis requires that the analyst be more than an observer. Although some judgment is employed in the other sections of job analysis . . . in order to state the job requirements . . . the analyst must make a detailed analysis and interpretation of the traits required of the worker for successful performance of the job.

COLLECTING INFORMATION

Job analysis involves collecting significant amounts of information—specifically information regarding job content, working environment, and worker requirements. There are a number of methods or techniques available for gathering information of this type. Regardless of the method used to gather the data, the following questions are useful in ascertaining the needed information.

First, the analyst must ask, "why?"

- Why is it necessary for the job to be performed?
- Why is the job done the way it is?
- Why is the job located organizationally where it is?
- Why is the job located physically where it is?

In any analysis, the most important question to ask is "why?" If a satisfactory response is given to this question, the second question to ask is "what?"

- What is happening at the workplace?
- What, specifically, is the worker doing?
- What are the work elements?
- Why are these elements being done?
- Why are they being done in that sequence?
- What are the job requirements?
- What are the performance expectations?
- What are the physical demands?
- What are the skill requirements?
- What are the mental requirements?
- What are the environmental requirements?

Each of these "what" questions, while necessary to gather the needed information, *must* be followed with the obligatory "why" question.

There are a variety of ways to gather the job analysis data. First of these is direct observation of the job, coupled with interviewing employees. "Experience has proven that the job analyst's personal interview with an employee benefits everyone concerned, even though it is somewhat more expensive. . . ." (Zollitsch and Langsner:281) Before any observations are made, the supervisors of the appropriate departments should be contacted. It is essential that supervisors provide their approval before any analysis begins. Once this permission has been obtained, the actual observation and interviewing can take place. While direct observation will provide the information about many of the tasks performed by the worker, it is the interview that will fill in the details.

The first step during the interview is to ask the worker to completely describe the major activities performed on the job. If the worker is cooperative, the answer to this question will provide significant information. If the worker requires additional questioning, asking the worker to describe all the activities done on a daily or less frequent basis may be helpful. It may also be helpful to have the employee describe a "typical" day on the job. Henderson suggests several questions that should be asked during the interview. (Henderson:163)

1. What is done?
2. To What is it done?
3. Why is it done?
4. How is it done?

Usually employees are more than willing to describe their job to an interested observer.

A successful interviewer will do the following while conducting the interview:

1. Work with the supervisor to identify an appropriate subject for the interview.
2. Establish an immediate rapport with the subject to be interviewed. Chances are the subject will be somewhat nervous, so it is advantageous for the interviewer to be able to put the subject at ease.
3. Follow a structured outline when questioning. If necessary, have questions prepared prior to the interview—and then stick to the questions.
4. Ask short–to the point–questions. Compound questions will not only be difficult for the employee to answer, but also will be less effective than simple and direct queries.
5. Permit the employee ample time to answer the questions. It is often very difficult for the person asking the question to keep quiet during the answer. This is essential though, and must be done.
6. Verify the information with the supervisor. Although it is convenient to blindly trust the worker, the information must be double-checked to assure its accuracy.

While the interview may be the most effective way to perform a job analysis, it is also very expensive.

The most popular method of gathering job information is the questionnaire. Questionnaires can get uniform results from all employees. If the questions are asked correctly, all workers, regardless of their ability to express themselves, will give consistent answers.

It is also conventional wisdom in the compensation field to request the employees' supervisor to review the job facts, approve them or augment them, and send the report to the job analyst. Questionnaires should be accompanied by letters to employees explaining the questionnaires and their use. Although the questionnaire is economical, there is the danger that a respondee will either not complete the questionnaire, complete it inaccurately, or take an excessively long time to return it.

While questionnaires are popular and interviews are generally deemed better, both methods are effective. As a matter of fact, both methods are acceptable, as long as accuracy of information and time consumption are considered. Questionnaires and interviews are not the only way though, of gathering information.

Another excellent source of job analysis information is the work measurement department's elemental descriptions used in setting time standards. These primarily describe the "best" way to perform a job, but they also list all the activities performed on a specific job. If these descriptions are available they provide an excellent source of information about the job. Regardless of how detailed the elemental breakdown is, each element must be logically defined, easily identified, and repeated on a more or less regular basis throughout the job cycle.

Another way of obtaining job information is in a conference with the supervisor. In order for this to be effective, the supervisor must be very familiar with the job being performed. It is usually productive for the employee whose job is being analyzed to participate in the interview. When this occurs the job analysis has been performed via interview, which was discussed earlier.

Some organizations use a diary or daily log to determine job activities. At the end of each work shift the employee reconstructs, from memory, all the activities that were performed that day. Variations, such as tape recorders and electronic data collectors are other ways of recording all the job activities.

Probably the very best way to gather job analysis information is to use all of the methods described. On a practical basis, though, the advice of Ghorpade and Atchison is applicable, ". . . choose the method that yields valid and reliable results in the context in which the study is being conducted . . . the efficacy of the methods utilized [should] be judged in the cold light of empirical results, rather than tradition or results." (Ghorpade and Atchison:140) Job analysis is a skill that is developed with practice. Some guidelines that are applicable regarding the conduct of a job analysis follow:

1. Permission for the analysis should be obtained before making the study.

2. All studies should be performed so that the results obtained are consistent.
3. Data gathered should reflect the work as it is—not as it should be.
4. The process should be kept as informal and friendly as possible. Everyday etiquette must be observed with the job analysis, as it is with all work observations.

SUMMARY

Job analysis provides information about the work being performed in the organization. Specifically, it provides general information about a job, such as title and position within the organization. It also describes the work performed, the equipment used, the working environment expected, the performance required, and the skills necessary to perform the job. Job analysis provides the job description and specification and leads directly to the job evaluation system. From this the relative worth of the job can be established, and criteria can be developed for evaluating the individual worker's performance. Indeed the job analysis task is a very important task.

Review Questions

1. What is job analysis?
2. What are the four major uses of job analysis information?
3. What is a job description?
4. What does a job evaluation system do?
5. What is job pricing?
6. What is job classification?
7. What is performance appraisal?
8. Why is job analysis performed?
9. What is meant by organizational development? What relationship does it have to job analysis?
10. What are the administrative management functions?
11. What is recruitment? How is it related to job analysis?
12. What is orientation? How is it related to job analysis?
13. What is training? How is it related to job analysis?
14. What is the first step in job analysis?

15. What is the second step in job analysis?
16. Specifically, what information must be collected during a job analysis?
17. What is general identification information?
18. What is the job summary?
19. What is the work description in a job analysis?
20. What equipment type information should be collected during a job analysis?
21. What is meant by working environment?
22. How do standards relate to a job analysis?
23. What are job requirements?
24. What questions should be asked during a job analysis?
25. What are the different ways of collecting job analysis information? What are the advantages and disadvantages of each?
26. What should an interviewer do in order to make a job analysis interview successful?
27. What is the most popular method of gathering job analysis information?

References

Aft, Lawrence S., *Productivity, Measurement and Improvement*, Reston Publishing Company, Inc., Reston, Virginia, 1983.

Belcher, David W., *Compensation Administration*, Prentice-Hall, Inc., Englewood Cliffs, N.J., 1974.

Ghorpade, Jai and Atchison, T. J., "The Concept of Job Analysis: A Review and Some Suggestions," *Public Personnel Management Journal*, Volume 9, Number 3, 1980.

Henderson, Richard I., *Compensation Management: Rewarding Performance*, 4th edition Reston Publishing Company, Inc., Reston, Virginia, 1985.

Klinger, Donald E., "When the Traditional Job Description is Not Enough," *Personnel Journal*, April, 1979.

Patten, Thomas H., *Pay*, Free Press (MacMillan), New York, 1977.

Rendero, Thomasine, "Job Analysis Practices," *Personnel*, January-February, 1981.

Zalusky, John, "Job Evaluation: An Uneven World," *AFL-CIO American Federationist*, April, 1981.

Zollitsch, H. G. and Langsner, A., *Wage and Salary Administration*, Southwestern Publishing Company, Cincinnati, Ohio, 1970.

Case Study

INTRODUCTION

Mountain View College is a medium-sized, state-supported liberal arts college located in a rapidly growing Sunbelt city. Current enrollment is 2,300 full-time students, about 1,000 part-time students, and 100 or so transient students. The faculty consists of about 70 full-time and 50 adjunct members. For many years Mountain View College, or MVC, had all the trappings of a family organization. There was a loose administrative structure, with administrators, faculty, and staff all pitching in to get the job done. For years this was successful, however, two significant events occurred which had a lasting impact on MVC.

First, was the slow but steady growth of the college. While Mountain View was able to accommodate this growth for many years and continue as a "Mom and Pop" college, the growth finally forced the college into facing some organizational facts of life. Coupled with the slow and steady growth of the school was MVC's location in the Sunbelt. The rapid growth of this region made the school aware that its own expansion would probably parallel the region and its own city's growth.

Second, was the appointment of a new President who viewed it as his mandate to prepare the college, not only academically, but administratively and organizationally for the "challenge of growth." Not to mention having to comply with certain legal requirements, the future course of MVC was well planned. Part of the organizational work that had to be performed was the development of a compensation administration program.

After a great deal of study the President announced the general organization structure shown in the organization chart in Figure 2-1. While many of the positions at the college are professional, such as faculty members, department heads, division directors, librarians, and so forth, there are a substantial number of positions that should be covered by the compensation or wage and salary administration program. These are primarily the secretarial and clerical positions that exist in just about every function shown on the organization chart. These positions need virtually all of the components that a wage and salary program can provide.

Job descriptions, job specifications, standardized job titles, job evaluation, job classification, job pricing and assignment of a monetary value, and an employee evaluation system all need to be developed. The first step, as the President saw it, was to assign the task to the personnel director. She knew, after receiving the assignment, that this was a classic case for a textbook application of wage and salary administration fundamentals. At the conclusion of many of the following chapters, including this one, the work of MVC's personnel director will be described.

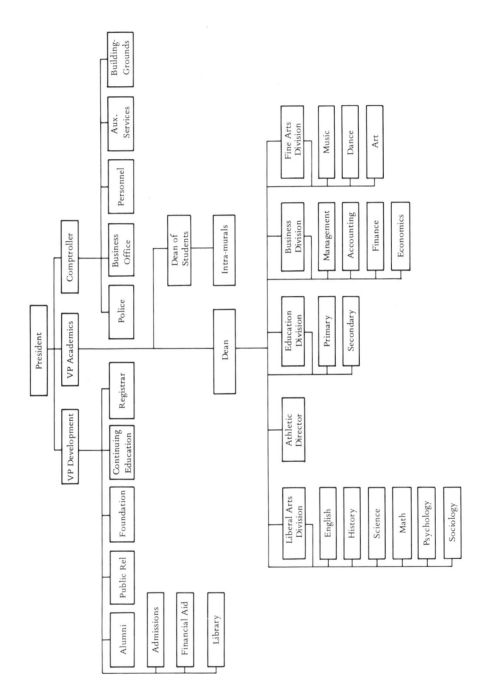

FIGURE 2–1. Mountain View College's Administrative Structure

MVC's JOB ANALYSIS

The first step in developing this program is the job analysis. The personnel director decided that the most effective method of gathering information would be with the interview. In order to assure that consistent information was gathered, she developed a checklist for the interviewer to follow during the course of the interview. Figure 2–2 shows the questions asked of each subject.

The information gathering began in earnest after a mass meeting of all college employees covered. Because MVC was relatively small, the personnel director decided to interview all covered employees, that is, all the secretarial and clerical personnel and their supervisors. At the conclusion of the interviews each employee and each supervisor signed off on the data collection form. Figure 2–3 shows a sample of the completed interview form.

At the conclusion of the interviews, the positions shown in Figure 2–4 were identified as being inclusive of all the secretarial and clerical positions at MVC. The data collected while performing the job analysis were used to develop the job descriptions for the College. These will be presented at the end of the next chapter.

Mountain View College – Clerical Job Analysis

General Information   Date _____

Title _____ Department _____

Pay _____ Reports to _____ Title _____

Nature and Purpose
Why is job performed? What happens if it is not?

What tasks are performed on the job? What are the most important? What is the relative frequency of each?

What tools and equipment are used on this job?

What standards, deadlines, goals, must be met? What are the consequences of not meeting these? How much guidance/direct supervision is given to/by?

Special education, training, experience requirements?

Special physical requirements?

Special environmental requirements?

Additional information about the job?

I have read the following information and believe that it correctly reflects upon the job I perform at Mountain View College.

_____   _____
Employee   Supervisor

FIGURE 2–2. MVC Job Analysis Questionnaire

Mountain View College – Clerical Job Analysis

General Information   Date __5·30__

Title __DEPARTMENTAL SECRETARY__   Department __MATH__

Pay __$14,200__   Reports to __DEPARTMENT HEAD__   Title __DEPT. HEAD__

Nature and Purpose

Why is job performed? What happens if it is not?

TYPES CORRESPONDENCE, REPORTS, AND EXAMINATIONS FOR DEPARTMENT, ACTS AS RECEPTIONIST. WORK IS UNDONE IF NOT TYPED OR TESTS ARE WRITTEN BY HAND BY INSTRUCTORS.

What tasks are performed on the job? What are the most important? What is the relative frequency of each?

TYPING (60%)
REPRODUCTION (20%)
FILING (5%)
MAIL SORTING (5%)

What tools and equipment are used on this job?

TYPEWRITER
COLLATOR
MIMEOGRAPH MACHINE

What standards, deadlines, goals, must be met? What are the consequences of not meeting these? How much guidance/direct supervision is given to by?

MUST MEET ARTIFICALLY IMPOSED DEADLINES OR ELSE REPORTS/ TESTS ARE NOT READY ON A TIMELY BASIS.

Special education, training, experience requirements?

HIGH SCHOOL DIPLOMA.
MUST TYPE AT 60 WPM.

Special physical requirements?

NONE

Special environmental requirements?

NONE

Additional information about the job?

MUST BE ABLE TO DEAL WITH STUDENTS.

I have read the following information and believe that it correctly reflects upon the job I perform at Mountain View College.

_____   _____
Employee   Supervisor

FIGURE 2–3(a).   Sample Completed Job Analysis Questionnaire

Mountain View College – Clerical Job Analysis

General Information   Date *1-1-84*

Title *CLERK*   Department *ADMINISTRATION RECORDS*

Pay _____ Reports to *CHRIS HOLLIS*   Title *ASSOCIATE DIRECTOR OF ADMISSIONS*

Nature and Purpose
Why is job performed? What happens if it is not?

THE JOB IS PERFORMED TO INSURE THE PROCESSING OF FRESHMAN AND TRANSFER STUDENT APPLICATIONS. FAILURE TO PERFORM THIS JOB WILL RESULT IN LATE ADMISSIONS.

What tasks are performed on the job? What are the most important? What is the relative frequency of each?

THE MAJOR TASK IS PROCESSING APPLICATIONS 25% OF THE TIME. OTHER TASKS INCLUDE ANSWERING INFORMATION PHONE CALLS 10% OF THE TIME AND WORKING AT THE ADMINISTRATION WINDOW 15% OF THE TIME.

What tools and equipment are used on this job?

TYPEWRITER
COPIER
ADDING MACHINE

What standards, deadlines, goals, must be met? What are the consequences of not meeting these? How much guidance/direct supervision is given to/by?

DEADLINES IMPOSED BY SUPERVISOR.
JOB NEEDS VERY LITTLE SUPERVISION.

Special education, training, experience requirements?

HIGH SCHOOL DIPLOMA.
TYPING.
COMMUNICATIVE SKILLS.

Special physical requirements?

40% STANDING, 40% SITTING, WALKING

Special environmental requirements?

NORMAL OFFICE ENVIRONMENT - STANDARD WORKING HOURS.

Additional information about the job?

MUST BE WILLING TO HELP WITH STUDENT PROBLEMS.

I have read the following information and believe that it correctly reflects upon the job I perform at Mountain View College.

_____   _____
Employee   Supervisor

FIGURE 2–3(b).   Sample Completed Job Analysis Questionnaire

Mountain View College – Clerical Job Analysis

General Information   Date _1-1-84_

Title _CLERK (JUNIOR)_ _____ Department _RECORDS_ _____

Pay _____ Reports to _JOHN MORGAN_ ___ Title _ASSOCIATE REGISTRAR_

Nature and Purpose

Why is job performed? What happens if it is not?

TO MAINTAIN & PROCESS STUDENT RECORDS. FAILURE TO PERFORM THIS JOB WILL DELAY OTHER JOBS IN THE REGISTRAR'S OFFICE.

What tasks are performed on the job? What are the most important? What is the relative frequency of each?

50% OF THE TIME IS SPENT SENDING OUT TRANSCRIPTS, VERIFICATION FORMS AND ASSISTING THE REGISTRAR'S SECRETARY. OTHER DUTIES INCLUDE TYPING, FILING, AND PROCESSING PETITIONS AND REPORTS.

What tools and equipment are used on this job?

STANDARD OFFICE EQUIPMENT.
3M MICROFILM MACHINE.

What standards, deadlines, goals, must be met? What are the consequences of not meeting these? How much guidance/direct supervision is given to/by?

DEADLINES MUST BE MET ACCORDING TO THE JOB PERFORMED.
JOB NEEDS VERY LITTLE SUPERVISION.

Special education, training, experience requirements?

HIGH SCHOOL DIPLOMA.
TYPING.
GENERAL OFFICE KNOWLEDGE.

Special physical requirements?

20% WALKING, 40% SITTING, 40% STANDING.

Special environmental requirements?

NORMAL OFFICE ENVIRONMENT- STANDARD WORKING HOURS.

Additional information about the job?

MATURITY REQUIRED IN CONFIDENTIAL MATTERS.

I have read the following information and believe that it correctly reflects upon the job I perform at Mountain View College.

_____   _____
Employee   Supervisor

FIGURE 2–3(c).   Sample Completed Job Analysis Questionnaire

Mountain View College – Clerical Job Analysis

General Information   Date _1-1-84_

Title _CLERK_ _____ Department _REGISTRAR'S OFFICE_ ____

Pay _____ Reports to _JOHN MORGAN_ ____ Title _ASSOC. REGISTRAR_

Nature and Purpose

Why is job performed? What happens if it is not?

THE JOB IS PERFORMED TO KEEP STUDENTS' RECORDS CHANGE FORMS UPDATED AND TO PROCESS ALL ON-CAMPUS MAIL OF THE SUPERVISOR.

What tasks are performed on the job? What are the most important? What is the relative frequency of each?

60% OF THE TIME IS SPENT PROCESSING DROP FORMS, WITHDRAWAL FORMS, AND PERMANENT RECORD CARDS. OTHER DUTIES INCLUDE HANDLING DEPARTMENTAL MAIL & ASSISTING STUDENTS AT THE OFFICE WINDOW.

What tools and equipment are used on this job?

STANDARD OFFICE MACHINES

What standards, deadlines, goals, must be met? What are the consequences of not meeting these? How much guidance/direct supervision is given to/by?

DEADLINES SET BY SUPERVISOR.
JOB NEEDS VERY LITTLE SUPERVISION.

Special education, training, experience requirements?

HIGH SCHOOL DIPLOMA
CLERICAL FIELD EXPERIENCE (2 YEARS).
EDUCATION FIELD EXPERIENCE PREFERRED.

Special physical requirements?

40% SITTING, 40% STANDING, 20% WALKING.

Special environmental requirements?

Additional information about the job?

MUST WORK WELL WITH OTHERS.

I have read the following information and believe that it correctly reflects upon the job I perform at Mountain View College.

_____   _____
Employee   Supervisor

FIGURE 2-3(d).   Sample Completed Job Analysis Questionnaire

Mountain View College – Clerical Job Analysis

General Information   Date *1-1-84*

Title *SECRETARY*   Department *PUBLIC RELATIONS*

Pay _____ Reports to *ED JONES*   Title *DEAN OF STUDENT AFFAIRS*

Nature and Purpose
Why is job performed? What happens if it is not?

THE JOB IS PERFORMED TO HANDLE GENERAL TYPING AND FILING AS NEEDED BY THE ALUMNI AND PR OFFICE.

What tasks are performed on the job? What are the most important? What is the relative frequency of each?

ABOUT 3/4 OF THE DAY IS SPENT TYPING AND ONE HOUR PER DAY IS SPENT FILING. OTHER DUTIES INCLUDE NEWSPAPER RESEARCH AND TELEPHONE ANSWERING.

What tools and equipment are used on this job?

STANDARD OFFICE EQUIPMENT

What standards, deadlines, goals, must be met? What are the consequences of not meeting these? How much guidance/direct supervision is given to/by?

DEADLINES SET BY SUPERVISOR.
JOB REQUIRES VERY LITTLE SUPERVISION.

Special education, training, experience requirements?

HIGH SCHOOL DIPLOMA.
COLLEGE ENGLISH HELPFUL.

Special physical requirements?

75% SITTING.

Special environmental requirements?

SMALL OFFICE - STANDARD WORKING HOURS.

Additional information about the job?

MUST BE ABLE TO DEAL WITH ALL LEVELS OF PEOPLE.

I have read the following information and believe that it correctly reflects upon the job I perform at Mountain View College.

_____   _____
Employee   Supervisor

FIGURE 2–3(e). Sample Completed Job Analysis Questionnaire

Mountain View College – Clerical Job Analysis

General Information   Date _1-1-84_

Title _SECRETARY_   Department _DEAN OF STUDENT AFFAIRS_

Pay _____   Reports to _ED JONES_   Title _DEAN OF STUDENT AFFAIRS_

Nature and Purpose

Why is job performed? What happens if it is not?

JOB IS PERFORMED TO AID THE DEAN OF STUDENT AFFAIRS AND TO PROVIDE SUPPORT TO THE ATHLETIC DEPARTMENT AND CLINIC.

What tasks are performed on the job? What are the most important? What is the relative frequency of each?

35% OF THE TIME IS SPENT TYPING, 25% OF THE TIME IS SPENT ON STUDENT AFFAIRS. OTHER TIME IS SPENT ON PROVIDING AID TO THE ATHLETIC DEPARTMENT & CLINIC ALONG WITH OTHER MISCELLANEOUS DUTIES.

What tools and equipment are used on this job?

STANDARD OFFICE EQUIPMENT

What standards, deadlines, goals, must be met? What are the consequences of not meeting these? How much guidance/direct supervision is given to/by?

NEEDS VERY LITTLE SUPERVISION. OFTEN MAKES OWN DECISIONS TO COMPLETE A JOB.

Special education, training, experience requirements?

_HIGH SCHOOL DIPLOMA.
SECRETARIAL EXPERIENCE (3-4 YEARS)_

Special physical requirements?

50% SITTING - 50% STANDING/WALKING

Special environmental requirements?

SINGLE OFFICE AREA, STANDING WORKING HOURS

Additional information about the job?

CONFIDENTIALITY REQUIRED ON STUDENT MATTERS.

I have read the following information and believe that it correctly reflects upon the job I perform at Mountain View College.

_____   _____
Employee   Supervisor

FIGURE 2–3(f).   Sample Completed Job Analysis Questionnaire

Mountain View College – Clerical Job Analysis

General Information

Date _____

Title *SECRETARY* _____ Department *DEPARTMENT OF ADMISSIONS AND REGISTRAR'S OFFICE*

Pay _____ Reports to *KATHY BRADBURN* Title *DIRECTOR OF ADMISSIONS AND REGISTRAR*

Nature and Purpose

Why is job performed? What happens if it is not?

JOB IS PERFORMED TO ASSIST THE DIRECTOR OF ADMISSIONS BY HANDLING ALL TYPING AND ORDERING AS NEEDED BY THE ADMISSIONS OR REGISTRAR'S OFFICE.

What tasks are performed on the job? What are the most important? What is the relative frequency of each?

40% OF THE TIME IS SPENT HANDLING GRADUATION MATTERS AND 20% OF THE TIME IS SPENT TYPING. OTHER DUTIES INCLUDE ORDERING FORMS AND SUPPLIES, HANDLING TIME CARDS FOR EMPLOYEES & SUPERVISING EMPLOYEES IN RECORDS.

What tools and equipment are used on this job?

STANDARD OFFICE EQUIPMENT.

What standards, deadlines, goals, must be met? What are the consequences of not meeting these? How much guidance/direct supervision is given to/by?

STANDARDS, DEADLINES, AND GOALS MUST BE MET REGARDING GRADUATION. NO SUPERVISION.
GIVEN SUPERVISION OVER RECORD EMPLOYEES.

Special education, training, experience requirements?

HIGH SCHOOL DIPLOMA
BUSINESS COLLEGE (2 YEARS)
FIVE YEARS EXPERIENCE.

Special physical requirements?

STANDING, SITTING AND WALKING AS NECESSARY.

Special environmental requirements?

NORMAL OFFICE · STANDARD WORKING HOURS.

Additional information about the job?

MUST WORK WELL WITH OTHERS.

I have read the following information and believe that it correctly reflects upon the job I perform at Mountain View College.

_____ _____
Employee   Supervisor

FIGURE 2–3(g). Sample Completed Job Analysis Questionnaire

Mountain View College – Clerical Job Analysis

General Information   Date _1-1-84_

Title _SECRETARY_____ Department _DEAN'S OFFICE_____

Pay _____ Reports to _DR. DEAN HARRIS___ Title _DEAN OF COLLEGE_

Nature and Purpose
Why is job performed? What happens if it is not?

JOB IS PERFORMED TO ASSIST THE DEAN IN ALL COLLEGE FUNCTIONS.

What tasks are performed on the job? What are the most important? What is the relative frequency of each?

ALL DUTIES ARE OF EQUAL IMPORTANCE. THEY INCLUDE PLACING &
ANSWERING PHONE CALLS FOR THE DEAN, MAKING APPOINTMENTS,
COMMITTEE WORK, AND ASSISTING OTHER DEPARTMENTS.

What tools and equipment are used on this job?

TYPEWRITER, DICTATOR MACHINE, COPIER, WORD PROCESSOR.

What standards, deadlines, goals, must be met? What are the consequences of not meeting these? How much guidance/direct supervision is given to/by?

DEADLINES AND GOALS ARE SET BY THE DEAN.
JOB NEEDS NO SUPERVISION.
OFTEN MAKES INDEPENDENT DECISIONS.

Special education, training, experience requirements?

HIGH SCHOOL DIPLOMA.
JUNIOR COLLEGE OR BUSINESS SCHOOL PREFERRED.
OFFICE EXPERIENCE (2 YEARS)

Special physical requirements?

STANDING, SITTING AND WALKING AS REQUIRED.

Special environmental requirements?

OFFICE ENVIRONMENT- STANDARD WORKING HOURS.

Additional information about the job?

MUST WORK WELL WITH OTHERS.

I have read the following information and believe that it correctly reflects upon the job I perform at Mountain View College.

_____   _____
Employee   Supervisor

FIGURE 2–3(h).   Sample Completed Job Analysis Questionnaire

Mountain View College – Clerical Job Analysis

General Information   Date *1-1-84*

Title *LIBRARY ASSISTANT*   Department *LIBRARY*

Pay _____ Reports to *JANE REED* Title *LIBRARY DIRECTOR*

Nature and Purpose

Why is job performed? What happens if it is not?

JOB IS PERFORMED TO INSURE THE PROPER HANDLING AND PROCESSING OF LIBRARY RECORDS.

What tasks are performed on the job? What are the most important? What is the relative frequency of each?

MAJOR DUTIES INCLUDE 30% MAINTAINING THE LISTINGS OF NEWLY PUBLISHED BOOKS, 20% SUPERVISING CATEGORIZING OF INCOMING BOOKS, AND 20% BOOKKEEPING.

What tools and equipment are used on this job?

TYPEWRITER.
REPRODUCTION MACHINES.

What standards, deadlines, goals, must be met? What are the consequences of not meeting these? How much guidance/direct supervision is given to/by?

DEADLINES SET BY SUPERVISOR.
NEEDS VERY LITTLE SUPERVISION.

Special education, training, experience requirements?

HIGH SCHOOL DIPLOMA.
TWO YEARS OF COLLEGE.
FIVE YEARS EXPERIENCE.

Special physical requirements?

EQUAL TIME SPENT SITTING, STANDING AND WALKING.

Special environmental requirements?

LIBRARY ENVIRONMENT-SOME NIGHT & WEEKEND DUTY.

Additional information about the job?

RESPONSIBLE FOR OPERATION OF LIBRARY ON SELECTED EVENINGS.

I have read the following information and believe that it correctly reflects upon the job I perform at Mountain View College.

_____   _____
Employee   Supervisor

FIGURE 2–3(i). Sample Completed Job Analysis Questionnaire

Mountain View College – Clerical Job Analysis	

General Information   Date _1-1-84_

Title _LIBRARY ASSISTANT_   Department _LIBRARY_

Pay _____ Reports to _JANE REED_ Title _LIBRARY DIRECTOR_

Nature and Purpose

Why is job performed? What happens if it is not?

JOB IS PERFORMED TO HANDLE MUSIC ROOM FUNCTIONS AND ASSIST IN CATALOGING BOOKS.

What tasks are performed on the job? What are the most important? What is the relative frequency of each?

MAJOR DUTIES INCLUDE 30% MANNING DESK IN MUSIC ROOM, 15% ASSISTING CATALOGER & FILING. OTHER DUTIES INCLUDE MANNING FRONT LIBRARY DESK, PREPARING ACQUISITIONS & MAINTAINING MUSIC EQUIP.

What tools and equipment are used on this job?

TYPEWRITER.
XEROX COPIER.
STEREO EQUIPMENT.

What standards, deadlines, goals, must be met? What are the consequences of not meeting these? How much guidance/direct supervision is given to/by?

DEADLINES SET BY SUPERVISOR.
JOB NEEDS LITTLE SUPERVISION.

Special education, training, experience requirements?

HIGH SCHOOL DIPLOMA.
BUSINESS SCHOOL PREFERRED.
LIBRARY EXPERIENCE (1 YEAR).

Special physical requirements?

MOSTLY STANDING & WALKING.

Special environmental requirements?

OFFICE ENVIRONMENT - STANDARD WORKING HOURS.

Additional information about the job?

MUST WORK WELL IN COLLEGE LIBRARY ENVIRONMENT.

I have read the following information and believe that it correctly reflects upon the job I perform at Mountain View College.

_____   _____
Employee   Supervisor

FIGURE 2–3(j).   Sample Completed Job Analysis Questionnaire

Mountain View College – Clerical Job Analysis

General Information   Date _1-1-84_

Title _ACCOUNTANT_____ Department _BUSINESS OFFICE_____

Pay _____ Reports to _JEFF MARTIN_____ Title _ACCOUNTANT III_

Nature and Purpose

Why is job performed? What happens if it is not?

  JOB IS PERFORMED TO KEEP ALL RECORDS UPDATED FOR DEPARTMENTAL EQUIPMENT

What tasks are performed on the job? What are the most important? What is the relative frequency of each?

  84% OF THE TIME IS SPENT ON PROCESSING REQUESTS FOR PURCHASES OF SUPPLIES AND EQUIPMENT. OTHER DUTIES INCLUDE PROCESSING TRAVEL REQUESTS AND MAINTAINING MAINTENANCE CONTRACTS.

What tools and equipment are used on this job?

  STANDARD OFFICE EQUIPMENT

What standards, deadlines, goals, must be met? What are the consequences of not meeting these? How much guidance/direct supervision is given to by?

  DEADLINES SET BY SUPERVISOR.
  JOB REQUIRES ALMOST NO SUPERVISION.

Special education, training, experience requirements?

  HIGH SCHOOL DIPLOMA.
  BUSINESS SCHOOL (2 YEARS). NOTARY PUBLIC CERTIFICATION
  BOOKKEEPING EXPERIENCE (2 YEARS).

Special physical requirements?

  LARGE PERCENTAGE OF TIME SITTING.

Special environmental requirements?

  PRIVATE OFFICE - STANDARD WORKING HOURS.

Additional information about the job?

  CONSIDERABLE INITIATIVE REQUIRED.

I have read the following information and believe that it correctly reflects upon the job I perform at Mountain View College.

_____   _____
Employee   Supervisor

FIGURE 2–3(k).   Sample Completed Job Analysis Questionnaire

"I don't know either Botkins, but it's right here in your job description."

Chapter Three

JOB DESCRIPTIONS AND SPECIFICATIONS

INTRODUCTION

The direct objective of performing the job analysis is the creation of the job description. Each employee in an organization is entitled to know exactly what he or she is expected to do, how well it is to be done, and how performance compares against the standards for the job. The vehicle to present this information is the job description. A job description is defined as a body of information compiled from job analysis, presented in organized statements that identify and describe the contents of a specific job or position. It details the tasks involved for a proper conception and a complete understanding of the job.

The job description is often expanded to include the job specification. Job specifications indicate requirements of the job regarding the various factors normally found in the job, such as skill, effort, responsibility, and so forth. These factors may be used to determine the relative worth of a job or to identify the individuals who might be best qualified for the job. Although technically there may be a distinction between job descriptions and job specification, they often are combined in one document.

USES OF JOB DESCRIPTIONS

Job descriptions have many uses within an organization. A framework of three major categories for classifying the functions of job descriptions is useful. These categories are for personnel uses, for legal compliance uses, and for collective bargaining purposes.

The personnel uses of job descriptions refer, generally, to the staffing requirements of an organization. Specifically, these may include some or all of the following:

1. Manpower Requirements—Job descriptions list the requirements and duties of jobs within the organization. If properly written using the job analysis information, the descriptions will contain the tasks that should be performed, as well as the performance standards for the jobs. A combination of this information, the standards and the job duties, translates into the number of positions required to complete the required work. These manpower requirements are based on the work that should be done, not necessarily the work that is currently being performed.

2. Hiring—Job descriptions are most useful in matching job applicants with duties they are capable of performing. "If the skills are adequately represented in a job description, an employment interviewer can more easily match an applicant's qualifications with a job calling for the applicant's skill levels. (Walsh:3)

3. Orientation—It is generally acknowledged that an employee's orientation to a new job is an excellent predictor of an employee's success with the organization. It is important that the employee know exactly what is expected (performance wise) when taking on a new job. Although managers often assume that employees know what is expected, and although employees often assume that managers know what is expected, this is not often the case. According to James Evered, Corporate Director of Human Resources for Redman Industries, "Usually an employee's perception of the job's responsibilities fails to match the manager's perception." (Evered:14) By providing the job description to the employee during orientation this difficulty can be eliminated.

4. Training and Development—The job description defines duties and responsibilities of the job. Individuals who assume new jobs, whether through promotion or by joining the organization, must be given the skills required to perform the job. The job description, by specifying the objectives of the job, provides the needed framework for the effective design of a training program. Also, when jobs change over time, perhaps for technological reasons, the differences between the old and new job descriptions identifies those skills that the individual must upgrade through training and development.

5. Authority and Responsibility—A job description provides a useful way to define the limits of effort, authority, and respon-

sibility for each job. Without a carefully designed set of controls, these areas may overlap and cause confusion and potentially serious conflicts in the operation of an organization. The job descriptions show the relationship between various jobs within a company.

6. Wage Structure—One of the most important uses of job descriptions is as the basis for the job evaluation system. This establishes, through a variety of methods, the relative worth of the job to the organization. Once this is established, the absolute worth of the job can be determined by wage surveys. (Later chapters will detail both the job evaluation process and the compensation survey techniques.)

The second major classification for uses of job descriptions is complying with legal requirements. There are several Federal Statutes that require the use of job descriptions for compliance.

1. Fair Labor Standards Act[1]—One of the provisions of this Act is identifying exempt and nonexempt positions. There are a number of limitations placed on jobs in these respective categories. When an organization classifies jobs in these categories, the job descriptions provide justification for these classification decisions. (Henderson:42–43)

2. Equal Pay Act[2]—People performing the same work for the same organization must receive the same pay. The job description is the vehicle for determining if the same work is being performed. A well-written job description will clearly identify the levels of skill, responsibility, experience, and so on that determine whether two jobs are the same or different.

3. Civil Rights Act Title VII[3]—The equal employment opportunity provisions of this law can best be complied with by using the job descriptions to show that there are no discriminatory requirements in the organization's jobs. If the job descriptions make no requirements regarding race or sex or any of the other conditions of potential discrimination, then none should be assumed.

4. OSHA[4]—Job descriptions generally include statements about the health and safety requirements for a job. By noting that certain tasks face unusual safety, environmental, or health

---

1. Refer to Chapter One.
2. Refer to Chapter One.
3. Refer to Chapter One.
4. Refer to Chapter One.

risks, the organization becomes responsible for either their elimination or the protection of the worker.

The third classification for the uses of job descriptions is the industrial or labor relations area.

1. Equal Pay—Labor unions have consistently been among the most vocal proponants of equal pay for equal work. Although included in legislation, this concept is one that labor unions fight for. It does encourage labor relations peace if individuals performing the same work, as substantiated in the job description, earn the same pay.
2. Grievances—Employees often will complain and file formal grievances when their performance appraisal is less than they anticipated. Properly written job descriptions, which include performance expectations, certainly make the identification of acceptable individual performance much easier to identify.

WRITING JOB DESCRIPTIONS—FORMAT

There are almost as many different ways to prepare job descriptions as there are organizations using job descriptions. While many more specific elements will be identified, there are three key types of information found in all job descriptions. The first category of information is concerned with the *what* and *why*, or the missions of the job, and its place in the workflow. The second category deals with depicting *how* the work gets done. The coverage here would encompass the tasks performed; types and levels of contacts with data, people, and things; the decisions required; and the processes and methods used. The final category would deal with the *where*, or the environmental context of the job, and the resultant demands on the worker.

The overriding guidelines in preparing job descriptions are to keep them simple, clear, and complete. It is good practice to have the job description as complete as possible. Union representatives will generally want the description written as tightly as possible, with clear lines differentiating one job from another so that duties can be clearly identified. Clarity is also important. Because job descriptions will be used by all levels of an organization, it is critical that the descriptions be understood by everyone. They must be written in plain, everyday English.

Although different organizations may have different formats for their job descriptions, all the jobs within a specific organization should have the same format. The following sections will suggest and describe the basic information that should be included in a job description. While some items may be combined, they will each be considered individually here.

Title: Job titles should be descriptive, meaningful, and consistent for comparable positions within the organization. There are a number of standard titles for certain types of work. The Department of Labor categorizes jobs into thousands of occupations (with titles) in the *Dictionary of Occupational Titles.* A job which primarily is responsible for supervising employees involved in assembling personal computers would logically be called an "assembly supervisor" or "electronic assembly foreman." The title should be descriptive and should reflect the position of the job on the organizational chart. Generally, the higher the job appears, the more "glamorous" the title should be.*

Job Function: A summary statement describing the function of the job should be provided. This gives an overview of what the job primarily consists of. For example, if the job title is assembly supervisor, the functional statement might read as follows:

"Assembly Supervisor: Under the direction of the plant manager the assembly supervisor directs and coordinates an assigned group of assemblers, and is responsible for meeting production schedules, quality requirements, and budget targets while maintaining the safe operation of the assembly operations."

Duties/Responsibilities: This section includes the complete listing of duties, responsibilities, and relationships for the job. The duties should be included in a logical format. Three general methods of organization each with its own advantages and limitations are often used.

Sometimes, the most frequently performed task is listed first, followed by the remaining tasks listed in order of descending frequency. This should indicate that the most important functions are listed first. However, just because a function is performed frequently does not necessarily mean that this task is really important. For example, an accounting clerk

---

*Case 3–2 uses DOT job descriptions for a large manufacturing facility.

might sharpen her pencil quite often, but that activity is surely not the most important one performed. Another way of listing the duties and responsibilities is sequentially. The various tasks included in a job are listed in the order that they occur. While valuable for standards developing, this particular way of organizing material leaves the determination of importance to the discrimination of the individual. A third method of listing the duties and responsibilities is by listing them in order of importance rather than by frequency. By showing the most important task first, the order transmits information about the true nature of the job.

Sometimes this part of the job description is called the job summary. Regardless of the format, this part of the job description provides a word picture of the major functions encompassed by the job.

Accountabilities: Besides listing the tasks performed, the job description should include the accountabilities, responsibilities, or specific expectation for performance for the job. The accountabilities section of a job description briefly describes the major results achieved in the satisfactory performance of the job responsibilities and duties. These standards might include items such as how well, how often, how acceptably, and how accurately certain tasks must be performed.

Specifications: The job specification identifies the special requirements of a job. Special skill and environmental conditions are identified in this part of the job description. If a special skill is required on a particular job, then that job would be worth more to the organization than some other job might be.

Within any job description there may be a temptation to also include a disclaimer section with a clause such as, "and other duties as assigned." This is extremely poor policy, as this catch-all clause is too vague to be meaningful. It also permits supervision to include any and all other activities it wants to. A statement of this type is no more than a manager's license to misuse his or her people. It is his or her way of preventing an employee from saying, 'that's not my job.' A complete job description, with sections for title, job function, duties/responsibilities, accountabilities, and specifications, should cover all expected job activities. As duties are added or deleted, the job description should be updated to reflect these changes.

WRITING JOB DESCRIPTIONS—MECHANICS

In order to be useful, a job description must be a clearly and concisely written description of the sections described above. Clarity of expression and simplicity of language are most important. Although this sounds like a straightforward assignment, it is most difficult. As any experienced communicator knows, it is quite easy to ramble and speak or write at length on a topic, but it is far more difficult to speak or write concisely and to the point.

The most important point about a job description is that the descriptions must be completely understood by all parties concerned. Some helpful lists of explicit words are shown in Figure 3–1.

For example, a clerk who files reports accurately should know what is expected. Qualifying words should make the meaning even clearer. The clerk who receives financial reports, organizes them alphabetically, and inserts them in file drawers without error knows explicitly what performance should be produced. The clearer the language, the clearer will be the information communicated.

SUMMARY

Job descriptions are valuable. In order to be effective as a management tool they must be complete and well-written. Including the correct information, as described in this chapter, will provide for a complete description. Writing descriptions that effectively communicate is more difficult, but just as important to the proper use of the job description. Figure 3–2 shows an example of two job descriptions used by a large corporation.

Following this chapter are some examples of job descriptions for Mountain View College. As can be seen, these include the required information and also are explicit in transmitting their meanings.

Helpful Terminology for Analyzing Jobs and Preparing Job Descriptions and Specifications

Action Words: (Verbs)

accounts for	details	lifts	repairs
acts	determines	maintains	requests
adjusts	directs	makes	reworks
analyzes	discovers	manipulates	reviews
answers	drafts	marks	schedules
applies	drives	mixes	secures
approves	estimates	observes	selects
arranges	examines	obtains	sells
assigns	figures	operates	sets
assists	files	orders	shoots
cares for	finds	organizes	sits
carries	follows	performs	sketches
checks	formulates	places	stamps
cleans up	gauges	plans	stands
climbs	handles	prepares	stores
compares	inspects	processes	supervises
composes	installs	proposes	systematizes
computes	instructs	pulls	takes
conducts	interprets	pushes	teaches
constructs	investigates	reads	totals
controls	issues	receives	types
coordinates	itemizes	recognizes	uses
decides	judges	records	walks
designates	keeps	refers	works
designs	lays out	removes	writes

Things Acted Upon: (Nouns)

assemblies	fittings	methods	service manuals
blueprints	formulas	models	sketches
books	gauges	orders	specifications
castings	graphs	parts	standards
cars	handbooks	patterns	supplies
charts	instruction manuals	problems	subassemblies
correspondence	instruments	processes	tables
decisions	letters	products	technical literature
diagrams	machines	records	telephones
drawings	manuals	reference books	templates
equipment	materials	reports	tools
errors	memos	requisitions	trucks
			working drawings

Qualifying Words: (Adjectives)

accurate	dirty	hot	strong
adequate	dry	humid	sufficient
average	dusty	inside	suitable
cold	effective	kind	superior
complex	efficient	noisy	uncomfortable
correct	excessive	normal	weak
cramped	extreme	outside	wet
difficult	high	proper	

FIGURE 3–1. Terminology Used to Analyze Jobs and Prepare Job Descriptions

JOB DESCRIPTION

Job Title: Preventive Maintenance Technician

General Summary:

Under the general supervision of the Plant Engineer, initiate and maintain the Preventive Maintenance Program for all machines and machine tools at the plant.

Principal Duties and Responsibilities:

1. Set up and maintain a Preventive Maintenance Program to reduce machine downtime and maintenance costs.
2. Supervise preventive maintenance inspections including the part specifications, generation of work orders and post-repair inspections for all preventive maintenance repair.
3. Aid in trouble-shooting for any break down maintenance as required.
4. Provide preventive maintenance training for all electrical and mechanical personnel.

Related Duties:

1. Set up preventive maintenance inspection program checklist for preventive maintenance inspections.
2. Analyze maintenance work orders for recurring problems and solutions to same.
3. Supervise preventive maintenance inspections on machines and machine tools by established schedules.
4. Plan and schedule all preventive maintenance repair work.
5. Research and requisition repair parts as required for preventive maintenance repair work.
6. Aid in machine design and modifications which improve machine performance and capabilities.
7. Inspect completed preventive maintenance repair work to insure that quality maintenance has been performed.
8. Establish and maintain thorough records for all machine repair work.
9. Establish and maintain maintenance cost records for analysis.

Qualifications:

1. Minimum of two years electronics training preferably possessing an Associate Degree in Electronics.
2. Hydraulics training from a recognized hydraulics training program.
3. Minimum of five years of CNC machine tool repair experience.
4. Machinist, NC programming and tooling experience desirable.

FIGURE 3–2(a). Typical Job Description

JOB DESCRIPTION

Job Title: Lift Truck Operator

General Summary:

Under general supervision of shift supervisor, operates the lift truck to support the various manufacturing operations.

Principal Duties and Responsibilities:

1. Retrieves and transports raw materials on a timely basis to each machine according to production order or verbal instruction.
2. Positions raw materials at the desired location to prevent undue delays.
3. Checks raw materials for correct size, amount, type, and degree of quality prior to delivering it to the specified location.
4. Retrieves and transports finished products to specified or predetermined location. Performs a variety of tasks to include:
   a. Stacking or placing material in inventory.
   b. Loading and/or unloading trailers, railcars, and/or other similar shipping vehicles.

Related Duties

1. Conducts daily maintenance checks on lift trucks and fills out maintenance checklist form. Maintenance check includes water level, brakes, oil level, horn, fuel, and any other items on checklist.
2. Performs minor maintenance tasks on lift trucks such as: adding oil, water, brake fluid, and fuel as required.
3. Responsible to observe company safety rules and maintain good housekeeping at all times.
4. Report all needed repairs and adjustments to supervisor.
5. Perform other duties equal to or less than the above duties.

Skills and Abilities Required:

1. Must be able to operate a lift truck.
2. Must satisfactorily complete the Lift Truck Training Program.
3. Must be able to read a micrometer and identify the various types of materials and products required in the specific department of assignment.
4. Must be familiar with the various manufacturing and supporting area locations as related to respective department operations.

FIGURE 3–2(b). Typical Job Description

Working Conditions:

1. Frequently exposed to noise, dust, heat, cold, and fumes.
2. Continuous riding on solid tires against concrete floor.
3. Frequently getting on and off the lift truck.

Equipment Used:

1. Lift truck

FIGURE 3–2(b). Typical Job Description *(continued)*

Review Questions

1. What is a job description?
2. What is a job specification?
3. What are the management uses of job descriptions?
4. What are the legal uses of job descriptions?
5. What are the industrial relations uses of job descriptions?
6. What are the three major categories of information found in a job description?
7. What main principle should be followed in writing job descriptions?
8. What are the headings typically found in a job description?

References

Evered, James, "How to Write a Good Job Description," *Supervisory Management*, April, 1981.

Ghorpade, Jai and Atchison, Thomas J., "The Concept of Job Analysis: A Review and Some Suggestions," *Public Personnel Management Journal*, Volume 9, Number 3, 1984.

Henderson, R., *Compensation Management*, Reston Publishing Company, Inc., Reston, Virginia, 1985.

Klinger, Donald E., "When the Traditional Job Description is Not Enough," *Personnel Journal*, April, 1979.

Walsh, William J., "Writing Job Descriptions: How and Why," *Supervisory Management*, February, 1972.

Zalusky, John, "Job Evaluation: An Uneven World," *AFL-CIO American Federationist*, April, 1981.

Zollitsch, H.G. and Langsner, A., *Wage and Salary Administration*, Southwestern Publishing Company, Cinncinnati, 1970.

Case Study (Mountain View College, continued)

JOB DESCRIPTIONS

     Using the results of the job analyses performed earlier, the personnel director for Mountain View College prepared the job descriptions for the positions indicated at the end of the preceeding chapter. These job descriptions are found on the following pages. It should be noted that the language used in these job descriptions remains consistent from one job description to the next. This is critical and cannot be over-emphasized.

JOB DESCRIPTION AND SPECIFICATION

Job Title: *Departmental Secretary*

Department: *Math*   **Reports to:** *Department Head*

Summary of Job Activities: *Types correspondence, reports, and examinations for department head and departmental faculty. Answers telephone, sorts mail, reproduces exams, and deals with students as they enter the departmental office.*

Major Duties:

60%	*typing*
20%	*reproduction*
10%	*working with faculty/students/telephone*
5%	*filing*
5%	*mail sorting*

Education Requirements: *High School diploma*

Training and Experience Requirements: *Must type at 60cwpm*

Working Conditions: *Typical office; daily hours from 8 am to 5 pm, five days per week*

Equipment: *Standard office equipment;*
Typewriter, Automatic collator, Mimeograph machine

Initiative: *Must be able to handle student problems in absence of department head or other faculty member; Requires very little supervision*

JOB DESCRIPTION AND SPECIFICATION

Job Title: *Records Clerk*

Department: *Registrar*   **Reports to:** *Associate Registrar*

Summary of Job Activities: *Handles, maintains, and processes student records.*

Major Duties:

25%	*send out transcripts and verification forms*
20%	*assist registrar's secretary*
15%	*filing*
10%	*type transfer credit evaluations*
10%	*process graduation petitions and type graduation letters*
10%	*process continuing education transcripts*
5%	*post grade changes to student records*
3%	*microfilm student records*
2%	*type transit letters*

Education Requirements: *High School diploma*

Training and Experience Requirements: *One year's prior office experience; must type at 50cwpm*

Working Conditions: *Typical office; daily hours from 8 am to 4:30 pm, five days per week*

Equipment: *Standard office equipment plus 3M microfilm machine*

Initiative: *Good judgment and maturity required in handling confidential matters; requires little supervision*

JOB DESCRIPTION AND SPECIFICATION

Job Title: *Clerk*

Department: *Admissions*   **Supervisor:** *Associate Director of Admissions*

Summary of Job Activities: *Admissions clerk processes applications of freshmen and transfer credit students to school.*

Major Duties:

8%	*open all mail and distribute to records and admissions sections*
10%	*answer phone calls, provide information*
15%	*work at information window*
5%	*type answers to incoming mail about school*
5%	*type immigration forms for foreign national students*
5%	*set up student departmental rolls for graduation*
5%	*schedule supervisor's appointments*
5%	*mail school catalogs*
5%	*handle SAT test procedures*
2%	*post student grades to transcripts*
25%	*process applications*
5%	*process readmission applications*
1%	*relieve switchboard operator*
4%	*answer questions during registration*

Education Requirements: *High school graduate*

Training and Experience Requirements: *Type at 50cwpm, communication skills, general knowledge of office equipment*

Working Conditions: *Typical multiperson office; daily hours from 8 am to 4:30 pm, five days per week*

Equipment: *Photocopier, typewriter, adding machine, standard office equipment*

Initiative: *Helps students with problems; requires some supervision*

JOB DESCRIPTION AND SPECIFICATION

Job Title: *Clerk*

Department: *Registrar's Office*   **Reports to:** *Associate Registrar*

Summary of Job Activities: *Updates and completes all student records change forms required. Processes all on-campus mail for the supervisor. Assists students at the office information window and via telephone.*

Major Duties:

20%	*process class drop forms*
20%	*process student withdrawal forms*
20%	*process and updates permanent record cards*
15%	*handle departmental on-campus mail*
10%	*assist students at information window*
5%	*answer telephone*
10%	*substitute for other absent employees in registrar's office*

Education Requirements: *Business school graduate*

Training and Experience Requirements: *Minimum of two years' experience in clerical field*

Working Conditions: *Typical office; daily hours from 8 am to 4:30 pm, five days per week*

Equipment: *Standard office equipment*

Initiative: *Must work with and assist students; requires some supervision*

JOB DESCRIPTION AND SPECIFICATION

Job Title: Secretary

Department: Public Relations   **Reports to:** PR Director

Summary of Job Activities: General typing, filing, reproduction, hosting visiting dignitaries.

Major Duties:

60%	typing
5%	newspaper research
5%	filing
10%	telephone answering
20%	hosting/planning media events with PR Director

Education Requirements: High School diploma

Training and Experience Requirements: Two years of college; type at 60cwpm

Working Conditions: Cramped office; daily hours from 8 am to 5 pm, five days per week

Equipment: Typical office equipment

Initiative: Must be able to deal with all levels of people.
Must greet and host campus dignitaries including presidents, mayors, deans, governors, and media representatives; requires little supervision.

JOB DESCRIPTION AND SPECIFICATION

Job Title: *Secretary*

Department: *Dean of Student Affairs*   **Reports to:** *Dean*

Summary of Job Activities: *Secretary to dean of student affairs types correspondence, reports, and minutes of student activity committees. Provides additional secretarial support to intramural athletic program. Deals with student emergencies.*

Major Duties:

35%	*typing correspondence, memos, and various reports*
25%	*screening telephone calls; handling inquiries from students, parents, and public*
10%	*maintaining student information files for students, fraternities and sororities, and student clubs*
15%	*maintaining records for the intramural athletic program*
15%	*locating students for emergency calls*
	validating student i.d. cards
	substituting for switchboard operator in emergencies

Education Requirements: *High School diploma*

Training and Experience Requirements: *Five or more years' experience as a secretary*

Working Conditions: *Typical office; daily hours from 8 am to 5 pm, five days per week*

Equipment: *Standard office equipment*

Initiative: *Judgment and maturity required in handling confidential and sensitive matters involving students; requires very little supervision.*

JOB DESCRIPTION AND SPECIFICATION

Job Title: *Secretary*

Department: *Registrar*   **Reports to:** *Registrar*

Summary of Job Activities: *Secretary to registrar performs all normal secretarial duties and assists the registrar with routing administrative matters.*

Major Duties:

40%	*orders diplomas, prepares graduation programs, and assists in graduation exercises*
10%	*supervisor to other employees in records*
5%	*orders office supplies and forms*
20%	*typing*
5%	*handles time card data*
10%	*works with associate registrar in developing registration procedures*
10%	*processes minutes of faculty meetings*

Education Requirements: *Two years of business college*

Training or Experience Requirements: *Five or more years' experience; type at 50cwpm*

Working Conditions: *Typical office; daily hours from 8 am to 5 pm, five days per week*

Equipment: *Standard office equipment*

Initiative: *Must work well with others, must occasionally act in the registrar's absence, must be able to supervise other clerical and student help.*

JOB DESCRIPTION AND SPECIFICATION

Job Title: Secretary

Department: Academic Dean   **Reports to:** Dean

Summary of Job Activities: Functions as secretary to the dean of the college. Serves as secretary to the entire academic organization within the college. Performs standard secretarial duties in this role.

Major Duties:

5%	answers and places phone calls for the dean
5%	logs in daily mail and distributes it to appropriate administrators
5%	makes all appointments for the dean
35%	types reports, budgets, memos, and general correspondence
5%	prepares campus-wide reports and reproduces and distributes these reports
5%	maintains policy and procedure notebooks
15%	maintains files
10%	assists academic divisions as necessary
10%	prepares committee reports for dean
5%	operates switchboard if necessary

Education Requirements: Associate Degree

Training and Experience Requirements: Two years' office experience; shorthand, type 60cwpm

Working Conditions: Typical office; daily hours from 8 am to 5 pm, five days per week

Equipment: Standard office equipment plus word processor

Initiative: Resourceful, practical, able to grasp new methods. Must be able to work well with others; represents dean to visitors upon their arrival; requires very little supervision.

JOB DESCRIPTION AND SPECIFICATION

Job Title: *Library Assistant*

Department: *Library*   **Reports to:** *Library Director*

Summary of Job Activities: *Maintains music room equipment and supplies, assists in cataloging books and other reading material, performs duties associated with circulation desk operation.*

Major Duties:

30%	*staffs front desk in music room*
5%	*prepares acquisitions forms for records/tapes*
5%	*catalogs records/tapes*
5%	*maintains (provide for maintenance) music room equipment*
5%	*maintains alumni donor records*
5%	*prepares thank you letters for donations*
15%	*assists in cataloging incoming books and reading material*
30%	*staffs circulation desk*

Education Requirements: *Two years of college*

Training and Experience Requirements: *One year experience in library related work; knowledge of typing*

Working Conditions: *Typical office-type environment; daily hours from 9 am to 6 pm, five days per week*

Equipment: *Standard office equipment; high fidelity and stereo equipment*

Initiative: *Capable of working with minimal supervision. Must adjust to changes as they occur.*

JOB DESCRIPTION AND SPECIFICATION

Job Title: Library Assistant—Senior

Department: Library   **Reports to:** Library Director

Summary of Job Activities: Processes all book acquisitions and maintains pertinent records, maintains library financial records, serves as liaison for interlibrary loan program.

Major Duties:

10%	maintains listing of newly published books
10%	maintains requests from faculty for selected publications
10%	orders publications
20%	supervises cataloging of incoming books
20%	performs bookkeeping services for library
15%	maintains microfiche for interlibrary loan programs
10%	staffs circulation desk
5%	recommends procurement of additional material for library

Education Requirements: Two years of college

Training and Experience Requirements: Five years' experience in related field; basic typing skills of 30cwpm; basic bookkeeping skills

Working Conditions: Excellent environment; must work split schedule with night duty and weekend duty as well

Equipment: Typewriter and other standard office equipment

Initiative: Responsible for supervision of student assistants. Responsible for operation of library in absence of library director.

JOB DESCRIPTION AND SPECIFICATION

Job Title: *Accountant*

Department: *Business Office* **Reports to:** *Accounting Supervisor*

Summary of Job Activities: *Makes all necessary transactions and keeps all records for supplying all college departments with equipment and funding necessary for their operation.*

Major Duties:

84%	*processes all requests for purchases of supplies and capital equipment*
5%	*processes all requests for authority to travel and travel expense statements*
4%	*prepares student salary check information*
3%	*maintains service contracts on office equipment for the college*
1%	*places employment advertisements*
1%	*arranges for postage permits*
1%	*prepares cash deposit records for registration fee payments*
1%	*maintains petty cash system*

Education Requirements: *Two years of business school*

Training and Experience Requirements: *Two years' bookkeeping experience; certification as notary public*

Working Conditions: *Typical office; daily hours from 8 am to 4:30 pm, five days per week*

Equipment: *Standard office equipment*

Initiative: *Considerable initiative required since work is done almost entirely without supervision.*

Case Study 3–1

LIFETIME INSURANCE COMPANY

Upon being promoted to supervisor of the Industrial Claims Department, J. Williams discovered that her secretary was indispensible to the operation of the office. The secretary, because of her individual competence, skill, and initiative had assumed more difficult duties, in terms of skills and responsibilities, than the existing job description required. She had made herself invaluable to running the department and to the success of Williams on her new job. Williams recognized this and immediately began working to upgrade her secretary's job to the position of Administrative Assistant.

As the first step in the process Williams obtained a job description of an Administrative Assistant in another department and rewrote her secretary's job description so that it sound exactly like the Administrative Assistant's. The second step was to document the activities the secretary had performed that were in line with the new job description. After the package was prepared it was submitted to the Wage and Salary Administrator.

Williams was upset to learn that the upgrade had been denied.

Discussion

1. Why might the request have been denied?
2. What might Williams have done to assure the upgrade?
3. Is this "job building" an understandable part of a supervisor's job? Why?
4. How does job building harm wage and salary structures?
5. How can Lifetime Insurance ensure that there will be no further job building?
6. What effect does job building have on the wage structure, especially regarding other departments?

Case Study 3–2

JOB DESCRIPTION EXERCISE

Listed below are some of the various job titles found in a manufacturing plant. Use the DICTIONARY OF OCCUPATIONAL TITLES to prepare job descriptions for these positions.

Assembler	Plater
Finisher	Quality Control Inspector
Grinder	Repairman
Light Assembler	Senior Clerk
Line Inspector	Senior Inspector
Machine Operator	Setup Man
Maintenance Man	Shipping Clerk
Material Handler	Utility Operator

"Turner, you'll be playing a pivotal role in our organization."

Chapter Four

JOB EVALUATION

INTRODUCTION

Job analysis and the preparation of job descriptions are important parts of determining the relative worth of jobs to an organization. Job evaluation is the actual process that determines the jobs' values. There are many techniques used to evaluate jobs. All of them have in common an underlying assumption that this relative value of the job can be ascertained from information contained in the job description. Each of the methodologies, to some degree, is also subjective. Regardless though of the techniques used, the purpose of job evaluation is to determine what the rate of pay for one job should be in proper relation to the rates of pay for other jobs in the same plant or organization.

This chapter will examine four of the frequently used methods of job evaluation. Two of these are non-quantitative: the ranking method and the job classification method. Two are quantitative in nature: the factor comparison method and the point method. Each of these methods evaluates the jobs and not the people. Each of these methods of job evaluation requires a good, well-written, job description for the job being evaluated.

RANKING METHOD

Job ranking is the simplest of all the job evaluation methods. Using the job descriptions developed by the wage and salary analyst, each job within the organization is compared to every other job in the organization. The relative worth of the jobs are compared based on the entire job. The ranking is commonly performed by top management based on its perception of the relative value of the job to the organization. The results of the process are the same as if each job were described on an index card and the evaluator arranged the cards so that the most valuable job was on top and the least valuable on the bottom. The jobs would be compensated based on their relative position in this stack.

As with each of the methods of job evaluations, there are advantages and disadvantages to using each. The simplicity of the ranking method makes it easily understood both by local union officers and by the membership and makes it hard for the company or its consultant to confuse them with technical jargon. Another advantage is that it works well where there are just a few jobs that must be evaluated. In a small organization where almost all the employees know almost all the jobs, consensus can usually be reached quite quickly regarding the relative standing of each job. Ranking, once the job descriptions are prepared, is also an inexpensive way to evaluate jobs. Finally, by considering the whole job rather than breaking its content into factors, this method helps to ensure that nothing of significance is overlooked.

Some disadvantages to job ranking include the fact that the ranking is completely subjective. Different people within an organization have different perceptions of different jobs' relative worth based primarily upon their position within the organization. Whether the production worker who assembles the product or the salesperson who sells it is more important depends, naturally, on who is evaluating. (Is it more important to sell the product or have the product to sell?) Job ranking is difficult when there are many jobs that need to be ranked. Even with well-written job descriptions it may be difficult for the evaluator to really know all of the jobs in a large organization. A third disadvantage of ranking is that ranking does not measure nor indicate the distance between jobs ranked. When pay is determined a more precise measure of the relative worth of jobs may be required. "For example, the ranking of a janitor, a laborer, and a tool and die maker might create an impression that the differences between the janitor and the laborer are the same as the differences between the laborer and the tool and die maker." (Zalusky:14)

JOB CLASSIFICATION

The second non-quantitative method for job evaluation is the job classification method. When this method is used the first step is to determine a number of labor grades or classifications within which to group jobs. Each job in a particular class would be worth the same amount, or have the same relative worth, to the organization. The second step is to identify a number of typical, representative, or "key" jobs. These benchmark jobs, which everyone in the organization is familiar with, serve as standards for all the jobs in the organization. After the key jobs are identified, these jobs are ranked according to their relative worth. This ranking is similar to the ranking performed in the ranking method of job evaluation. Once the key jobs are ranked according to relative worth, the remaining jobs are classified as being the "same as" one of the key jobs. For example, "in simplest terms, three labor grades could be defined as unskilled, semi-skilled, and skilled, and use janitor, drill press operator, and machinist as [key job] examples. It would be fairly easy to slot the laborer, fork-lift operator, and electrician into the appropriate labor [and pay] grade using this simple plan." (Zalusky:14) Most job classification systems set up twelve to fifteen job categories.

Advantages of this job evaluation method include the ease in understanding by all employees. It is especially effective in small firms because it is also easy to use. It also uses the entire job and would not overlook certain aspects of the job. Revision can be easily accomplished. Finally, the job evaluation system, because it uses the company's benchmark jobs, generally meets the needs of the organization.

There are also disadvantages to using the job classification evaluation system. First of these is that the selection of number of different categories and the ranking of the key jobs is subjective. The ability to show jobs correctly depends upon the job descriptions. The blanket ranking of a job has few concrete and consistent factors to justify the ranking. Second, some jobs may fall into more than one job classification. Some duties may be highly skilled as, for example, the maintenance position that must repair broken electrical equipment but which also must sweep floors. Finally, as the organization grows, there may be new jobs that don't fit any of the existing categories or the volume of jobs created may exceed the job knowledge of the evaluator.

Non-quantitative job evaluation procedures can be useful in small organizations or when jobs logically arrange themselves in groupings. However, not all organizations' jobs fit these special conditions. Two systems have been developed that attempt to remove some of the subjectivity from the evaluation process. This is done by the use of numerical, or quantitative evaluation.

FACTOR COMPARISON METHOD
(KEY JOB METHOD)

The factor comparison method provides a quantified method for establishing the relative worth of the key jobs. All other jobs are compared to the key jobs based on subdivisions, or factors, that are present in all jobs being evaluated. A number of steps are involved in using the factor comparison method.

First of these is the identification of the key jobs. Key jobs have the following characteristics:

1. Key jobs must be representative of the jobs found within the organization. They must be selected from all the jobs found in the company, both high and low paid. They must be paid fairly.
2. Key jobs should be jobs that are well-known throughout the organization. These jobs should be familiar to everyone within the company.
3. The job descriptions for these key jobs must be available, complete, and up to date.

Second, after the key jobs are identified, the factors must be determined. Factors are components of jobs that are believed to be present, to some extent, in all the jobs in an organization. The factors most frequently used are mental requirements, skill requirements, physical requirements, responsibility, and working conditions. Each application would have its own number of factors. Some, such as the U.S. Government Job Classification Method, use as few as three factors: difficulty, responsibility, and qualifications. Some systems use as many as seven factors, but the five mentioned: mental requirements, skill requirements, physical requirements, responsibility, and working conditions are most frequently used.

Once the factors have been determined they must be defined. The definitions must be understood and agreed upon by all people performing the evaluation.

Third, after the factors are identified and defined, the key jobs are evaluated. Each key job is examined to determine, relatively speaking, how much of each factor is present in each job as compared with the other key jobs. The key jobs are ranked on a factor by factor basis. For example, an organization which had three key jobs and used a five-factor system would rank each of the jobs, from top to bottom, for each of the factors. The final ranking might look as shown in Figure 4–1.

The fourth step in job evaluation using the factor comparison method is the conversion of the ranking into dollars. This process uses the existing wage rates for the key jobs. The rates are proportioned based upon the ranking of the factors. For example, if job A in Figure 4–1 is paid $11.00 per hour, then the mental factor is worth (3/11) of $11.00, or $3.00. Similarly, if job B normally earns $8.00 per hour, then this factor is worth (2/10) of $8.00, or $1.60. For job C, paid at the rate of $4.50 per hour, the mental factor is

Key Job No.	Factor Mental	Skill	Physical	Responsibility	Conditions	Total
A	3	3	1	3	1	11
B	2	1	3	2	2	10
C	1	2	2	1	3	9

(3 is top ranking)

FIGURE 4–1. Sample Key Job Rankings

	Graded Money Rates					
Key Job No.	Factor Mental	Skill	Physical	Responsibility	Conditions	Total
A	3.00	3.00	1.00	3.00	1.00	11.00
B	1.60	.80	2.40	1.60	1.60	8.00
C	.50	1.00	1.00	.50	1.50	4.50

FIGURE 4–2. Graded Money Rates

worth (1/9) of $4.50, or $.50. These graded money rates can be similarly calculated for each factor for each of the key jobs. This is shown in Figure 4–2.

After the graded money rates are determined, the fifth step is to evaluate all the other jobs in the organization. In this process each job is compared to the key jobs, on a factor by factor basis, to determine which job it most closely resembles. The graded money rates for each job are then matched with the appropriate factors and the pay, or relative worth, of the job is determined.

For example, using the job evaluation system shown in Figures 4–1 and 4–2, a fourth job, job D, was evaluated based on the five factors. It was decided that the mental requirements for this job most closely resembled job B; the skill requirements were closest to A; the physical requirements closest also to A; responsibility was also comparable to A; and working conditions were similar to C. Job D would be paid (and worth) the following:

Mental Requirements	$1.60
Skill	3.00
Physical	1.00
Responsibility	3.00
Working Conditions	1.50
	$10.10 per hour

This analysis must be performed for each job in the organization.

Advantages of using the Factor Comparison Method include the fact that each of the factor comparison methods is developed specifically for the organization using it. The use of the benchmark or key jobs as a basis for comparison is also an advantage. Finally, the relative ease in use does not require the organization to maintain a highly trained specialist to evaluate jobs.

A number of disadvantages have also been suggested. The major disadvantage of the factor comparison type of plan is that it is complex and expensive to construct. A second disadvantage lies with the key jobs. In order for this type of plan to cover all the appropriate jobs in an organization, there must be a reasonable number of key jobs that can be identified as being representative of the work done in the organization. There is also the problem of job content changing over time. If key jobs change, then the pay scales for these jobs become suspect as the wage determinant for the other jobs. A final disadvantage is the subjectivity in ranking the job factors. This may be difficult to explain, and in the final analysis, depends upon the job evaluator's judgment.

POINT METHOD

The fourth method of job evaluation, and the most widely used method, is the point plan. The quantitative plan attempts to limit the amount of subjectivity required in evaluating jobs.

The point plan uses factors, as described in the factor comparison method of job evaluation. Instead of comparing factors on a job-by-job basis, the factors are subdivided into what are known as degrees. Degrees show to what extent a factor is present in a particular job. Degrees are stated so explicitly that judgment should not be required to place factors in the appropriate degrees. The factors used in the point plan are usually more specific than the five factors commonly used in the factor comparison method. These five may be stated as major factors with further subdivisions or subfactors used. Figure 4–3(a), the American Association of Industrial Management Job Evaluation Plan, shows some typical factors used in point plans of job evaluation. These factors need to be selected based on the general nature of the jobs that will be evaluated.

The following are descriptions of factors as originally described in the American Association of Industrial Management (National Metal Trades Association) Job Evaluation Plan.

EDUCATION: This factor measures the basic trades training or knowledge or "scholastic contact" essential as background or training preliminary to learning the job duties. This job knowledge or background may have been acquired either by formal education or by training on jobs of lesser degree or by any combination of these approaches.

EXPERIENCE: This factor measures the minimum length of time it would take a "normal qualified" person working under "normal" supervision to attain quality and quantity performance standards. Do not include scholastic or job knowledge considerations which have been rated under Education or any additional time after competency is reached.

INITIATIVE AND INGENUITY: This factor measures the independent action, use of judgment, the making of decisions and the amount of resourcefulness and planning the job requires as determined by the complexity of the duties performed.

PHYSICAL DEMAND: This factor measures the kind, amount, and frequency of the physical effort required to perform all the job duties; and the work position in which the effort is applied in handling material, parts, tools, equipment, and in operating equipment, machines, processes, and apparatus. Periods of physical inactivity must be taken into consideration.

MENTAL OR VISUAL DEMAND: This factor measures the degree of mental and/or visual fatigue sustained through the application of mind and eye in performing all of the job duties. Consider the volume and complexity of the work, cycle of application of mental and visual faculties and the intensity of such application.

RESPONSIBILITY FOR EQUIPMENT OR PROCESS: This factor measures the responsibility for preventing damage, due to employee's mistake or carelessness, to the equipment or process used in the performance of the job. Consider the PROBABLE amount of damage resulting from improper handling, set-up, operation, etc., for any one mishap.

RESPONSIBILITY FOR MATERIAL OR PRODUCT: This factor measures the responsibility for preventing loss which may result from negligent inspection or testing; from spoilage or wastage of raw, in process and finished materials; or from damage to physical facilities being installed, moved, or maintained. Consider the PROBABLE amount of loss before detection and correction in any one operation, or within any one work day or within the inspection period if shorter than one work day in any lot or run. Take into account the quantity, weight, or volume involved, the extent of spoilage, wastage or damage and the possibility of salvage, all in terms of manufacturing costs. Do not use either maximum or minimum, but an average based on normal expectation.

FIGURE 4—3(a). AAIM Job Factors

RESPONSIBILITY FOR SAFETY OF OTHERS: This factor measures the responsibility for carefulness to prevent injury to others which the nature of the job places upon the employee, after making allowance for and giving consideration to the fact that safety devices provided and furnished by the Company are to be properly used and that published safety rules are to be adhered to. Injury to the employee on the job being rated is credited under Hazards. Consider: Can the employee on the job injure others through careless operation of the machine, inattention or thoughtlessness; failure to safeguard work area or warn others of hazards? If so, how and the PROBABLE extent of such injury?

RESPONSIBILITY FOR WORK OF OTHERS: This factor measures the responsibility incident to the job for setting up and checking the work of others, assisting and instructing them, and directing and maintaining the flow of their work. It is not intended to appraise supervisory responsibility for results.

WORKING CONDITIONS: This factor measures the surrounding or physical conditions under which the job must be done and the extent to which they make the job disagreeable. Consider the presence, relative amount of, and continuity of exposure to dust, dirt, heat, fumes, cold, noise, vibration, water, oil, etc.

HAZARDS: This factor measures the hazards connected with the job after making allowances for all protective devices that have been installed or furnished and for compliance with prescribed safety rules and regulations. Consider the material handled; the tools, equipment or apparatus used; the work locations; the utilization of the safety devices provided; and the PROBABLE extent of injury should an accident occur.

Reprinted with permission AAIM Headquarters Willow Grove, Pennsylvania

FIGURE 4—3(a).   AAIM Job Factors *(continued)*

The following describe the degrees associated with the American Association of Industrial Management (National Metal Trades Association) Job Evaluation Plan Factor for INITIATIVE AND INGENUITY.

1st Degree

Requires the use of little judgment to follow instructions, using simple equipment in performing duties where the employee is told what to do and has little or no choice as to the procedures used in achieving results.

2nd Degree

Requires the use of some judgment to comply with instructions and standard procedures, methods or practices involving the making of minor decisions.

3rd Degree

Requires the use of judgment to plan, perform, and make decisions as to the sequence of set-ups, operations and processes within the limitations of recognized or standard methods and procedures.

4th Degree

Requires the use of considerable judgment to plan and perform unusual and difficult work where only general methods are available, and the making of broad decisions involving considerable initiative and ingenuity.

5th Degree

Requires the use of outstanding judgment, initiative and ingenuity to work independently toward ultimate objectives on very involved and complex jobs, to devise methods and procedures to meet unusual conditions and to make original contributions to solution of complex problems.

Reprinted with permission AAIM Headquarters Willow Grove, Pennsylvania

FIGURE 4–3(b).   AAIM Job Evaluation Degrees

After the factors have been selected and defined, the degrees of each factor must also be defined (Figure 4–3(b)). Subjective words or phrases such as "some education" must be avoided. For example, a factor of education may be defined as:

Education: Number of years of formal schooling required for the individual to meet the minimum entry-level requirements of the job.

The degrees need to be stated explicitly, such as:

First Degree: Grade School Diploma

Second Degree: High School Diploma

Third Degree: Business School or Vo-Tech Diploma

Fourth Degree: Associate Degree from Accredited College

Fifth Degree: Bachelor's Degree from Accredited College

Sixth Degree: Master's Degree from Accredited College

Seventh Degree: Earned Doctorate

The lowest degree should include the minimum qualifications needed by an individual to work for the organization. There should not be any open ended degrees. (Although in practice this is sometimes necessary.) Experience may have the highest degree of "20 or more years performing comparable work."

Once all the factors are known (there may be as many as 15 or 20 factors in a point plan, although 7 to 10 is much more common) and the degrees are defined, the factors and degrees are weighted, or assigned points. A judgment must be made regarding the relative worth of each factor. For example, education may be worth 20%, skill 40%, experience 15%, and so forth. Weights are often expressed as percentages of the total available and converted to points. (Zalusky:16) Thus, the total points assigned to the first degree often total 100 (it is convenient). Points are assigned to higher degrees by one of two generally followed conventions.

Each succeeding degree may show its points increasing by an arithmetic or geometric progression. When an arithmetic progression is used the points increase by a constant amount from degree to degree. For example, a factor worth 20 points in degree 1 may increase by a constant factor of 20 points—and may be worth 40 points in degree 2; 60 points in degree 3; and so on. The total points for the degree would increase in a corresponding fashion. The first degree would total 100 points, the second 200 points, etc.

When a geometric progression is used the points increase by a constant ratio from degree to degree. This yields a larger spread in possible points. For example, if a ratio of 2 is used, and the weight of the first degree is 15 points for a given factor, the weight of the second degree would be two times that, or 30 points. The same factor would be applied between the second and third degrees. The weight for the third degree would be twice the weight for the second, or 60 points. Similarly, the fourth degree would be two times the third, or 120 points. Correspondingly, the total for each degree would be twice the preceeding, or 100, 200, 400, 800, and so forth.

USING THE POINT PLAN

Once all of the factors and degrees have been defined and the points assigned to each of these, the point plan is ready to be used. Before a wholesale evaluation of jobs is performed it is advisable to evaluate, on a trial basis, a number of representative and key jobs. If the plan is properly designed then the relative standing of these key jobs should not be altered. If there is an extreme reordering of the jobs, then the job evaluation system must be revised. If the evaluations are within expectations, then the point plan can be implemented.

The following steps are often followed when jobs are evaluated with the point plan. First of all, the job description for each of the jobs is examined to make sure that it is an accurate description of the work being performed. Then each job is examined, on a factor-by-factor basis, to determine which degree that job fits into for each factor. The results of this analysis should be documented. Using complete and well-written job descriptions makes this justification fairly easy. For example, if a job description specifies that a four-year accounting degree is required for a particular job, then the justification for assigning that job to the corresponding degree in the education factor would be as follows:

Factor/Degree	Points	Justification
Education/5	60	Four-year college degree required

A similar justification should be performed for each job for each factor. The factor/degree definitions, when combined with the job descriptions, virtually remove judgment from the evaluation process. Figure 4–4 shows a job description (a) and evaluation (b).

After each job is evaluated for each degree, the assigned points can be totaled. After all the jobs are evaluated the point totals show the relative worth of each job. The clerical and secretarial jobs at Mountain View College that were described at the end of Chapter Three are evaluated at the end of this chapter. In the next chapter the process of converting the points into absolute worth, or dollars, will be examined.

Often the factor and degree definitions, along with the job descriptions and the factor/degree evaluations, comprise what is known as the job evaluation manual. The complete manual includes the data on pricing the jobs as well as the evaluation information compiled thus far.

The point plan of job evaluation has its advantages and disadvantages. On the positive side is the consistency of job evaluations. Because the factors and degrees are so well defined, there is little room for subjective judgment in evaluating jobs. Everyone who reads the same job descriptions and the same factor/degree definitions should evaluate the jobs the same way. A second advantage often cited is that jobs are evaluated before the jobs are assigned monetary values. This can remove money from the evaluation process and make the job evaluation process less "emotional."

A third advantage is that by the selection of the appropriate numbers of factors and degrees the system can be tailored to fit each individual organization. Most authorities believe there is less chance of making rating errors or manipulating the ratings because the ratings and their basis can be easily understood by most employees.

Among the disadvantages is that the plans must be tailored for each organization. Although organizations such as American Association of Industrial Management—AAIM (formerly known as the

Job Rating Standard

Blanko Corporation   Code No. ___x 100_____
Anytown, U.S.A.
                                                          Total Points __281_____

Job Title __Grinder—Rough (Castings)_____

Department __49—Grinding_____ Section __Foundry_____

| Job Description | Grinds gates, fins, burrs, roughness, etc., from a wide variety of castings such as small blanks attachments to large commercial castings using stand grinder. Checks castings to determine size and type of grinding wheel to use, to perform specified operation according to previous instructions and with proper wheel, first sounding for cracks, places safety washer correctly, and tightens retaining nut. Dresses wheel when necessary with a star wheel dresser to obtain proper wheel surface, and adjusts rest to proper height and distance from wheel to accommodate size of work, or compensate for wheel wear.

Shovels castings into pan at machine and manually holds casting between rest and wheel manipulating part in most efficient manner to remove excessive metal. Places ground castings in barrel, and when completed separates grinder's and packer's tickets, places packer's ticket on barrel and rolls barrel out to be trucked to next operation. Occasionally uses hand air grinder for setting types of grinding and burring such as large flat hard iron plates, and inside of scoops and toehr castings that can not be reached by conventional stand grinder. |

Factor	Rating	Basis of Rating

FIGURE 4–4(a).   Job Description

Job Rating Standard

Blanko Corporation

Anytown, U.S.A.

Code No. __x 100__

Total Points __281__

Job Title __Grinder – Rough (Castings)__

Department __49 – Grinding__   Section __Foundry__

	Factor	Rating	Basis of Rating
SKILL	1 General Knowledge	1 (5)	Requires the ability to understand English, understand and carry out specific oral instructions and recognize signs.
	2 Experience	4 (48)	Requires 6 to 9 months experience to perform routine semi-skilled work of grinding fins, burrs, gates, etc., from a wide variety of Blanko attachments and castings using various sizes and types of grinding wheels on stand grinder and hand air grinder.
	3 Judgment	3 (21)	Some judgment required on standardized rough grinding operations where variations in location of burrs, fins, gates, etc., on a wide variety of Blanko attachments and castings. Involves making decisions such as correct grinding wheel to use, distance between wheel and rest and type of rest best suited for job and maximum production.
	4 Initiative & Ingenuity	2 (14)	Performs work of grinding gates, fins, burrs, etc., off castings, according to limited detailed instructions in following standard grinding methods but makes occasional changes in grinding rests and set-ups to grind castings in more efficient manner.
	5 Manual Dexterity	4 (24)	Considerable manual skill and speed in the use of fingers, hands, and arms on repetitive operations of holding castings between rest and grinding wheel and manipulating part in most efficient manner and against wheel without use of grinding rest and burring of Blanko attachment where burrs are ground off by rapid touching of head and open end on side of wheel.
	6 Accuracy	2 (16)	Moderate accuracy required in performance of rough grinding duties involving removal of fins, burrs, gates, etc., from a wide variety of castings where care must be taken to insure removal of the proper amount of metal.
	7 Physical Activity	4 (28)	Sustained repetitive physical activity in manipulating Blanko attachments and castings between rest and wheel and burring of Blanko attachments and castings on wheel when rest is not used. Requires manual pressure for all types of grinding.
	8 Strength	5 (25)	Requires the strength and physical activity to constantly handle castings weigh-weighing up to 5 lb. and lift 30 to 50 lb m

(See Figure IV for Job Description)

FIGURE 4–4(b).   Using the Point Plan

81

National Metal Trades Association, the National Electrical Manufacturers' Association, and the Life Office Management Association, among others, have developed uniform point plans, these must be modified for each organization that uses them. This may require a substantial investment, as compared with other methods of job evaluation. Another disadvantage is the relatively large amount of managerial time required to evaluate the jobs. The documentation required in the job manual—justifying the degree for each factor for each job, can be costly to compile. Finally, after a point plan is established it is difficult to change or modify. Small changes tend to disrupt the entire structure and may affect many jobs. Most organizations, it has been argued, are hesitant to rock the boat over small changes in scale definition or weights. Actually the point system accommodates new jobs very easily and also changes in content.

SELECTING A METHOD
OF JOB EVALUATION

The four common methods of job evaluation: ranking, classification, factor comparison, and the point plan have been examined. Each has its advantages and disadvantages. The following section suggests a method for selecting the job evaluation procedure that best fits an organization's needs.

Before any job evaluation plan can be selected, some important points need to be emphasized.

1. Jobs peculiar to some industries hold an established hierarchical position in the wage structure that must be accommodated by whatever evaluation plan is used. (For example, the job of stringer in the piano industry is expected to rate highly among production jobs.)
2. A job evaluation plan must give at least some consideration to the dominant employers in a given city or area.
3. The influence of any single employer dominating a small community must be considered in the selection of a plan.

Remembering these special influences the following criteria have been suggested to try to guide the selection process.

- *Validity*—The technical soundness of the plan is important. The system used must evaluate jobs consistently. If employees complain about inconsistencies, then obviously the system is not evaluating jobs validly. It depends on basis of complaints.

- *Practicality*—The method used must fit the organization. Just because the wage and salary analyst knows one system really well does not mean it will fit the jobs within an organization. It would be a waste of resources, for example, for a mail house employing 10 people to use a point plan with 11 factors and 6 degrees.
- *Acceptability*—Whatever plan is adopted it must be acceptable to workers, the union, and management. While union attitudes will be examined in more detail later in this chapter, the highly complex methods make employees suspicious of management. For any system to work it must be understood by first-line management so that these supervisors can explain and, if need be, defend the system.
- *Maintainability*—The system, even though it may be designed by competent consultants, must be maintained by the organization's personnel. There must be present, within the organization, people competent to operate and maintain the system after the consultants leave.
- *Applicability*—The system that is selected must apply to the jobs within the organization. There are plants that have been specifically designed for general-salaried jobs, supervisory jobs, accounting positions, and technical positions. Just because a system is available does not mean that all the jobs in the organization will automatically fit that system.

All job evaluation systems have the same objective: to ensure that jobs are paid commensurate with their status in the organizational hierarchy. The system selected should fit the needs of the organization using it. If the factors of validity, practicality, acceptability, maintainability, and applicability are considered, then a job evaluation method that is workable can be installed and used by an organization.

UNIONS AND JOB EVALUATION

"Unions are faced with two basic questions when dealing with job evaluation . . . . First, whether job evaluation will enhance or limit collective bargaining on basic wages issues; second, whether job evaluation helps equal pay for work of comparable value." (Zausky: 20) Although some unions, such as the United Steel Workers, have successfully used job evaluation in their collective bargaining agreements, organized labor has voiced a number of specific concerns about job evaluation over the years.

The two most critical problems unions voice regarding job evaluation are first, that the plan is not understood by the employees and second, that the plan is not kept up to date. Other concerns stated by various labor officials include the following:

- Job evaluation alone does not give a sufficient basis for setting relative job values.
- Job evaluation is unsound because the relative values of jobs cannot be determined from the job duties alone.
- Point rating plans are frequently objectionable because they attempt to eliminate the use of judgment.
- Poorly written job descriptions and specifications are used as the basis for evaluation. They describe what should be rather than what really is.

But despite these concerns, unions have very seldom really opposed job evaluation, provided it is not used as the sole criteria for establishing wages or as a substitute for the process of collective bargaining. It is important that job evaluation be differentiated from job pricing in the minds of the labor leaders. There must be a relationship developed between jobs before the dollar worth of the jobs is established. This dollar worth can be established in a variety of ways, including collective bargaining, as long as the hierarchy of positions is maintained.

SUMMARY

Job evaluation is the process of determining the relative worth of the jobs within an organization or within one type of job classification, such as general production work. The relative worth of the jobs is determined from the results of the job analysis. This is or must be documented in the job description. The relative standing of the jobs is then used as the basis for determining the appropriate pay levels of the positions evaluated. It must be remembered that job evaluation is a tool—not an end in itself. Every plan is a subjective creation that can yield unacceptable results. But when properly developed and used, job evaluation provides valuable and necessary information for the wage and salary administration function.

Review Questions

1. What is job evaluation?
2. Describe the job ranking method of job evaluation.

3. Discuss the advantages and disadvantages of the ranking method of job evaluation.
4. Describe the job classification method of job evaluation.
5. Discuss the advantages and disadvantages of the classification method of job evaluation.
6. What is a benchmark job?
7. What is a key job?
8. Describe the factor comparison method of job evaluation.
9. Discuss the advantages and disadvantages of the factor comparison method of job evaluation.
10. What are three characteristics of key jobs?
11. What are factors?
12. Describe the point system of job evaluation.
13. What is a degree?
14. How are points assigned to degrees in the point plan of job evaluation?
15. What is a job evaluation manual?
16. What criteria must be considered when selecting a job evaluation method?
17. How do unions view job evaluation?
18. Which method of job evaluation is the most widely used?

References

Akalin, M.T. and Hassan, M. Z., "How Successful is Job Evaluation—A Survey," *IE*, March, 1971.

Hay, Edward N., "The Attitude of the American Federation of Labor on Job Evaluation," *Personnel Journal*, volume 26, 1947.

Janes, Harold D., "Union Views on Job Evaluation: 1971 vs 1978," *Personnel Journal*, February, 1979.

Risher, Howard, "Job Evaluation: Mystical or Statistical," *Personnel*, September-October, 1978.

Saver, R.L., "Selecting the Best Job Evaluation Plan," *IE*, March, 1971.

Zalusky, John, "Job Evaluation: An Uneven World," AFL-CIO *American Federationist*, April, 1981.

Zollitsch, H.G. and Langsner, A., *Wage and Salary Administration*, Southwestern Publishing Company, Cincinnati, 1970.

Case Study (Mountain View College, continued)

MOUNTAIN VIEW COLLEGE

> Mountain View College elected to use the point plan of job evaluation to determine the relative worth of the secretarial/clerical jobs at the college. Because these jobs are similar in nature, this is an appropriate use of this type of system.
>
> The following factors were selected as being applicable to these jobs: education; experience and training; skill; working conditions; supervision; initiative and ingenuity; and interpersonal relations. For each of the factors six degrees were defined. Each of these factors, its degrees, and its definitions is shown on the following pages.

Factor 1: Education

> **Definition:** This factor describes the minimum educational requirements necessary for the worker to successfully perform the job. The education is the result of a formal school program at an accredited institution.

Degree	Requirements	Points
1st	No education required	10
2nd	Elementary school diploma required	12
3rd	High school diploma required	14
4th	Business school/VoTech diploma required	16
5th	Associate Degree required	18
6th	Bachelor's Degree required	20

Factor 2: Experience and Training

> **Definition:** This factor describes the minimum prior experience required or the amount of on-the-job training required for the worker to successfully perform the job. Work performed during this training must be of a high enough quality to justify the continued employment of the worker.

Degree	Requirements	Points
1st	Three months or less	30
2nd	Over three months but less than one year	36
3rd	Over one year but less than three years	42
4th	Over three years but less than four years	48
5th	Over four years but less than five years	54
6th	Over five years; must be capable of training others in the same job	60

Factor 3: Skill

Definition: *This factor describes the basic skills required for the worker to successfully perform the job. Skills must produce work that meets minimum performance standards.*

Degree	Requirements	Points
1st	Routine clerical operations such as filing, sorting, and collating written material	20
2nd	Use of standard office equipment such as calculators, adding machines, photocopying machines and reproduction equipment where routine of operations is well defined	24
3rd	Use of standard office equipment for clerical work which requires high speed and accuracy or where the routine is not well defined	28
4th	Clerical work which includes dictation and stenographic duties, composition of letters for superior's signatures, schedule and arrange appointments, and is proficient at operating all standard office equipment including electric and electronic typewriters	32
5th	Clerical work as described in 4th degree but also must be able to operate word processing equipment	36
6th	Highly specialized clerical work involving accounting practices as well as all clerical and stenographic work described through the 5th degree	40

Factor 4: Working Conditions

Definition: *This factor describes the environmental conditions under which work is normally performed. Also included are expected working hours.*

Degree	Requirements	Points
1st	Normal office environment with standard working hours	5
2nd	Occasional exposure to noise and temperature changes with standard working hours	6
3rd	Normal office environment with split shift day/night working hours	7
4th	Occasional exposure to noise and temperature changes with split shift day/night working hours	8
5th	Constant exposure to noise and temperature changes with standard working hours	9
6th	Constant exposure to noise and temperature changes with split shift day/night working hours	10

Factor 5: Supervision

Definition: *This factor describes the amount of immediate supervision and monitoring required for the individual to successfully perform the job.*

Degree	Requirements	Points
1st	Requires constant supervision	5
2nd	Requires supervision 75% of the time [most]	6
3rd	Requires supervision 50% of the time [some]	7
4th	Requires supervision 25% of the time [little]	8
5th	Requires supervision 10% of the time [very little]	9
6th	Requires supervision 0% of the time [none]	10

Factor 6: Initiative and Ingenuity

Definition: *This factor describes the amount of initiative (or self-reliant judgment) the worker requires to perform the job. The factor also describes the ability of the worker to make decisions and handle exceptions to standard procedures as they arise.*

Degree	Requirements	Points
1st	No decisions required; Must have either verbal or written procedures for all possible activities	20
2nd	Occasional minor or routine decisions according to predefined decision criteria	24
3rd	Frequent minor or routine decisions made according to predefined decision criteria	28
4th	Occasional independent or non-routine decisions made when no procedure exists to handle the situation	32
5th	Frequent independent or non-routine decisions made when no procedure exists to handle the situation	36
6th	Requires significant ingenuity and initiative to handle a complex and difficult job. Makes many independent decisions when no procedure exists to handle the situation	40

Factor 7: Interpersonal Relations

Definition: *This factor describes the amount of interaction with visitors, students, faculty, administrators, or co-workers other than the immediate supervisor required during the normal course of the work performed.*

Degree	Requirements	Points
1st	No interaction at all	10
2nd	No more than 5% of time	12
3rd	No more than 10% of time	14
4th	No more than 15% of time	16
5th	Frequent (up to 50% of time)	18
6th	Constant (over 50% of time)	20

The factors/degrees and points assigned are summarized below. Note that an arithmetic progression is used to increase points by degrees within each factor. The weightings for the first degree were arbitrarily selected by the analyst who designed the plan for MVC. This was undoubtedly based on judgment, experience, and her perceptions about the relative importance of each factor.

Factor	Degree					
	1st	2nd	3rd	4th	5th	6th
1	10	12	14	16	18	20
2	30	36	42	48	54	60
3	20	24	28	32	36	40
4	5	6	7	8	9	10
5	5	6	7	8	9	10
6	20	24	28	32	36	40
7	10	12	14	16	18	20
Totals	100	120	140	160	180	200

To illustrate the use of the job evaluation system, the jobs that were described at the end of the preceeding chapter are evaluated on the following pages (Figure 4–5(a–k)). Naturally there are many more secretarial and clerical jobs at the college, and all would have to be evaluated in practice. However, since this representative sampling has been developed, it should permit the illustration of the job evaluation system in operation.

Job Title: *Departmental Secretary*

Department: *Math Department*

Total Points: _134_

Factor	Degree	Points	Justification
1	2	12	*high school diploma*
2	1	30	*no prior experience specified*
3	4	32	*includes stenographic duties*
4	1	5	*normal office/standard hours*
5	5	9	*very little supervision*
6	4	32	*handle in absence of department head*
7	3	14	*10% of time interacting*

FIGURE 4–5(a). Job Evaluation

Job Title: *Clerk*

Department: *Records*   Total Points: __*141*__

Factor	Degree	Points	Justification
1	3	14	*high school diploma required*
2	2	36	*one year experience preferred*
3	4	32	*typing, general office knowledge*
4	5	5	*typical office/normal hours*
5	4	8	*requires little supervision*
6	4	32	*good judgment required*
7	3	14	*assist registrar's secretary*

FIGURE 4–5(b). Job Evaluation

Job Title: *Junior Clerk*

Department: *Records*

Total Points: <u>*128*</u>

Factor	Degree	Points	Justification
1	*3*	*14*	*high school graduate*
2	*1*	*30*	*no minimum specified*
3	*4*	*32*	*typing required*
4	*1*	*5*	*typical multi-person office*
5	*3*	*7*	*some supervision*
6	*2*	*24*	*10% of time information operator*
7	*4*	*16*	*10% of day on telephone*

FIGURE 4–5(c). Job Evaluation

Job Title: *Clerk*

Department: *Registrar's office*

Total Points: _144_

Factor	Degree	Points	Justification
1	3	14	*high school graduation required*
2	3	42	*two years of experience required*
3	4	32	*typing and all office machines*
4	1	5	*typical office/normal hours*
5	3	7	*some supervision required*
6	3	28	*fill in for other positions, assist with student problems*
7	4	16	*assist students, telephone relief*

FIGURE 4–5(d).   Job Evaluation

Job Title: *Secretary*

Department: *Public Relations*

Total Points: _146_

Factor	Degree	Points	Justification
1	3	14	high school diploma required
2	1	30	no minimum stated
3	4	32	typing, standard office equipment
4	2	6	cramped office
5	4	8	requires little supervision
6	5	36	must deal with all levels of visitors and handle visit arrangements
7	6	20	greet dignitaries, deal with many different people

FIGURE 4–5(e). Job Evaluation

Job Title: *Secretary*

Department: *Dean of Student Affairs*   Total Points: __170__

Factor	Degree	Points	Justification
1	3	14	*high school diploma required*
2	6	60	*over 5 years required*
3	4	32	*typing, standard office equipment*
4	1	5	*well-lighted single office*
5	5	9	*requires very little supervision*
6	4	32	*good judgment and maturity, handle student emergencies*
7	5	18	*frequent (40%) dealing with students*

FIGURE 4–5(f).   Job Evaluation

Job Title:: *Secretary*

Department: *Admissions*

Total Points: *175*

Factor	Degree	Points	Justification
1	4	16	2 years business school required
2	6	60	over 5 years required
3	4	32	typing, standard office equipment
4	1	5	typical office, good surroundings
5	6	10	required to supervise others
6	5	36	required to supervise others
7	4	16	15% of time

FIGURE 4–5(g). Job Evaluation

Job Title: *Secretary*

Department: *Dean's office*

Total Points: _164_

Factor	Degree	Points	Justification
1	5	18	*junior college required*
2	3	42	*2 years required*
3	5	36	*word processor use required*
4	1	5	*typical office area*
5	5	9	*requires very little supervision*
6	5	36	*resourceful, practical*
7	5	18	*20% of time*

FIGURE 4–5(h). Job Evaluation

Job Title: *Library Assistant*

Department: *Library*

Total Points: 144

Factor	Degree	Points	Justification
1	4	16	*business school required*
2	2	36	*1 year experience required*
3	2	24	*typing speed not required, standard office equipment used*
4	1	5	*excellent environment*
5	5	9	*work with minimal supervision*
6	5	36	*adjust priorities as required*
7	5	18	*40% of the time*

FIGURE 4–5(i). Job Evaluation

Job Title: *Library Assistant (Senior)*

Department: *Library*

Total Points: _169_

Factor	Degree	Points	Justification
1	3	14	*high school diploma required*
2	6	60	*5 years required*
3	3	28	*dictation and stenographic duties not required but standard office equipment operation is*
4	3	7	*excellent environment/split schedule*
5	6	10	*supervises others*
6	5	36	*supervises others*
7	3	14	*10% of time*

FIGURE 4–5(j). Job Evaluation

Job Title: *Accountant*

Department: *Business office*

Total Points: __*173*__

Factor	Degree	Points	Justification
1	4	16	*business school required*
2	3	42	*2 years required*
3	6	40	*bookkeeping requirements use acctg practices in addition to standard office equipment*
4	1	5	*comfortable private office*
5	6	10	*work completely without supervision*
6	6	40	*considerable initiative*
7	6	20	*over 50% of the time*

FIGURE 4–5(k). Job Evaluation

The possible range of points goes from a minimum of 100 to a maximum of 200. These jobs, ranging from the 128 for the junior records clerk to 175 points for the admissions secretary are representative of the positions within the college. The relative placement of the positions also seems to conform with employee expectations, since the Dean's secretary had an evaluation of 170 points and a departmental secretary had that position evaluated at 134 points. This fits within the hierarchy for the organization. Undoubtedly the President's and Vice President's secretary's positions would receive even higher job evaluations.

This evaluation information will be used by Mountain View College to set a pay scale for these positions. This process will be explained in the next chapter and will be illustrated at the end of the chapter when the case study continues.

Case Study 4—1

NATIONAL INDUSTRIES, INC.
ANALYZING, EVALUATING, AND COMPENSATING WORK*

Job Analysis Approaches at
Claremont College

National Industries, Inc., a large conglomerate with holdings in several major industries, acquired Claremont Commercial College in 1971. Located in northern Los Angeles, the school specialized in the secretarial and computer sciences. Its Management Institute, sponsored by companies in the area, provided continuing education for members of the companies.

With an administrative staff of 20 and a professional staff of some 60 full-time and part-time employees, the school was considered large for its type and reasonably profitable. Seniority was recognized and thus constituted a form of tenure.

In 1974, the salary budgets for teaching departments was increased by five percent. The president of Claremont asked area chairpersons (three) to make recommendations as to how the budget should be used in their area.

THE MANAGEMENT INSTITUTE

This department consisted of 18 full-time employees who taught both day and evening courses, plus a staff of 12 part-time people from industry who supplemented the full-time staff. The academic structure included the following:

Position	Number	Time Full	Time Part	Sex Male	Sex Female
Full professor	3	3	—	3	0
Associate professor	7	7	—	5	2
Assistant professor	10	6	4	7	3
Lecturer	6	1	5	5	1
Instructor	4	1	3	2	2
	30	18	12	22	8

Reprinted with permission from PERSONNEL MANAGEMENT: CASES AND EXERCISES by Elmer H. Burack; copyright 1978 by West Publishing Company. All rights reserved.

The chairperson of the Management Institute was somewhat unde-
cided as to what to recommend. In the past little thought had been given
to what constitutes the central responsibilities of these academic jobs or
how to judge performance.

Discussion

1. Identify a group of factors which you would consider to be
   main job functions for the academic staff.
2. Rank these in terms of their relative importance to the wel-
   fare and functioning of Claremont College.
3. State and clarify your assumptions regarding these factors.
4. In what way did your choice of factors reflect individual decisions to a. maintain affiliation? b. to join?
5. How would you contrast job evaluation with person evaluation or appraisal?

Case Study 4–2

*SANTO'S FOODS
JOB EVALUATION APPROACHES**

By 1970, Santo's Foods, a regional food chain, operated over 50 stores
in the Ohio and Pennsylvania areas. Stores varied in size from 15,000
to over 50,000 square feet and multishift employment (full-time plus
part-time) from 20 to over 70 people. Although the stores varied greatly
in size, they all contained a common core of supervisory personnel. Key
supervisory personnel titles and a brief description of their responsibilities follow:

Night Manager: Assistant to store manager; functions as
store manager in absence of store manager and carries out
orders to accomplish tasks as communicated by store
manager.

Meat Manager: Duties related to running of meat department; directs purchasing and cutting supervisor; displays
supervision. Level of education necessary to sustain decision-
making ability along trade lines; planning an essential
factor in the successful operation of this department where
theft, spoilage, and high costs are considerations.

*Reprinted with permission from PERSONNEL MANAGEMENT: CASES AND EX-
ERCISES by Elmer H. Burack; copyright 1978 by West Publishing Company. All
rights reserved.

Service Manager: *Customer relations are important. Duties include supervision of up-front operations, check-outs, bottle returns, coordination of employees, other customer-related services. Trains own people.*

Canned Goods Manager: *Maintenance of store appearance; displays; shelf-stock rotation; responsible for up-to-date pricing. Planning is essential to display and coordination of activities with other departments. Trains own people.*

Produce Manager: *Packaging of fresh fruits and vegetables; maintaining stock, and hiring help as needed. Trains own people.*

Dock Supervisor: *Unloading and checking in of all goods received at the store. Storage of all goods.*

Variations in store size, location, and so forth, at times posed unique problems of management for a particular store not encountered in other stores. For example, the quality of community relationships in a large suburban store were of some importance for store image and acceptance in the community. The "community" for city stores largely related to their immediate neighborhood.

Discussion

1. *Prepare summary job descriptions for each of these key supervisors and store managers.*
2. *Prepare a point evaluation scheme based on functional approaches (100 points) and apply it to the supervisory jobs and that of the managers. Be sure to state your assumptions regarding factors selected and points assigned.*
3. *Use the critical incidents technique* to prepare descriptions of the jobs of store manager and department manager. Describe and justify your assumptions.*
4. *Propose a 100-point evaluation scheme based on the "dimensions of managerial positions" or some other standardized job evaluation scheme. Apply the plan to all of the managerial positions.*

---

*The critical incidents technique is a work-oriented description of what a person actually does on the job. Categories are then established and the list of incidents sorted into these categories of related items. Managerial positions could involve 80 or so "incidents" and these in turn might be sorted into 5 to 10 categories. Critical incidents are also described as "behaviorally anchored" work descriptions.

Case Study 4–3

THE CASE OF THE HEATED FURNACE REPAIRMAN*

Workers in a number of job classifications at the Littleton Steel Company had been disgruntled for some time over what they held were wage inequities between their jobs and other jobs in the company. By far the most vocal were the 23 holders of the job classification "furnace repairman," who argued that the conditions under which they had to work warranted top wages in the mill. What the job amounted to was for the worker to don asbestos clothing, crawl into a furnace in which the temperature had been allowed to cool to around 180°F., dig out bricks that had deteriorated under up to 3000°F. operating temperatures, and cement in new bricks. The workers were in a furnace for 15 minutes, then were out for 30 minutes to recuperate from the heat exposure. There was no disagreement by anybody that it was a miserable job.

Ray Miller, personnel director of Littleton Steel, and Harry Frank, job analyst, had recognized for some time that the grade system of job evaluation that the company used was inadequate for the number and varieties of jobs in a steel mill. The many complaints by workers that their jobs were unfairly rated induced Miller to request sufficient funds to design and install a more comprehensive system. Upon approval of his request, he held a meeting with the union stewards to let them know that the company was going to try to do something about the alleged inequities. He went a further step and invited the stewards to select three of their number to make up an ad hoc job evaluation committee with him, Frank, and another management representative. The purpose of the committee was to select a new system, and then to re-evaluate every job in the mill. Concurrent with the study of various possible systems was a review and updating of all job descriptions.

The committee finally selected a point system tailored after the one approved by the National Metal Trades Association, but with the wording of the gradations, or degrees, for each element written in the context of steel mill work. The committee then spent almost one year in careful reevaluation of each job. Particular attention was given to such jobs as furnace repairman, where gross misjudging of worth under the old system was claimed.

When the final scores for each job were tabulated, it was found that the new system established the relative worth of furnace repairman one classification lower than it had been under the old system. The immediate response of the furnace repairmen was to file a formal grievance, after which a meeting was arranged between the union grievance committee and the ad hoc job evaluation committee, not including the union members.

From MANAGEMENT: FUNCTIONS AND MODERN CONCEPTS by Clayton Reeser. Copyright 1973 by Scott, Foresman and Company. Reprinted with permission.

Joe Graber represented the furnace repairmen and was supported by the two shop stewards and the local union business agent. The meeting had not even been called to order when Graber burst out, "Miller, you and the rest of these fancy pants guys had better learn to crawl in a furnace because I and the rest of the gang are going to walk out."

The business agent, Bob Chewning, said calmly, "Now let's not talk about walking out. We're here to learn if your job was not properly evaluated."

Ray Miller first went over the table of point values for each of the factors considered important in steel mill jobs (Table 4-3-1). He was about to go over the way the committee had evaluated the job of furnace repairman, starting with the factors where the job had received a high number of points, but Graber beat him to it.

"How about working conditions and hazards?" he demanded. "How did you rate the jobs on those?"

"Furnace repairman was rated at the 5th Degree for working conditions, which is 50 points, or maximum," said Miller. "It also received the maximum points for hazards, but the 5th Degree for this element is only 25 points. This is because our safety program has eliminated really serious hazards, as is testified to by Littleton's extremely low accident rate. Another element for which the job of furnace repairman received the maximum number of points was physical demand, which is also 50 points at the 5th Degree. So you can see that everything that you claim makes your job worth more has been agreed to by the evaluation committee."

Table 4-3-1.   Littleton Steel Company Job Evaluation System Point Values for Job Factors

Factors	1st Degree	2nd Degree	3rd Degree	4th Degree	5th Degree
Skill					
1. Education	14	28	42	56	70
2. Experience	22	44	66	88	110
3. Initiative	14	28	42	56	70
Effort					
4. Physical Demand	10	20	30	40	50
5. Mental Demand	5	10	15	20	25
Responsibility					
6. Equipment	5	10	15	20	25
7. Material	5	10	15	20	25
8. Safety of Others	5	10	15	20	25
9. Work of Others	5	10	15	20	25
Job conditions					
10. Working conditions	10	20	30	40	50
11. Hazards	5	10	15	20	25

"Now for the factors where furnace repairman did not receive a high evaluation," Miller continued. "It was rated at the 1st Degree for education."

"As I only have an 8th-grade education myself, I guess I can't complain about that," conceded Graber.

Miller went on, "There are four new men on the job who are doing satisfactory work with experience that compares to the 2nd Degree, so we think that is a fair rating. About the only initiative that is required for the job is deciding whether a brick has started to crumble, so it is also rated at the 2nd Degree for that element. For the three skill factors, furnace repairman has 86 points out of a possible 250 points."

"Do you see anything unfair about this, Joe?" asked Chewning.

"No, but I know the job isn't being paid enough," said Graber.

"To continue," said Miller, "the job was rated at the 1st Degree for mental demand. It was rated fairly high, at the 3rd Degree, for both responsibility for equipment and for material, but at the 1st Degree for responsibility for safety of others and work of others. To summarize, the job received a total of 256 points out of a maximum of 500 points. These 256 points places it in the fifth highest classification in the mill, which means that it is considered to be an important job to the company."

"Not important enough to be paid what it is worth," said Graber heatedly. "I might admit that the job rates are low on some of those things, but not enough points are given for others like working conditions."

"That is a matter of opinion," said Miller.

"Yeah, and my opinion is as good as yours. The boys and I are walking out," shouted Graber.

"Oh no, you're not," was Chewning's response to this outburst.

Discussion

1. Suppose you were in your early sixties and the chief executive and a large stockholder of a company whose stock was on the stock exchange. What would be your inclination for setting the amount of your own salary? How would the amount affect your subordinate managers?

2. What reason would there be for a company's having a different evaluation system for factory, clerical, and technical jobs?

3. In the case above, what were some evidences of good judgment shown by Ray Miller in implementing an improved job evaluation system?

4. What foreseeable problem came up in explaining the evaluation of the furnace repairman job to Joe Graber?

5. What have you noticed to be an obvious result of Ray Miller's careful planning for the implementation of the job evaluation system?

Case Study 4—4

DOGWOOD DOORS

A prefabricated door manufacturing firm was faced with a union certification election. In an attempt to combat the union's major campaign point—unequal pay for equal work—the company has adopted the AAIM job evaluation system. In addition to the factors offered in the AAIM evaluation system, Dogwood has added factors for creativity, loyalty, punctuality, and dedication to the company. The union has countered the adoption of this system by pointing out that these three additional factors rate the individual rather than the jobs performed, and is merely the company's attempt to reward loyal (anti-union) employees. The union is even threatening to report this to the NLRB as a violation of the National Labor Relations (Taft Hartley) Act.

Discussion

1. Comment on the job evaluation system Dogwood has adopted.
2. Does the union have a valid position?
3. What might the company have done instead to reward employees who have done a commendable job?

Case Study 4—5

NORTHERN AIRLINES

Northern Airlines, a commuter airline serving the Northeast, has had a dismal profit picture in recent years. The newly hired president has, after intensive study, concluded that the poor profit picture was due to the high wages paid to the union employees. Furthermore, the president is convinced that the high wages are in large part due to the relatively poor working conditions. As a result of this study, he has recommended that Northern purchase a completely new fleet of aircraft. This will result in the "conditions" factor of the job evaluation system to be re-evaluated for all jobs and should give the lowest degree rating for all the jobs. This will have the result of lowering all the employees' pay and reducing the operating costs for the Airline. The interest and depreciation charges should minimize the cost of purchasing the airplanes.

Before implementing this plan the president has asked you, as an impartial expert in wage and salary administration, to comment on the proposal. Be prepared to justify your comments.

Case Study 4–6

DOLLY'S DINER

Dolly has decided to open a brand new old-fashioned diner featuring home-cooked fast food just like Mom used to make. Dolly plans to employ a cook, two waiters, and a dishwasher. She will serve as the hostess.

Discussion

1. Recommend a suitable job evaluation method for use in the diner.
2. How will this system work if Dolly's becomes a franchise operation?
3. What assumptions were required?

Case Study 4–7

POINT RATING ASSIGNMENT (A)

Listed below are various job titles and summary descriptions for positions found in a large aircraft manufacturing plant. Use these job descriptions and the AAIM job evaluation plan to evaluate these jobs and find the appropriate relative level (point total) for each. Be sure to justify your evaluation.

Aircraft-and-Engine Mechanic: Services, repairs, and overhauls aircraft and aircraft engines to ensure airworthiness: Repairs, replaces, and assembles parts, such as wings, fuselage, tail assembly, landing gear, control cables, propeller assembly, and fuel and oil tanks, using tools, such as power shears, sheet metal breaker, arc and acetylene welding equipment, rivet gun, and air or electric drills to rebuild or replace airframe or its components. Consults manufacturers' manuals and airline's maintenance manual for specifications and to determine feasibility of repair or replacement according to malfunction. Examines engines for cracked cylinders and oil leaks and listens to detect sounds of malfunctioning, such as sticking or burnt valves. Tests engine operation, using testing equipment, such as ignition analyzer, compression checker, distributor timer, and ammeter to locate source of malfunction. Replaces worn or damaged components, such as carburetors [CARBURETOR MAN (air trans.)], superchargers, and magnetos [IGNITION SPECIALIST (air trans.)], using handtools. Removes engine from aircraft, using hoist or forklift truck. Disassembles and inspects parts for wear, warping, or other defects. Repairs or replaces defective engine parts and reassembles and installs engine in aircraft. Adjusts and repairs electrical wiring system and aircraft accessories and instruments [INSTRUMENT MAN]. Inspects, services, and repairs pneumatic and hydraulic systems. Performs miscellaneous duties to service aircraft, including flushing crankcase, cleaning screens, greasing moving parts, and checking brakes. May be required to hold airframe or power plant mechanic's license issued by Federal Aviation Agency.

Aircraft-and-Engine Mechanic Helper: Assists AIRCRAFT-AND ENGINE MECHANIC in servicing, repairing, and overhauling aircraft and aircraft engines by performing any combination of following duties: Adjusts and replaces parts, such as control cables, fuel tanks, spark plugs, and tires, using mechanics' handtools. Disconnects instruments, ignition system, and fuel and oil lines. Aids in dismantling engines. Cleans engine parts with solvents. Aids in assembling engines, control cables, and aircraft sections, such as tail assemblies and wing sections. Inflates tires, fills gasoline tanks and oil reservoirs, and greases aircraft with grease gun. Performs other duties as assigned.

Aircraft Mechanic, Armament: Assembles, installs, tests, and adjusts guns, power-driven turrets, and bomb racks in aircraft, according to specifications, using handtools and measuring instruments: Bolts gun turrets to aircraft, using handtools. Cleans, oils, and assembles gun parts, and attaches accessories to guns, such as sights, firing devices, and mounting frames, using gauges and handtools. Drills bolt holes in gun mounts in aircraft or armament sections and bolts guns to mounts, using handtools, scale, and square. Installs armament sections in aircraft, using handtools and hoist. Connects cables to turrets and guns for electrically controlled equipment, such as ammunition-loading, sighting, and firing devices, using ring locks, cotter keys, threaded connectors, and turnbuckles. Installs bomb release mechanisms and bomb racks in aircraft, using metal pins and spring connectors. Aligns battery of stationary guns to obtain specified convergence of fire, using sighting devices and handtools. *Fires guns and operates bomb release mechanisms on firing range or on test flights to ensure specified operation.*

Aircraft Mechanic, Electrical and Radio: *Lays out, assembles, and installs radio and electrical systems in aircraft and missiles, according to specifications, using handtools and precision testing equipment: Assembles units, such as switches, electrical controls, and junction boxes, and connects them to major units, such as radio systems, instruments, magnetos, and inverters, using handtools and soldering iron. Lays out installation of major units in aircraft, using scribe, scale, and protractor. Installs and connects units, according to wiring diagrams, using handtools and soldering iron. Tests units, using equipment, such as circuit continuity tester, oscilloscope, and voltmeter, and adjusts or repairs malfunctioning units.*

Aircraft Mechanic, Heat and Vent: *Lays out, assembles, installs, and tests heating and ventilating systems in aircraft, according to specifications, using handtools, machines, and test equipment: Lays out location of assemblies and parts, such as heaters, superchargers, ducts, outlets, valves, and fittings on aircraft, using layout tools, such as scribers, rules, steel tape, and center punches. Fabricates parts, such as brackets, stiffeners, patches, and shims, using metalworking machines, such as power shears, punches, arbor presses, and drill presses. Lays out trim lines on surface of parts. Bolts, screws, or clamps parts and assemblies in place for welding. Performs functional test of assembled systems in aircraft or in major units, such as fuselage, wings, or tail sections, to determine that system operates according to specifications.*

Aircraft Mechanic, Plumbing and Hydraulics: *Lays out, assembles, installs, and tests plumbing and hydraulic systems in aircraft and missiles, following engineering sketches or blueprints: Lays out location of parts and assemblies, such as pumps, valves, fuel and oil lines, landing-gear actuating mechanisms, and braking systems, on aircraft or missile, following blueprints and using ruler and chalk. Drills mounting holes in frame. Operates machines, such as arbor press, power shear, and punch press, to fabricate parts, such as brackets, stiffeners, patches, and shims. Screws or bolts parts and assembles to structures, such as fuselage, wings, or tail, or clamps parts in place for welding. Turns setscrews and* *jam nuts to adjust actuating cylinder throws, valves, locks, and booster pumps. Performs functional tests of installed systems under simulated flight conditions to determine that systems meet specifications.*

Airplane Woodworker: *Fabricates and assembles wooden airplane and glider parts to form major units, such as spars, wings, fins, and fuselage sections, following blueprints and templates, using handtools, power tools, and measuring instruments: Cuts and shapes parts, using power tools, such as saw, planer, shaper, and router. Positions parts in jigs or structural framework and verifies assembly dimensions, using scales, templates, gauges, straightedge, and square. Trims parts to obtain specified fit, using rasp, scrapers, and plane. Fastens parts together and installs reinforcement members, such as stiffeners, gussets, stays, and braces, using glue, nails, screws, and bolts. Glues wooden skin to framework and sands surface to smooth finish. May install plywood skin on metal frame of fuselage and be designated* Skin Man, Wood.

Assembler, Aircraft Power Plant: *Assembles engines and auxiliary parts and installs them in aircraft, using handtools and following specifications: Positions engine in engine mount bolted on portable stand, using chain hoist. Bolts and clamps engine auxiliaries, such as carburetors, generators, fuel and oil pumps, and magnetos, in position, using handtools. Connects electric cables to terminals and tightens bolts and clamps supporting cable system, using handtools and soldering iron. Hoists engine and attached mount to position in fuselage or wing, and bolts mount to firewall of airplane. Installs insulation around engine and clamps or screws connections of wiring system, fuel and oil lines, pressure gauges, and engine control rods to corresponding fittings on firewall. Turns turnbuckles and setscrews to adjust engine controls after engine is installed. Positions propeller, using hoist, and aligns and bolts it to engine, using handtools. May uncrate engines and clean parts with solvent and airhose before fastening them in mount.*

Assembler, Aircraft, Structures and Surfaces: *Assembles tail, wing, and fuselage sections of airplanes and missiles from subassemblies, such as frames, bulkheads, doors, stabilizers, and landing gear, following blueprints and using handtools and measuring instruments: Positions subassemblies in jigs or fixtures in relation to each other, using* *measuring instruments, such as templates, protractors, and dividers following blueprint station lines and index points. Drills, reams, and countersinks holes in subassemblies, using power drill. Bolts, rivets, or tack-welds assemblies together, using rivet gun, welding equipment and handtools. Shapes adjoining edges to specifications, using tinsnips and files, and verifies tolerances between edges, using gauges and calipers. Locates holes to be drilled in structure for installation of parts, such as engine cowl, bomb-bay doors, wing nacelle, and wiring, using jigs, templates, scales, and square. Drills holes in structure and attaches brackets, hinges, braces, clips, and tubing to secure subassemblies and parts. Installs such units as doors, sheet metal and glass sections, landing gear, rudder, and elevators, and connects them to controls with pulleys and cables, using riveting gun, power drill, and handtools. Fits sheet metal sections to skeleton frame for covering and reinforcement.*

Baling-Machine Operator: *Tends machine to compress and bind paper, cloth, or other loose materials to facilitate handling: Trucks or carries materials to baling machine. Places materials in compression chamber of baling machine with materials by hand or by dumping from an overhead floor. Moves lever or electric switch, causing ram to compress material. Threads tie-bands around bale and tightens them by twisting or clamping ends. Opens compression chamber doors and removes bale from machine. May truck bales to storage place, weigh bales, and record their weights. May line compression chamber of baling machine with paper, burlap, or other covering before baling. May sew or tie wrapping in place after baling, and stencil bales.*

Bench Grinder: *Moves metal objects, such as castings, billets, machine parts, sheet metal subassemblies, or arrowheads, against abrasive wheel of bench grinder to grind, smooth, or rough-finish objects to specifications: Clamps workpiece in workholder or jig, or holds it in hands, and feeds it against rotating grinding wheel to remove excess metal, scratches, or burrs. Examines or measures workpiece for conformance to standards. May position workpiece in automatic feed mechanism. May select and mount abrasive wheels of different grit size to grinder to obtain specified finish of workpiece. Guides dressing tool across wheel to true surface. Replaces worn wheels, using wrench. May start pump and direct coolant flow against wheel.*

Bench Mechanic, Steel Weld: *Bolts, rivets, or tack-welds together parts of airplanes, such as motor mounts, cockpit cowlings, and cockpit enclosures, to temporarily or permanently unite them: Ascertains from blueprints the most advantageous system of assembly. Examines supplementary parts for defects, using squares, micrometers, and rules to test measurements. Places parts in jig or fixture to ensure proper relative fit of piece at all points. Makes adjustments, using mallets and files, to improve the juxtaposition of parts. Secures pieces together with bolts, rivets, or temporary spring fasteners, or temporarily welds them. Reshapes and straightens fittings warped by heat of welding process by measuring amount of deformation, using micrometers, calipers, squares, and rules, and hammering and bending parts to desired shape. May fit and assemble parts without aid of jigs or fixtures when building equipment for new aircraft types. May use common metalworking machines, such as drill presses and honing machines.*

Bending-Machine Operator: *Sets up and operates machine to bend metal structural shapes, such as bars, rods, angles, pipes, and tubes, to angle or contour specified by work order, drawings, templates, or layout: Selects and bolts holding clamp, die block, and guide clamp to machine. Positions and clamps end stops on machine to set specified location of bend. Inserts or screws plug stops into guide wheel to set specified degree of bend. Positions workpiece against end stop. Locks holding clamp and guide clamp onto workpiece. Lubricates workpiece with oil. Starts turntable that draws workpiece through guide clamp around die block until stopped by plug stops or until dial indicator points to specified degree of bend. May slide mandrel into tubing instead of using guide clamp. May preheat workpiece, using hand torch or heating furnace. May use hand-powered bending machine for short runs. May fill tubes or pipe with sand, resin, or lead to prevent wrinkling or collapsing. May heat tube, using torch, and manually bend tube or pipe around forming blocks. May flare tube ends, using tube flarer and cut metal stock to length, using power shears or saws.*

Tends machine that bends metal structural shapes, such as bars, rods, angles, and tubes to specified angle or contour: Positions workpiece against end stops. Locks holding clamp and guide clamp onto workpiece. Lubricates workpiece with oil. Pulls lever or depresses pedal to activate turntable which draws workpiece through guide clamp and around die block until stopped by plug stops. May slide mandrel into tubing instead of using guide clamp. May use hand-powered bending machine. May perform such fabricating tasks as flaring tube ends, using tube flarer, or cutting metal stock to length, using power shears or saws.

Carpenter, Maintenance: *Constructs and repairs structural woodwork and equipment in an establishment, working from blueprints, drawings, or oral instructions: Builds, repairs, and installs counters, cabinets, benches, partitions, floors, doors, building framework, and trim, using carpenter's handtools and power tools. Installs glass in windows, doors, and partitions. Replaces damaged ceiling tile, floor tile, and sheet plastic wall coverings. May build cabinets and other wooden equipment in carpenter shop, using woodworking machines, such as circular saw, bandsaw, and jointer. May install window shades, venetian blinds, curtain rods, and wall fans for tenants.*

Electrical-Discharge-Machine Set-Up Operator: *Sets up and operates one or more electrical-discharge machines to shape metal workpieces to specifications, following standard charts and manuals, and applying knowledge of electrical-discharge machining processes and methods, electric currents and circuitry, metal properties, and shop mathematics: Examines blueprint of product and plans operations. Positions and secures workpiece on machine table with clamps, vise, or fixture. Positions and secures electrode in holder on surface plate, verifying concentricity, alignment, and depth with measuring instruments, such as calipers and dial indicators. Mounts electrode and holder on machine spindle, verifying alinement of electrode and workpiece, using measuring instruments. Positions gage blocks, dial indicator, and spindle stop on machine so that descending electrode will stop at specified depth when indicator feeler point touches gauge blocks. Turns valve to adjust flow of dielectric coolant over electrode and workpiece or to immerse them in circulating bath. Reads charts to ascertain such settings as electric current and electrode feed rate and turns controls to these settings. Starts machine and observes beginning of operation. May move controls to rotate electrode or workpiece. May inspect completed workpiece visually and with templates and other measuring instruments. May compute settings from specifications and knowledge of machine capacities. May give* TOOL MAKER *specifications, such as allowances between blueprint dimension and dimensions of electrode to be made.*

Electronics Assembler, Developmental: *Assembles or modifies prototypes or final experimental assemblies of electronic equipment, such as missile control systems, radio and test equipment, computers, and machine-tool numerical controls, using handtools and electronic test equipment, and following schematic or assembly drawings, sketches, and wiring diagrams: Installs components such as switches, coils, transformers, relays, transistors, and potentiometers, in assemblies, using handtools, power drills, and soldering iron. Routes and solders wires to components in assembly to form circuitry. Solders cable wires to specified terminals to connect circuits and subassemblies. Installs cables and wire harnesses to connect assemblies with power source, switch panels, and junction boxes. Assembles and laces cables* [CABLEMAKER *(elec. equip.; electronics)*]. *Tests continuity of circuits, using circuit analyzer. May assemble breadboard (experimental) layouts of electronic circuits to prove engineering design. May instruct workers in techniques of wiring and soldering.*

Foreman: *Supervises and coordinates activities of workers engaged in one or more occupations: Studies production schedules and estimates man-hour requirements for completion of job assignment. Interprets company policies to workers and enforces safety regulations. Interprets specifications, blueprints, and job orders to workers, and assigns duties. Establishes or adjusts work procedures to meet production schedules, using knowledge of capacities of machines and equipment. Recommends measures to improve production methods, equipment performance, and quality of product, and suggests changes in working conditions and use of equipment to increase efficiency of shop, department, or work crew. Analyzes and resolves work problems, or assists workers in solving work problems. Initiates or suggests plans to motivate workers to achieve work goals. Recommends or initiates personnel actions, such as promotions, transfers, discharges, and disciplinary measures. May train new workers. Maintains time and production records. May estimate, requisition, and inspect materials. May confer with other* FOREMEN *to coordinate activities of individual departments. May confer with workers' representatives to resolve grievances. May set up machines and equipment. When supervising workers engaged chiefly in one occupation or craft, is required to be adept in the activities of the workers supervised. When supervising workers engaged in several occupations, is* *required to possess general knowledge of the activities involved.*

Grinder Set-Up Operator, Gear, Tool: *Sets up and operates gear-grinding machine with special indexing equipment to grind precision and master gears, usually on custom basis, analyzing specifications and deciding on tooling according to knowledge of gear grinding procedures: Studies blueprints to visualize grinding to be done and plans sequence of operations. Computes machine indexing ratios and cam dimensions for specified spacing and contour of gear teeth, using shop mathematics. Selects index plate, cams, grinding wheel, feed rates, grinding speed, and depth of cut, according to computations, gear specifications and knowledge of gear design, metal properties, and abrasives. Positions and secures index plate, cams, and grinding wheel in machine, using wrenches. Sets up automatic dressing device to dress wheel to specified profile. Moves controls to set synchronized rotation speeds and feed rates. Positions and secures workpiece on mandrel between centers or in chuck, and turns handwheels to position workpiece and wheel, verifying positions with thickness gauges and dial indicator and by reading micrometer dial on machine. Turns valve handle and directs flow of coolant against wheel and workpiece. Moves controls to index workpiece and feed wheel to workpiece, adjusting depth of cut in part by sight and feel. Verifies dimensions of ground workpiece for conformance to specifications, using specialized gear inspection devices, such as gear measuring wires and involute checker. May grind nonmetallic materials. May be required to have experience with particular type of gear, kind of computation, precision level, or type or trade name of machine.*

Heat Treater: *Controls heat-treating furnaces and quenching equipment to alter physical and chemical properties of variety of metal objects by methods of controlled heating and cooling, such as hardening, tempering, annealing, case-hardening, and normalizing: Determines temperature and time of heating cycle, and type and temperature of quenching medium to attain specified hardness, toughness, and ductility of parts, using standard heat-treating charts, knowledge of heat-treating methods and equipment, and properties of metals. Adjusts furnace controls, observing pyrometer, to bring furnace to prescribed temperature. Loads parts into furnace. Removes parts after prescribed time and quenches in* *water, oil, brine, or other bath, or allows parts to cool in air. May test hardness of parts* [HARDNESS INSPECTOR]. *May set up and operate die-quenching machine to prevent parts from warping during quenching. May set up and operate electronic induction equipment to heat objects.*

Controls one or more furnaces to heattreat metal objects according to specifications: Places parts in racks, trays, or baskets, and places them on conveyor or loads them directly into furnace. Adjusts furnace temperature, observing pyrometer, to heat metal to prescribed temperature. Sets speed of conveyor for prescribed time cycle or records time that parts are to be removed from furnace. Removes parts after prescribed time and quenches them in water, oil, or other media, or allows them to cool in air. May test hardness of parts [HARDNESS INSPECTOR]. *May feed die-quenching machine to prevent parts from warping during quenching operation. May degrease or remove scale from parts. May draw wire or sheet metal through furnace and attach to winding mechanism that pulls metal through furnace.*

Helper: *A worker who assists another worker, usually of a higher level of competence or expertness, by performing a variety of duties, such as furnishing another worker with materials, tools, and supplies; cleaning work area, machines, and equipment; feeding or offbearing machine; holding materials or tools; and performing other routine duties.*

Inspector, Assemblies and Installations: *Inspects assemblies, such as wings, body sections, flap and tail assemblies, joining of subassemblies into major structures, and complete aircraft for adherence to sequence of operation and for correctness of assembly, according to blueprints, drawings, and production and inspection manuals: Examines cables for kinks, cracks, and loose connections. Inspects alignment of parts, using templates, check jigs, and sight levels. Verifies location, size, shape, reaming, and countersinking of bolt and rivet holes, using ball gauges, templates, and calipers. Inspects assembly of mechanical equipment, such as landing gear struts and wing flap and rudder actuators, for tolerance of fit, using micrometers, calipers, and verniers. Examines installation of engines, mechanical equipment, plumbing lines and tanks, wiring shields, and brackets in subassemblies and aircraft structures to verify location and fastening and to determine surface defects, such as scratches and cracks. Examines fit and seal of windows and doors and installation of bulkheads, seats, instrument panels, and* *decorative panels. Examines installation of floor and wall coverings and upholstery to verify color, quality, and fit of material. Writes inspection reports.*

Jig Borer, Tape Control: *Sets up and operates tape-controlled single-spindle jig borer to face, drill, ream, and tap metal castings: Positions holding fixture on indexing table and adjusts clamps of fixture to secure casting in position specified on process sheet. Pushes button to zero indexing table and console at established locating point. Positions control tape in reader at zero point and starts machine that automatically positions indexing table through predetermined code punched in tape. Calculates travel of cutting tool required to touch top of casting and selects precision blocks which equal that distance. Places blocks under dial indicator to set machine for depth of cut. Turns handwheel to lower cutting tool and dial indicator. Stops wheel when needle on dial indicates cutting tool has machined casting to specified depth. Presses buttons to record dimension on console for subsequent automatic machining process and to advance tape. Verifies dimension of holes, using specified gauges.*

Machine Try-Out Man: *Sets up and operates prototype metalworking machines, such as lathe, milling machine, or forging press, to verify conformance to operating specifications: Installs dies or cutting tool in machine, following blueprints, and using handtools and measuring instruments. Sets controls to regulate speed of feed, depth of cut, or length of ram stroke according to type of machine being tested. Operates machine to obtain sample piece. Verifies conformance of workpiece to specifications, using measuring instruments, such as calipers, micrometers, and gauges. Adjusts machine setup to conform with operating specifications. Notifies supervisor of malfunctions or problems with setup.*

Machinist: *Sets up and operates machine tools, and fits and assembles parts to make or repair metal parts, mechanisms, tools, or machines, applying knowledge of mechanics, shop mathematics, metal properties, and layout machining procedures: Studies specifications, such as blueprint, sketch, or description of part to be replaced, and plans sequence of operations. Measures, marks, and scribes dimensions and reference points to lay out stock for machining [LAY-OUT MAN]. Sets up and operates lathe, milling machine, shaper, or grinder to machine parts to specifications, and verifies conformance of part to specifications, using measuring instru-*

ments [TOOL-MACHINE SET-UP OPERATOR]. *Positions and secures parts on surface plate or worktable with such devices as vises, V-blocks, and angle plates, and uses handtools, such as files, scrapers, and wrenches, to fit and assemble parts to assemblies or mechanisms. Verifies dimensions and alignment with measuring instruments, such as micrometers, height gauges, and gauge blocks. May operate mechanism or machine, observe operation, or test it with inspection equipment to diagnose malfunction of machine or to test repaired machine. May develop specifications from general description and draw or sketch product to be made.*

Milling-Machine Operator, Production: *Tends one or more previously set up milling machines to mill surfaces of metal workpieces to specifications on production basis: Positions and secures workpiece in fixture or feeding device. Starts machine, and turns handwheel to feed workpiece to cutter or vice versa or engages feeding mechanism. Changes worn cutters, using wrenches. Verifies conformance of work to specifications, using instruments, such as fixed gauges, calipers, and micrometers. May turn valve handle and direct flow of coolant against cutter and workpiece. May mill non-metallic materials, such as plastics. May be required to have experience with particular material or product, or with machine of particular size, type, or trade name, and be designated accordingly.*

Strip-Cutting-Machine Operator: *Tends machine that cuts rolls of textile material into narrow rolls of specified width: Lifts rolls of material onto machine bar and hammers wedge into core of roll to secure roll to bar. Turns handwheel to move rotary blade into cutting position, following markings on calibrated scale to obtain specified cutting width. Starts machine that rotates blade and roll in opposite directions. Presses lever to move rotating blade forward and cut through roll of material. Releases lever and positions blade for subsequent cut. Removes narrow rolls of material from machine and stacks rolls on shelf according to width.*

Tool-and-Die Maker: *Analyzes variety of specifications, lays out metal stock, sets up and operates machine tools, and fits and assembles parts to make and repair metalworking dies, cutting tools, jigs, fixtures, gauges, and machinists' handtools, applying knowledge of tool and die designs and construction, shop mathematics, metal properties, and layout, machining, and assembly procedures: Studies specifications, such as blueprints, sketches, models, or de-*

scriptions, and visualizes product. Computes dimensions, decides on machining to be done, and plans layout and assembly operations. Measures, marks, and scribes metal stock for machining [LAY-OUT MAN]. Sets up and operates machine tools, such as lathe, milling machine, shaper, and grinder, to machine parts, and verifies conformance of machined parts to specifications [TOOL-MACHINE SET-UP OPERATOR]. Lifts machined parts manually or with hoist, and positions and holds them on surface plate or worktable, using such devices as vises, V-blocks, and angle plates. Uses handtools, such as scrapers and abrasive stones, and power grinders to smooth flat and contoured surfaces and fit and assemble parts into assemblies or mechanisms. Verifies dimensions, alignments, and clearances, using measuring instruments, such as dial indicators, gauge blocks, thickness gauges, and micrometers. Dowels and bolts parts together, using handtools such as hammers and wrenches. May connect wiring and hydraulic lines to install electric and hydraulic components.

Tool Maker, Bench: Lays out, fits, and assembles parts to make and repair cutting tools, jigs, fixtures, gauges, or machinists' handtools, analyzing specifications according to knowledge of tool designs, shop mathematics, machining, and layout and assembly procedures: Studies blueprint, decides on machining to be done, and plans layout and assembly procedures. Measures, marks, and scribes metal stock to lay out for machining by other workers [LAY-OUT MAN]. Operates drill press to drill and tap holes in parts [DRILL-PRESS SET-UP OPERATOR, SINGLE SPINDLE]. Smooths and scrapes parts to fit, using handtools, such as files and scrapers. Positions and secures parts on surface plate with devices such as V-blocks, vises, and angle plates. Assembles parts into product, using tools, such as wrenches, hammers, and tweezers, and verifies dimensions and alignments, using measuring instruments such as micrometers, height gauges, and gauge blocks.

Case Study 4—8

POINT RATING ASSIGNMENT (B)

Use the job descriptions prepared in the job description exercise (3-2) and the AAIM point plan of job evaluation to evaluate the jobs listed. Be sure to justify your ratings.

"Ms. Beamish, the employees have requested another discussion of the company's pay grade structure."

Chapter Five

PRICING THE JOB

INTRODUCTION

Job evaluation, whether performed by the ranking, classification, factor comparison, or point method systems, determines the relative worth of jobs to the organization. While this is very important information it does not, except for factor comparison, establish the relative worth of the job in dollars. The compensation for each job must still be determined through a process that is called pricing the job.

The pricing procedure has several major steps. These include establishing pay grades, conducting wage surveys, developing a wage curve, and implementing a pay scale. Each of these major steps will be explained as it relates to the most commonly used job evaluation procedure, the point plan. At the end of the chapter the steps will be applied to the clerical jobs at Mountain View College.

ESTABLISHING PAY GRADES

Ideally, after each job in the organization has been evaluated and assigned a point total, the individual jobs can each be given a pay rate. This is difficult for several reasons. First is the magnitude of the work involved. If the organization has hundreds of jobs, most with different point totals, finding the comparable dollar value can be extremely difficult. Second, many questions have been raised about the accuracy or precision of the individual job evaluation. The potential for measurement errors always exists, and to specifically establish a pay rate for each job can cause inaccuracies. Third, there is the question of acceptability to the workers. It would be difficult to justify a pay difference of $.08 per hour for workers performing almost exactly the same work on similar machines just because one job had an evaluation 1 or 2 points higher than the other, especially if that difference were based on some minor consideration such as something to do with working conditions. The workers will accept the difference due to seniority or employee evaluation fairly readily, but not due to some small part of job evaluation.

To overcome these objections it is recommended that pay ranges or pay grades be established. A pay grade is an arbitrary grouping of jobs that have similar job evaluation scores. All the jobs that fall within a given pay grade should, if the job evaluations have been performed correctly, be "worth" the same number of dollars to the organization and be classified in the same pay grade.

The number of pay ranges that an organization needs depends on several factors. These include the number of jobs that have been evaluated, the organization's structure, and the possible number of points that jobs can be assigned. It would be a waste of effort for a system that evaluated 15 jobs to have 15 or 20 pay ranges. Each job would probably end up in its own grade, or probably worse still, all the jobs might end up in the same grade, and the problems associated with these outcomes have been discussed. There should be enough pay grades so that a reasonable number of jobs are found in most pay grades.

The hierarchical structure of the organization is an important factor in the structuring of pay grades. It would be unwise, especially for morale purposes, to have a supervisor's job and the people he or she supervises have their jobs in the same pay grade. In most situations supervisors need to earn more money than the people they supervise. Generally, the more organizational levels a company has, the more pay grades will be required. As an individual progresses through the organization, there are often concurrent progressions through higher pay grades.

The number of pay grades established also depends on the total possible points in the job evaluation system. If the system has a minimum possible evaluation of 100 points and a maximum of 1,000 points, there would more likely be more grades than on a system that went from 100 to 200 points. There must be a sufficient range of possible points within each pay grade so that enough similar jobs are placed within each pay grade. For example, if the possible points range from 100 to 1,000, 20 pay grades, each having 50 points may be logical. For the plan that goes from 100 to 200 points it may be more appropriate to have five pay grades of 20 points each, or four pay grades of 25 points apiece. The decision on number of pay grades should be logical and reasonable.

There is no "correct" number of pay grades, only an appropriate number.

Once the number of pay grades has been established, the size of the pay grades is automatically determined. Generally, it is advisable for all of the pay grades to be the same size, that is, to encompass the same number of points. The midpoint of each pay range is said to be the most representative of each pay grade.

ASSIGNING JOBS TO PAY GRADES

After the pay grades have been established and the upper and lower bounds, as well as the midpoints for each pay grade defined, the evaluated jobs must be assigned to pay grades. This is a straightforward matter of placing the job evaluation results in the appropriate category. After this is done the organization knows which jobs will have the same dollar value. This does not complete the pricing activity, though. At this point only the relative worth of the jobs is known. It still remains to set the absolute value, or a range of dollar values, for each of the pay grades and for the jobs within each of the pay grades.

DETERMINING WAGES

The actual amount paid to a job or assigned to a pay grade depends on many factors. Some of the key ones include wages paid by employers in comparable businesses, on both a local and national or regional level, the local cost of living, minimum acceptable wages, legal minimum wages, the organization's ability to pay, the productivity of the individual workers, and the supply and demand for certain types of employees or skill levels.

Certain industries have traditionally paid either above average or below average wages no matter where they are located. For example, aircraft manufacturers have tended to pay more than textile manufacturers. An aircraft manufacturer might have to pay comparable jobs more than a textile producer would in order to attract qualified personnel. Although the actual rate might vary by geographical region, the relationship would more than likely remain the same whether the companies were located in relatively higher paying California or relatively lower paying South Carolina.

The actual dollar amount must also reflect the local cost of living. As was stated above, certain regions of the country, such as California or New York, have higher costs of living than other regions, such as parts of the South. Payment must reflect the local situation.

Regardless of the living wages that should be paid, there must be a minimum wage established that will permit the recipient to maintain a household and find working more attractive than the alternative. There is also the legally mandated minimum wage, but in some instances this is not sufficient to attract and maintain qualified employees.

A very important consideration is the organization's ability to pay. Resources must be available to meet whatever payroll obligations are established. There must be a sufficient cash flow and revenue, that is, money coming into the organization to cover its obligations. Many businesses, large and small, fail each year simply because there was not enough money available. Recently, however, even such giant companies as Chrysler and Eastern Airlines have had to reduce wage payments in order to remain in business. Sometimes this shortage in cash flow is due to poor management; for example promising more than could realistically be paid, or offering an undesirable product or service in the market place. Sometimes it is caused by outside factors, such as the rapid rise in oil prices that was not anticipated by anyone.

The productivity of the workers and the resources also have an impact on the wage payments. In some instances, as with the incentive plans described in Chapter 7, there is a direct link between worker productivity and wages. It depends, of course, on how much of the job the worker controls and how much the production process controls. Although pay has often been determined, to an extent, by employee evaluation, continuing attention has to be given to relating wages to productivity.

A final significant factor regarding the money paid for particular jobs is the availability of the people with the required skills. While a particular job may not have the top point value for a particular company, the pay required to attract the required workers may have to compensate for a shortage of people with that skill. For example, in a particular company the jobs of toolmaker and senior machinist may both fall into the same pay grade or job classification, but within the community where the company is located there may be many machinists but few toolmakers available. The economics of supply and demand will force a higher wage payment for toolmakers if the company wants to fill the positions. Similarly, if there are many people available with a particular skill, then the market will force the wages for that skill down.

One additional factor that, to some extent also influences the financial worth of certain jobs is the community expectations. Certain jobs, such as those in the legal profession and medical profession (specifically lawyer and doctor) have traditionally been highly compensated. Others, such as teaching, have always been on the low end of the compensation scale. These community expectations or attitudes seem to override even the supply and demand of the market place.

The above factors are all important to consider when determining the absolute worth of jobs. Most organizations use the wage survey to help determine the appropriate level to set wages at in order to hire and retain competent employees and develop a pay structure.

WAGE SURVEYS

A wage survey is a statistical method employed to determine wages paid at a particular time in a particular geographic region for particular occupations. Wage surveys can take many forms. These include those done by the organization itself and those done by third parties. No matter who conducts the wage survey there is certain information that must be collected. This includes information about both the absolute pay and the fringe benefits offered to workers.

The absolute pay is the hourly or weekly wage rate paid to the employee. The fringe benefits include indirect pay such as pensions, paid vacations, sick leave, and insurance. While no two organizations have the same benefits package, it is part of the overall compensation and must be recognized when wage survey information is compiled. The wage survey should provide information that is needed and useful for base rates and additions to income.

When a company performs its own survey it must be careful to include the following information.

- Jobs that exist within the geographical area.
- Complete coverage of jobs found in the organization.
- Stability of work force surveyed.
- Organizations surveyed that have a significant number of employees.*
- Supply and demand factors regarding individual jobs.

---

*Often small organizations pay employees wages that are either much higher or much lower than the "going rate" for similar work.

The firms surveyed should be:

- Classified as local firms.
- Within a 50-mile radius of the company doing the survey.
- Producing a product or service similar to the organization doing the survey.

The specific data collected should include:

- Base rates for a variety of jobs.
- Average earned rate of pay for employees in various jobs.
- Minimum hiring rates for a variety of different jobs.
- Fringe benefits offered to employees.

When an organization conducts its own wage survey it should include the following information.

1. A cover letter thanking the other organization.
2. Instructions on completing the survey.
3. A list of job titles for benchmark jobs.
4. Questions regarding the nature of the compensation.
5. Questions about direct wages and fringe benefits.
6. General questions regarding company demographics.
7. Self-addressed, postage-paid envelopes.

When an individual company does its own survey there is always the possibility that invalid data will be collected. Because of this, many organizations elect to use commercially available wage surveys. Available wage surveys are provided by such diverse organizations as the U.S. Department of Labor's Bureau of Labor Statistics (BLS), the Bureau of National Affairs (BNA), the Administrative Management Society (AMS), the American Management Associations (AMA), the Federal Reserve System, the Institute of Industrial Engineers (IIE), Prentice-Hall, and so on. Some of the survey data, such as that provided by BLS, provides wage data on many different types of occupations on a geographical grouping. Others, such as the survey IIE annually prepares, relates specifically to the compensation of industrial engineers.

These surveys have the advantages of being relatively inexpensive, well summarized, and coming from large samples. The disadvantages of these include the fact that the user is unable to specify the jobs included, the user has no control over the sample, and the user cannot select the sample taken.

Despite the potential drawbacks, these are one of the most popular ways to collect wage data. Among the most popular of these survey methods is the survey conducted regularly by the Bureau of Labor Statistics for various geographic regions of the country. The government surveys employees within a region and tabulates, for certain standardized jobs, the wages paid. By comparing these standardized job descriptions with the organization's own job descriptions, key or benchmark jobs can be identified and the pay range determined. After several of these jobs have been identified, the pay ranges for all jobs can be established. The government uses the job descriptions found in the *Dictionary of Occupational Titles* as the basis for the jobs included. After the going rate for these representative jobs is determined, the wage curve can be established. Figure 5–1 shows the results of a 1983 wage survey for secretarial and clerical positions in the Atlanta, Georgia, metropolitan region.

WAGE CURVE

After the wages for certain key jobs in a given region are determined, these wages, including the corresponding fringe benefits, can be directly related to the job evaluation of the jobs in the organization. The surveyed jobs should, if the Bureau of Labor Statistics wage survey data is used, be based on the *Dictionary of Occupational Titles* job descriptions. This will assure that the organization's jobs are comparable to the ones covered by the survey. If other wage survey data is used, benchmark jobs must be identified. These require that job descriptions be readily available, and that these descriptions be well-written.

Quite literally, a graph, known as the wage curve, can be developed, showing the relationship between the job evaluation in points and the wage survey dollar values. The more points a job or labor grade has, the higher the possible pay should be. Figure 5–2 shows a possible wage curve. Depending on the number of points found within a labor grade, the wage curve can be modified as shown in Figure 5–3.

The dollars shown on the wage curve are the average for each labor grade. In reality, the wages paid for each labor grade present a range of values. The jobs within any labor grade *progress* through a sequence based on seniority and/or merit. The longer a job is held by an individual and the better that individual performs the job, the more the person should get paid.

The number of steps within a given pay grade should include provisions for seniority, merit, and other factors. Generally, pay ranges will overlap, allowing for a highly senior or competent employee in a lower pay grade to make as much or more than individ-

FIGURE 5–1. Average Weekly Earnings of Office, Professional, and Technical Workers, by Sex, in Atlanta, Ga., May 1983

Sex,[3] Occupation, and Industry Division	Number of Workers	Average (mean[2]) Weekly Hours[1] (standard)	Average (mean[2]) Weekly Earnings[1] (in dollars)[1]
Office occupations— men			
Messengers	91	39.5	203.00
Nonmanufacturing	86	39.5	202.50
Order clerks	431	40.0	285.50
Nonmanufacturing	354	40.0	290.50
Order clerks I	209	40.0	256.50
Order clerks II	222	40.0	313.00
Nonmanufacturing	193	40.0	312.00
Accounting clerks:			
Nonmanufacturing:			
Transportation and utilities	122	39.0	383.50
Accounting clerks II:			
Transportation and utilities	40	38.0	343.00
Accounting clerks III	66	39.5	355.00
Nonmanufacturing	63	39.5	354.50
Transportation and utilities	42	39.5	406.00

Sex,[3] Occupation, and Industry Division	Number of Workers	Average (mean[2]) Weekly Hours[1] (standard)	Average (mean[2]) Weekly Earnings[1] (in dollars)[1]
Stenographers I	208	38.5	319.50
Nonmanufacturing	208	38.5	319.50
Transportation and utilities	189	38.5	323.50
Stenographers II	509	39.0	415.00
Typists	508	38.5	221.50
Nonmanufacturing	377	38.0	208.00
Transportation and utilities	63	38.0	305.00
Typists I	358	38.5	203.00
Nonmanufacturing	300	38.0	196.00
Typists II	150	38.5	266.50
Nonmanufacturing	77	37.5	255.00
Transportation and utilities	38	37.0	277.00
File clerks	415	39.0	195.00
Nonmanufacturing	381	39.0	188.50
File clerks I	334	39.0	186.50
Nonmanufacturing	311	38.5	184.00
File clerks II	76	39.5	217.00
Nonmanufacturing	68	39.5	205.00

Sex,[3] Occupation, and Industry Division	Number of Workers	Average (mean[2]) Weekly Hours[1] (standard)	Average (mean[2]) Weekly Earnings[1] (in dollars)[1]
Accounting clerks III	1,405	39.5	282.00
Manufacturing	141	39.5	317.50
Nonmanufacturing	1,264	39.5	278.00
Transportation and utilities	195	39.5	385.50
Accounting clerks IV	621	39.0	332.50
Nonmanufacturing	578	39.0	324.50
Payroll clerks	590	39.5	264.50
Manufacturing	117	40.0	271.50
Nonmanufacturing	473	39.0	263.00
Key entry operators	2,481	39.0	247.00
Manufacturing	334	40.0	273.50
Nonmanufacturing	2,147	39.0	243.00
Transportation and utilities	210	39.0	324.00
Key entry operators I	1,790	39.0	229.50
Manufacturing	206	40.0	252.50
Nonmanufacturing	1,584	39.0	226.50
Transportation and utilities	113	38.5	301.50
Key entry operators II	691	39.5	293.00
Manufacturing	128	40.0	307.50

Occupation	Number of workers	Average weekly hours	Average weekly earnings
Accounting clerks IV:			
Nonmanufacturing	35	39.5	417.00
Transportation and utilities			
Office occupations—women			
Secretaries	3,608	39.0	338.50
Manufacturing	1,000	39.5	355.00
Nonmanufacturing	2,608	38.5	332.00
Transportation and utilities	509	38.5	426.00
Secretaries I	638	38.5	264.00
Manufacturing	177	39.5	282.00
Nonmanufacturing	461	38.0	257.00
Secretaries II	855	38.5	289.00
Manufacturing	206	39.0	307.00
Nonmanufacturing	649	38.5	283.50
Secretaries III	1,075	39.0	366.50
Manufacturing	323	40.0	405.00
Nonmanufacturing	752	39.0	350.00
Transportation and utilities	226	38.5	433.50
Secretaries IV	795	38.5	382.50
Manufacturing	209	38.5	360.00
Nonmanufacturing	586	38.5	390.00
Transportation and utilities	209	38.0	405.00
Secretaries V	245	38.5	441.00
Manufacturing	160	39.0	451.00
Nonmanufacturing	54	38.0	486.00
Stenographers	717	39.0	387.50
Switchboard operators	249	39.5	229.00
Nonmanufacturing	225	39.5	219.00
Transportation and utilities	45	39.5	290.50
Switchboard operator-receptionists	795	39.5	223.00
Manufacturing	137	40.0	240.00
Nonmanufacturing	658	39.5	219.50
Transportation and utilities	39	40.0	241.50
Order clerks	1,039	39.0	258.50
Manufacturing	368	40.0	262.00
Nonmanufacturing	671	39.0	256.50
Order clerks I	560	39.0	238.00
Manufacturing	172	39.5	253.50
Nonmanufacturing	388	39.0	231.00
Order clerks II	479	39.0	282.00
Manufacturing	196	40.0	269.50
Nonmanufacturing	283	38.5	291.00
Accounting clerks	4,855	39.0	272.00
Manufacturing	483	40.0	283.50
Nonmanufacturing	4,372	39.0	270.50
Transportation and utilities	868	39.0	360.00
Accounting clerks I	290	39.5	228.00
Nonmanufacturing	288	39.5	228.00
Accounting clerks II	2,478	39.0	257.00
Manufacturing	251	40.0	243.50
Nonmanufacturing	2,227	39.0	258.50
Transportation and utilities			
Stenographers	434	39.0	346.00
Nonmanufacturing	563	39.5	289.50
Professional and technical occupations—men			
Computer systems analysts (business)	851	38.0	615.00
Manufacturing	165	39.5	623.50
Nonmanufacturing	686	37.5	613.00
Computer systems analysts (business) I	222	37.5	514.50
Nonmanufacturing	221	37.5	514.50
Computer systems analysts (business) II	368	38.0	622.00
Manufacturing	52	39.5	622.50
Nonmanufacturing	316	37.5	622.00
Computer systems analysts (business) III	256	38.5	693.50
Manufacturing	107	39.5	627.00
Computer programmers (business)	839	39.0	454.00
Manufacturing	61	39.5	472.00
Nonmanufacturing	778	39.0	452.50
Computer programmers (business) II	386	39.0	444.50
Nonmanufacturing	364	39.0	445.50
Computer programmers (business) III	257	39.5	528.00
Nonmanufacturing	228	39.5	528.50
Computer operators	875	39.0	354.50
Manufacturing	133	40.0	415.00
Nonmanufacturing	742	38.5	343.50
Transportation and utilities	132	38.5	403.50

See footnotes at end of tables.

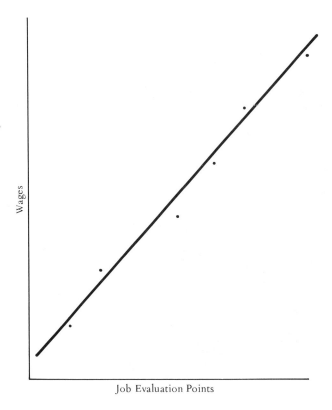

FIGURE 5–2.   Typical Wage Curve—Using Job Evaluation Points

uals in higher pay grades who are less senior or less competent. Figure 5–4 shows an example of the typical overlapping pay grades. It must be noted that once an employee reaches the top level of a pay grade that individual's pay can only be increased by an overall increase of the pay levels within the organization. Unless the individual is qualified in other respects, promotion to a higher pay grade should not be used as a tool for increasing the pay of an employee.

PAYING THE JOBS

Since all of the organization's jobs are classified by pay grade, depending on the points assigned, a pay range is established for each

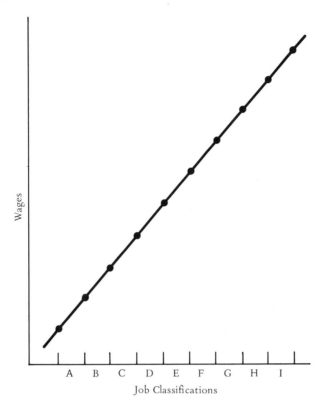

FIGURE 5–3. Typical Wage Curve—Using Job Classifications/Pay Grades

job. The various steps can be established and a pay rate established. Figure 5–5 shows the pay schedule for the U.S. Government, which uses a fairly large number of classifications. Figure 5–6 (a, b, and c) shows the jobs pay scale and job classifications for a large manufacturing organization. Most organizations explicitly establish the requirements for each step within a pay grade. "Actual range construction is an art; it is an iterative process in which the compensation analyst tries to meet the constraints of internal policy and still allows the organization to provide external equity." (Wallace:168) The organization's job manual might include detailed instructions descibing how an individual would progress through the various steps in a pay grade. Some steps would simply automatically be made the longer the individual performed the job satisfactorily, others would be the result of performance evalua-

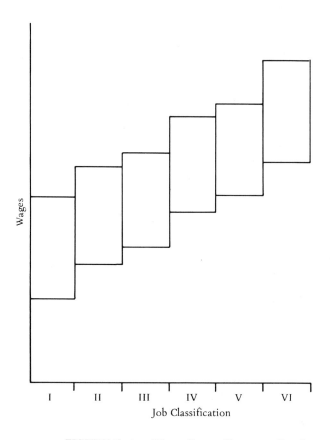

FIGURE 5–4.   Wage Curve Showing Overlapping Pay Grades

tion. Promotions, based on merit, might permit an employee to advance one or more pay grades.

ADJUSTMENTS TO THE STRUCTURE

When an organization applies the wage structure to existing jobs, there are three possible consequences. First, all jobs may fit perfectly. Second, some of the existing jobs may be underpaid. Third, some of the existing jobs may be overpaid.

If all the jobs are paid the correct amount the analyst can sit back, smile, and relax. When jobs are underpaid they should be, using an accelerated timetable, upgraded for payment at the cor-

General Schedule Pay System

	$8,342	$8,620	$8,898	$9,175	$9,453	$9,615	$9,890	$10,165	$10,178	$10,439
GS-1										
2	9,381	9,603	9,913	10,178	10,292	10,595	10,898	11,201	11,504	11,807
3	10,235	10,576	10,917	11,258	11,599	11,940	12,281	12,622	12,963	13,304
4	11,490	11,873	12,256	12,639	13,022	13,405	13,788	14,171	14,554	14,937
5	12,354	13,282	13,710	14,138	14,566	14,994	15,422	15,850	16,279	16,706
6	14,328	14,806	15,284	15,762	16,240	16,718	17,196	17,674	18,152	18,630
7	15,922	16,453	16,984	17,515	18,046	18,577	19,108	19,639	20,170	20,701
8	17,634	18,222	18,810	19,398	19,986	20,574	21,162	21,750	22,338	22,926
9	19,477	20,126	20,775	21,424	22,073	22,722	23,371	24,020	24,669	25,318
10	21,449	22,164	22,879	23,594	24,309	25,024	25,739	26,454	27,169	27,884
11	23,566	24,352	25,138	25,924	26,710	27,496	28,282	29,068	29,854	30,640
12	28,245	29,187	30,129	31,071	32,013	32,955	33,897	34,839	35,731	36,723
13	33,586	34,706	35,326	36,946	38,066	39,186	40,306	41,426	42,546	43,666
14	39,689	41,012	42,335	43,658	44,981	46,004	47,627	48,950	50,273	51,696
15	46,485	48,241	49,797	51,353	52,909	54,465	56,021	57,577	59,133	60,689
16	54,765	56,580	58,405	60,230	62,055	63,390	65,705	67,530	69,055	
17	64,142	66,280	68,418	70,656	72,694					
18	75,177									

Source: Federal Register, Vol. 46, No. 200, Friday, October 16, 1981, p. 50922.

FIGURE 5–5. U.S. Government GS Pay Schedule

Class 1

Assembly Helper
Laundryman
Duplicator Operator
Messenger
Typist

Class 2

General Clerk
Clerk Typist
Keypunch Operator

Class 3

Bonded Assembler
Fabrication Helper
Machine Shop Helper
Material Sorter
Milling Machine Operator C
Numbering Machine Operator
Service Worker

Class 4

Roll Operator B
Drill Operator
Components Tester
Maintenance Helper
Power Trucker
Service Attendant

Class 5

Burring Operator
Structure Sealer
Chemical Process Masker
Crane Rigger Helper
Detail Assembler
Drill Press Operator B
Drill Sharpener
Mechanic C
Plastic Parts Fabricator

Class 6

Painter
Prep Operator
Metal Baler
Cable Assembler
Decal Applier
Milling Machine Operator B
Portable Tool Repairman

Class 7

Assembler Installer
Brill Operator B
Bench Hand
Drop Hammer Helper
Electrical Assembler
Form Block Maker B

Class 8

Automatic Routing
    Machine Operator
Bonded Fabricator
Carpenter B
Chemical Processor
Circular Saw Operator
Drill Press Operator A

Class 9

Chauffeur
Concrete Finisher
Roll Operator A
Model Painter
Final Painter

Class 10

Drill Operator A
Bonded Autoclave Operator
Crane Rigger
Crater
PC Inspector
Mechanic B

Class 11

Assembler-Sheet Metal
Electronics Mechanic
Tank Installer
Grinder-Tool Cutter
Hydraulic Assembler
Milling Machine Operator A

Class 12

Continuity Checker
Horizontal Boring Mill Operator
Cable Splicer
Chemical Milling Mechanic
Die Cast Finisher
Engineer Lathe Operator
Bench Metal Worker

Class 13

Bench Machinist
Body Mechanic
Drop Hammer Operator
Electronics Technician
Form Block Maker A

Class 14

Checkout Mechanic
Heat Treater
Hydraulic Mechanic
Ultrasonic Inspector

Class 15

Cabinet Maker
Carpenter A
Precision Grinder
Inspector-Precision
Mechanic A
Set Up Man
Set Up Mechanic

FIGURE 5–6(a).   Jobs by Classification for a Large Manufacturing Organization

rect level. Care must be taken though, because when certain selected jobs are upgraded, there is a potential for morale problems with employees whose positions were not similarly adjusted.

Jobs that are overpaid are often called "red circle jobs" or "red circle rates." These jobs cannot be cut in pay without serious morale consequences. Instead, the jobs are generally given minimal or token increases at appraisal time until their pay falls within the specified range. If there are an excessive number of red circle rates, then the entire system of job evaluation will need a careful examination and potentially a complete restructuring.

The structure should be taken seriously, but not as an absolute straight jacket. Job evaluation is a tool, and wage survey data are estimates and averages. Building the structure is a matter of judgment, not a precise science.

JOB CLASS	MIN					MAX
15	10.96	11.24	11.29	11.57	11.63	11.91
14	10.74	11.05	11.06	11.37	11.39	11.70
13	10.54	10.86	10.86	11.18	11.19	11.51
12	10.39	10.70	10.72	11.03	11.04	11.35
11	10.31	10.61	10.62	10.92	10.94	11.24
10	10.22	10.51	10.53	10.82	10.85	11.14
9	10.12	10.42	10.46	10.72	10.73	11.03
8	10.02	10.29	10.32	10.59	10.63	10.90
7	9.00	9.30	9.61	10.21	10.51	10.82
6	8.91	9.20	9.50	10.08	10.37	10.67
5	8.82	9.11	9.41	9.97	10.26	10.56
4	8.75	9.04	9.34	9.90	10.19	10.49
3	8.69	8.98	9.28	9.85	10.14	10.44
2	8.67	8.96	9.26	9.78	10.07	10.37
1	8.62	8.90	9.19	9.67	9.95	10.24

FIGURE 5–6(b). Pay Grades for a Large Manufacturing Organization

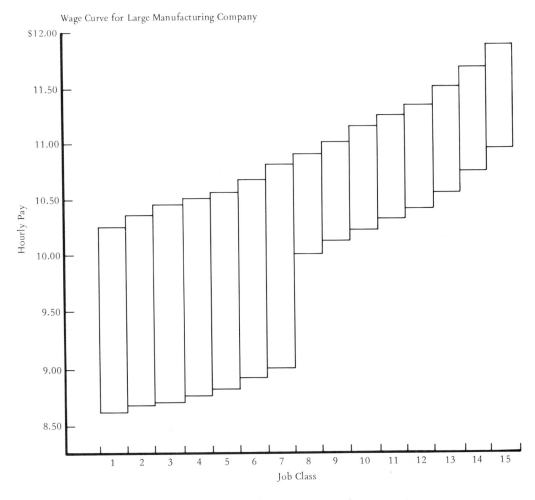

FIGURE 5–6(c).   Wage Curve for a Large Manfacturing Company

SUMMARY

Determining the absolute worth of the jobs within any organization depends on many factors, including comparable wages paid in the region and in the same type of business; the organization's ability to pay; and the supply and demand factors that influence the availability of certain skills. This wage data must be carefully coupled with the organization's job evaluation to develop a pay scale for the various jobs within the organization. Only after this is done can the pay level for the individuals in the organization be set.

Review Questions

1. What is a pay grade?
2. How are pay grades established?
3. How many pay grades should an organization have?
4. What factors influence the number of pay grades an organization uses?
5. How are jobs assigned to pay grades?
6. What factors influence the actual wage payments for pay grades?
7. Why might certain industries pay more than others for comparable worth?
8. Why are wages higher in certain regions of the country than in others?
9. How does supply and demand affect the wages paid for certain jobs?
10. What are some jobs that might be affected by the supply and demand factors?
11. What is a wage survey?
12. What are the various forms that a wage survey can take?
13. What are some typical fringe benefits offered to workers?
14. What types of information should be included on a wage survey?
15. What are some sources of wage survey data?
16. How are wage survey data related to an organization's jobs?
17. What is a wage curve?
18. How is a wage curve used to set pay rates?
19. How do pay ranges relate to the wage curve?
20. How do individuals progress through pay ranges?
21. How do individuals progress into a higher pay grade?
22. How do overlapping pay ranges affect the wage payments for an individual who has been promoted into a job with a higher classification?
23. How are underpaid jobs adjusted?
24. How are overpaid jobs adjusted?
25. What are red circle rates?
26. What problems result when out-of-line jobs are adjusted to comply with the wage scale?
27. How are wages increased for jobs that are on the top step of a particular pay range?

References

Belcher, David W., *Compensation Administration*, Prentice-Hall, Englewood Cliffs, NJ, 1974.

Chruden, H. and Sherman, A., *Managing Human Resources*, Southwestern Publishing Company, Cincinnati, 1984.

Henderson, R., *Compensation Management*, Reston Publishing Company, Inc., Reston, Virginia, 1985.

Patton, J., Littlefield, C. and Self, S., *Job Evaluation*, Richard D. Irwin, Homewood, Illinois, 1964.

Wallace, M.J. and Fay, C.H., *Compensation Theory and Practice*, Kent Publishing Company, Boston, 1983.

Zalusky, John, "Job Evaluation: An Uneven World," AFL-CIO *American Federationist*, April, 1981.

Zollitsch, H.G. and Langsner, A., *Wage and Salary Administration*, Southwestern Publishing Company, Cincinnati, 1970.

Case Study (Mountain View College, continued)

MOUNTAIN VIEW COLLEGE

The wage and salary administrator at Mountain View College elected to establish three pay classifications for the secretarial and clerical jobs found at the college. These were called job classes 1, 2, and 3. Job class 1, using the job evaluation system designed at the end of Chapter 5, included all jobs with 100 to 133 possible points, job class 2 had jobs with 134 to 167 points, and job class 3 contained 168 to 200 possible evaluation points. Figure 5–7 lists the job titles and shows the classification for the sample jobs that have been described in this continuing case study.

For convenience, MVC decided to use the wage survey data compiled by the Bureau of Labor Statistics and published in its area survey. Within the BLS data, three positions that have similar job descriptions to the jobs found in each of the college's three job classifications were identified. Figure 5–8 shows all the job descriptions, as prepared by BLS and published in the area wage survey, for the positions identified as secretary 1, secretary 2, and secretary 3. Pay special attention to the descriptions.

Figure 5–9 shows the weekly earnings of office workers in Atlanta for a variety of office workers. Note on the figure that the average weekly salary for secretaries in nonmanufacturing positions was, for the three positions, secretary I, II, and III, respectively, $257, $283.50, and $350. Figure 5–10 highlights the range of pay for each of these positions. This range was used by MVC to establish the pay ranges for each of the three job classes. Within each of these three classes it was decided to have five steps ranging from the minimum for each position, the entry level position, to the maximum. The entire pay scale is shown in Figure 5–11. It should be noted at this point that had their been more classifications MVC would have had to prepare a wage curve. As Figure 5–12 shows, the curve for the three positions is not really necessary, since it does not add very much to the available information. However, if there were 10 or 20 job classes, it would be most useful for sorting out the data required to prepare the pay scale shown in Figure 5–11.

Class 1	Class 2	Class 3
Junior Records Clerk	Departmental Secretary	Dean of Student Affairs
	Records Clerk	Secretary
	Registrar's Clerk	Admissions Secretary
	Public Relations Secretary	Dean's Secretary
	Library Assistant	Senior Library Assistant
		Accountant

FIGURE 5–7. MVC Jobs Arranged by Classification

Level of Secretary's Supervisor (LS)

LS-1

a. Secretary to the supervisor or head of a small organizational unit (e.g., fewer than about 25 or 30 persons); or

b. Secretary to a nonsupervisory staff specialist, professional employee, administrative officer or assistant, skilled technician or expert. (NOTE: Many companies assign stenographers, rather than secretaries as described above, to this level of supervisory or nonsupervisory worker.)

LS-2

a. Secretary to an executive or managerial person whose responsibility is not equivalent to one of the specific level situations in the definition for LS-3, but whose organizational unit normally numbers at least several dozen employees and is usually divided into organizational segments which are often, in turn, further subdivided. In some companies, this level includes a wide range of organizational echelons; in others, only one or two; or

b. Secretary to the head of an individual plant, factory, etc., (or other equivalent level of official) that employs, in all, fewer than 5,000 persons.

LS-3

a. Secretary to the chairman of the board or president of a company that employs, in all, fewer than 100 persons; or

b. Secretary to a corporate officer (other than chairman of the board or president) of a company that employs, in all, over 100 but fewer than 5,000 persons; or

c. Secretary to the head (immediately below the officer level) over either a major corporatewide functional activity (e.g., marketing, research, operations, industrial relations, etc.) or a major geographic or organizational segment (e.g., a regional headquarters; a major division) of a company that employs, in all, over 5,000 but fewer than 25,000 employees; or

d. Secretary to the head of an individual plant, factory, etc., (or other equivalent level of official) that employs, in all, over 5,000 persons; or

e. Secretary to the head of a large and important organizational segment (e.g., a middle management supervisor of an organizational segment often involving as many as several hundred persons) of a company that employs, in all, over 25,000 persons.

FIGURE 5–8.   BLS Job Descriptions

LS-4

a. Secretary to the chairman of the board or president of a company that employs, in all, over 100 but fewer than 5,000 persons; or

b. Secretary to a corporate officer (other than the chairman of the board or president) of a company that employs, in all, over 5,000 but fewer than 25,000 persons; or

c. Secretary to the head, immediately below the corporate officer level, of a major segment or subsidiary of a company that employs, in all, over 25,000 persons.

NOTE: The term "corporate officer" used in the above LS definition refers to those officials who have a significant corporatewide policymaking vote role with regard to major company activities. The title "vice president," though normally indicative to this role, does not in all cases identify such positions. Vice presidents whose primary responsibility is to act personally on individual cases or transactions (e.g., approve or deny individual loan or credit actions; administer individual trust accounts; directly supervise a clerical staff) are not considered to be "corporate officers" for purposes of applying the definition.

Level of Secretary's Responsibility (LR)

This factor evaluates the nature of the work relationship between the secretary and the supervisor, and the extent to which the secretary is expected to exercise initiative and judgment. Secretaries should be matched at LR-1 or LR-2 described below according to their level of responsibility.

LR-1

Performs varied secretarial duties including or comparable to most of the following:

a. Answers telephones, greets personal callers, and opens incoming mail;

b. Answers telephone requests which have standard answers. May reply to requests by sending a form letter;

c. Reviews correspondence, memoranda, and reports prepared by others for the supervisor's signature to ensure procedural and typographical accuracy;

d. Maintains supervisor's calendar and makes appointments as instructed;

e. Types, takes and transcribes dictation, and files.

FIGURE 5–8. BLS Job Descriptions *(continued)*

LR-2

Performs duties described under LR-1 and, *in addition* performs tasks requiring greater judgment, initiative, and knowledge of office functions including or comparable to most of the following:

a. Screens telephone and personal callers, determining which can be handled by the supervisor's subordinates or other offices;

b. Answers requests which require a detailed knowledge of office procedures or collection of information from files or other offices. *May* sign routine correspondence in own or supervisor's name;

c. Compiles or assists in compiling periodic reports on the basis of general instructions;

d. Schedules tentative appointments without prior clearance. Assembles necessary background material for scheduled meetings. Makes arrangements for meetings and conferences;

e. Explains supervisor's requirements to other employees in supervisor's unit. (Also types, takes dictation, and files.)

The following tabulation shows the level of the secretary for each LS and LR combination:

	LR-1	*LR-2*
LS-1	I	I
LS-2	II	III
LS-3	III	IV
LS-4	IV	V

STENOGRAPHER

(4623:Stenographer)

Primary duty is to take dictation using shorthand, and to transcribe the dictation. May also type from a written copy. May operate from a stenographic pool. May occasionally transcribe from voice recordings. (If primary duty is transcribing from recordings, see Transcribing-machine typist.)

NOTE: This job is distinguished from that of a secretary in that a secretary normally works as the principal office assistant performing more responsible and discretionary tasks.

FIGURE 5–8. BLS Job Descriptions *(continued)*

Stenographer I.

Takes and transcribes dictation under close supervision and detailed instructions. May maintain files, keep simple records, or perform other relatively routine clerical tasks.

Stenographer II.

Takes and transcribes dictation determining the most appropriate format. Performs stenographic duties requiring significantly greater independence and responsibility than Stenographer I. Supervisor typically provides general instructions. Work requires a thorough working knowledge of general business and office procedures and of the specific business operations, organizations, policies, procedures, files, workflow, etc. Uses this knowledge in performing stenographic duties and responsible clerical tasks such as maintaining follow-up files; assembling material for reports, memoranda, and letters; composing simple letters from general instructions; reading and routing incoming mail; answering routine questions, etc.

TRANSCRIBING-MACHINE TYPIST
(4623:Stenographer)

Primary duty is to type copy of voice recorded dictation which does *not* involve varied technical or specialized vocabulary such as that used in legal briefs or reports on scientific research. May also type from written copy. May maintain files, keep simple records, or perform other relatively routine clerical tasks. (See Stenographer definition for workers involved with shorthand dictation.)

TYPIST
(4624:Typist)

Uses a manual, electric, or automatic typewriter to type various materials. Included are automatic typewriters that are used only to record text and update and reproduce previously typed items from magnetic cards or tape. May include typing of stencils, mats, or similar materials for use in duplicating processes. May do clerical work involving little special training, such as keeping simple records, filing records and reports, or sorting and distributing incoming mail.

Excluded from this definition is work that involves:

a. Typing directly from spoken material that has been recorded on disks, cylinders, belts, tapes, or other similar media;

FIGURE 5–8.   BLS Job Descriptions *(continued)*

b. The use of varitype machines, composing equipment, or automatic equipment in preparing material for printing; and

c. Familiarity with specialized terminology in various keyboard commands to manipulate or edit the recorded text to accomplish revisions, or to perform tasks such as extracting and listing items from the text, or transmitting text to other terminals, or using "sort" commands to have the machine reorder material. Typically requires the use of automatic equipment which may be either computer linked or have a programmable memory so that material can be organized in regularly used formats or performed paragraphs which can then be coded and stored for future use in letters or documents.

Typist I

Performs *one or more of the following:* Copy typing from rough or clear drafts; or routine typing of forms, insurance policies, etc.; or setting up simple standard tabulations; or copying more complex tables already set up and spaced properly.

Typist II

Performs *one or more of the following:* Typing material in final form when it involves combining material from several sources; or responsibility for correct spelling, syllabication, punctuation, etc., of technical or unusual words or foreign language material; or planning layout and typing of complicated statistical tables to maintain uniformity and balance in spacing. May type routine form letters, varying details to suit circumstances.

FILE CLERK

(4696:File clerk)

Files, classifies, and retrieves material in an established filing system. May perform clerical and manual tasks required to maintain files. Positions are classified into levels on the basis of the following definitions:

File Clerk I

Performs routine filing of material that has already been classified or which is easily classified in a simple serial classification system (e.g., alphabetical, chronological, or numerical). As requested, locates readily available material in files and forwards material; and may fill out withdrawal charge. May perform simple clerical and manual tasks required to maintain and service files.

FIGURE 5–8. BLS Job Descriptions *(continued)*

FIGURE 5–9. Weekly Earnings of Office Workers in Atlanta, Ga., May 1983

Occupation and Industry Division	Number of Workers	Average Weekly Hours[2] (Standard)	Weekly Earnings (in dollars)[1] Mean[2]	Median[2]	Middle range[2]	120 and under 140	140–160	160–180	180–200	200–220	220–240	240–260	260–280	280–300	300–320	320–340	340–360	360–380	380–400	400–420	420–440	440–460	460–480	480–520	520–560	560 and over
Secretaries	3,929	39.0	344.00	330.00	274.00–403.50	—	—	26	61	106	265	314	321	309	379	352	276	218	246	215	228	112	94	253	108	46
Manufacturing	1,001	39.5	355.50	331.00	280.50–415.50	—	—	—	—	—	45	112	90	97	99	116	81	56	39	22	17	18	3	142	45	19
Nonmanufacturing	2,928	39.0	340.00	329.00	271.00–403.50	—	—	26	61	106	220	202	231	212	280	236	195	162	207	193	211	94	91	111	63	27
Transportation and utilities	509	38.5	426.00	435.00	379.00–466.50	—	—	—	—	—	—	—	—	7	24	29	31	40	39	29	119	36	48	69	33	5
Secretaries I	638	38.5	264.00	259.00	226.00–303.50	—	—	46	47	104	113	68	59	92	40	19	2	2	17	3	—	—	—	—	—	—
Manufacturing	177	39.5	282.00	271.00	247.50–310.00	—	—	—	—	31	27	39	23	22	15	18	2	—	—	—	—	—	—	—	—	—
Nonmanufacturing	461	38.0	257.00	243.50	216.00–300.00	—	—	46	47	73	86	29	36	70	25	1	—	2	17	3	—	—	—	—	—	—
Secretaries II	858	38.5	289.00	287.50	251.50–317.00	—	—	—	15	22	108	97	166	116	135	88	36	20	—	4	2	8	1	—	—	—
Manufacturing	206	39.0	307.00	291.00	271.00–327.00	—	—	—	—	—	11	18	47	39	27	24	3	15	—	2	2	—	—	—	—	—
Nonmanufacturing	652	38.5	283.50	279.00	245.00–313.50	—	—	—	15	22	97	79	119	77	108	64	33	5	—	2	—	8	1	—	—	—
Secretaries III	1,077	39.0	367.00	350.00	285.50–464.00	—	—	—	37	49	93	79	80	98	98	64	65	48	64	23	90	12	35	183	59	2
Manufacturing	324	40.0	405.50	494.00	289.50–494.00	—	—	—	—	2	62	4	19	14	—	19	17	—	48	—	—	—	—	—	31	2
Nonmanufacturing	753	39.0	350.00	339.00	279.00–426.00	—	—	—	37	47	31	75	61	84	—	45	48	—	—	—	—	—	—	—	28	—
Transportation and utilities	226	38.5	433.50	438.00	424.50–477.00	—	—	—	—	—	—	—	—	—	—	—	54	13	4	52	85	44	42	139	—	2
Secretaries IV	795	38.5	382.50	364.50	330.00–428.00	—	—	—	—	2	2	11	2	51	53	47	115	68	64	52	71	53	19	39	14	18
Manufacturing	209	38.5	360.00	339.50	318.00–367.00	—	—	—	—	—	1	—	16	36	17	35	27	10	—	7	7	1	—	1	—	6
Nonmanufacturing	586	38.5	390.00	380.50	335.00–435.50	—	—	—	—	2	1	6	2	35	36	80	41	54	45	70	71	51	19	38	14	12
Transportation and Utilities	209	38.0	405.00	401.00	362.00–446.50	—	—	—	—	—	—	—	—	7	9	14	24	29	16	32	27	13	6	13	12	2
Secretaries V	245	38.5	441.00	427.00	369.50–491.00	—	—	—	—	—	—	—	3	—	1	11	37	18	13	33	15	14	27	28	19	●26
Nonmanufacturing	160	39.0	451.00	461.50	369.50–507.00	—	—	—	—	—	—	—	3	—	1	—	29	11	1	22	2	6	24	27	19	15
Transportation and utilities	54	38.0	486.00	481.00	455.50–530.00	—	—	—	—	—	—	—	—	—	—	—	1	1	—	4	2	6	12	12	13	3
Stenographers	736	39.0	386.50	379.50	329.50–477.00	—	2	2	2	11	21	42	25	53	52	33	215	4	6	25	25	42	175	1	—	—
Stenographers I	221	38.5	320.50	329.50	276.00–360.00	—	2	2	10	17	32	32	13	21	38	9	60	2	6	1	1	1	4	1	—	—
Nonmanufacturing	221	38.5	320.50	329.50	276.00–360.00	—	2	2	10	17	32	32	13	21	38	9	60	2	6	1	1	1	4	1	—	—
Transportation and utilities	194	38.5	323.50	330.00	276.00–360.00	—	2	2	10	17	19	19	5	21	38	6	58	1	6	1	1	1	4	1	—	—
Stenographers II	515	39.0	415.00	433.00	379.50–485.00	—	—	—	1	—	4	10	12	32	14	155	2	—	2	—	24	41	171	—	—	—
Typists	518	38.5	223.50	217.00	175.00–248.00	42	42	51	39	38	112	38	10	8	17	4	13	6	6	—	—	2	1	7	—	—
Nonmanufacturing	386	38.0	211.00	189.00	167.00–210.50	42	42	49	29	28	63	9	8	6	14	4	12	6	6	—	—	2	—	3	—	—
Transportation and utilities	63	38.0	305.00	322.00	224.50–360.00	—	—	2	12	5	3	9	4	3	7	4	12	6	6	—	—	—	—	3	—	—
Typists I	363	38.5	204.00	187.00	167.00–227.00	42	42	39	38	56	16	17	3	3	8	4	13	6	—	—	2	—	1	4	—	—
Nonmanufacturing	304	38.0	197.50	176.00	167.00–200.50	42	42	37	28	28	5	12	1	2	8	4	12	6	—	—	2	—	—	4	—	—
Typists II	155	39.0	268.50	248.00	230.50–284.00	—	—	2	12	56	22	21	5	5	12	—	13	—	—	2	—	—	—	4	—	—
Nonmanufacturing	82	37.5	259.50	230.50	230.50–315.00	—	—	2	12	35	3	4	2	2	12	—	12	—	—	2	—	—	—	3	—	—
Transportation and utilities	38	37.0	277.00	280.50	199.50–360.00	—	—	2	12	1	31	2	2	3	4	—	12	—	—	2	—	—	—	3	—	—
File clerks	441	38.5	197.00	173.00	160.00–220.00	22	72	63	77	39	44	24	13	—	12	4	2	2	—	—	—	1	—	6	—	—
Nonmanufacturing	406	39.0	191.00	172.50	160.00–201.00	22	72	62	80	39	43	20	13	—	12	4	2	2	—	—	—	1	—	3	—	—
File clerks I	356	38.5	186.50	172.00	160.00–199.00	6	72	73	72	16	12	12	23	—	12	8	13	6	6	—	—	—	—	—	—	—
Nonmanufacturing	333	38.5	184.00	172.00	160.00–199.00	6	72	72	72	16	12	12	23	—	12	8	12	6	6	—	—	—	—	—	—	—
File clerks II	80	39.5	230.50	228.00	182.50–228.00	16	4	4	8	4	32	3	—	—	—	4	2	2	—	—	—	—	2	3	—	—
Nonmanufacturing	71	39.5	217.50	228.00	161.50–228.00	16	4	4	8	4	31	1	—	—	—	2	2	2	—	—	—	—	2	3	—	—
Messengers	240	39.0	209.50	193.00	176.00–215.50	—	37	63	77	39	3	4	13	7	1	8	8	2	6	3	3	—	—	—	—	—
Nonmanufacturing	222	38.0	209.00	193.00	176.00–210.00	—	37	62	70	34	1	4	13	7	1	8	8	2	6	3	1	—	—	—	—	—
Transportation and utilities	26	37.5	253.50	229.00	179.00–327.50	—	—	7	4	2	1	1	1	1	—	8	8	—	—	1	—	—	—	—	—	—
Switchboard operators	281	39.5	239.50	211.50	172.00–300.00	1	37	62	33	16	9	16	9	19	45	11	11	—	—	1	8	9	—	9	—	—
Nonmanufacturing	257	39.5	231.50	196.00	172.00–294.00	1	37	62	33	10	8	14	7	17	33	2	4	1	—	1	7	7	—	5	—	—
Transportation and utilities	50	39.5	313.00	280.00	240.00–358.00	—	—	7	2	2	2	2	1	2	6	6	2	1	—	7	7	5	—	5	—	—

[1] Weekly Earnings (in dollars).
[2] Standard hours / Mean / Median / Middle range.

147

Position	Minimum	Mean	Maximum
Secretary I	216.00	257.00	300.00
Secretary II	245.00	283.50	313.50
Secretary III	279.00	350.00	426.00

FIGURE 5–10.   Pay Ranges for Job Classes

Pay Grade	Step 1	2	3	4	5
1	216	237	258	279	300
2	245	262	279	296	313
3	279	314	349	384	419

FIGURE 5–11.   Pay Scale for Job Classes

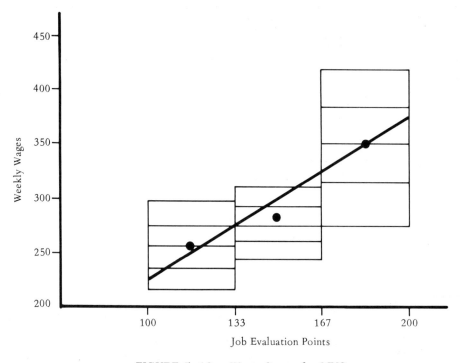

FIGURE 5–12.   Wage Curve for MVC

Case Study 5—1

THE PAY DIFFERENTIAL*

"No way those guys in Chicago are worth 30 cents an hour more than we are," Mike Brown said. Mike was the business manager of the Federated Association of Machinists, Local 467.

"You know that the Chicago area is a lot more expensive to live in than Bedford, Mike," Dirk Samson said. Dirk was vice president of labor relations for the Amalgamated Steel Fabrication Company, which had plants in both places.

"So what else is new? We work on the same machines—we produce the same output per worker. We should get paid the same. You guys are taking us."

"No, we're not. You know that our rate is 10 cents an hour over any other place in Bedford already."

"So what? That town only has a handful of machinists besides us, and they're non-union to boot. Come on, Dirk, face up to it. You've got a sweet deal, and I noticed your profits went up 20 percent last year besides. The boys here are upset, and this could get to be a sticky issue when the contract expires next year."

"I've got the figures right here, Mike. The cost of living in Bedford is 96, compared to 107 in Chicago. Actually you fellows are in better shape than those guys up there."

"Whose figures, Dirk—the Bureau of Labor Statistics? Those things are loaded, and you know it. Try telling one of my boys that it costs less to live here, and he'll laugh at you."

"You used those BLS figures last year to prove that the cost of living went up enough to justify an increase, Mike. They were okay then."

"I still say that we should equalize the rates. We do the same work, so we should get the same pay."

"It costs us more in Bedford."

"I thought you said it was cheaper, Dirk."

"It is for a family, but not for a company. Look where the place is— way out in southern Indiana. We have higher power costs, bigger transportation expenses, more telex costs—"

"That's your problem, Dirk. Our boys feel that it costs them more to live in Bedford. They're right, too—have you tried to own a house here or buy some groceries? The cost of living is way up."

"It's up everywhere, Mike, but Bedford's a totally different labor market than Chicago. You know that. You just can't compare the two."

"We're doing it, and we don't like what we see. Equal pay, equal work—that'll be the demand in the next contract. You may as well get ready for it."

---

*From Donald P. Crane, PERSONNEL, pp. 303–304. Copyright 1974 by Wadsworth, Inc. Reprinted by permission of Kent Publishing Company, 20 Park Plaza, Boston, MA; a division of Wadsworth, Inc.

Discussion

1. If you were a mediator (impartial third party) at the next contract bargaining session, what data would you want to work out this differential question? Why?
2. Give all arguments for equal pay for the union's negotiator. Do these seem reasonable?
3. Give all arguments for a pay differential for the company's negotiator. Do these seem reasonable?
4. Who is right?

Case Study 5–2

SALARY ADJUSTMENT: EQUITY AND MORALE*

It was faculty salary increase time. Dr. John Suverman, Dean of the Pharmacy College, had recently sent notices of salaries for the forthcoming year to all of his members.

Since he was new to the Dean's job, Suverman had asked University President Hadley what information to include in salary announcement letters. He was particularly concerned if he should inform each faculty member of the average increases for the entire college and for the University so that each professor would be able to compare an individual salary with the average.

President Hadley told Suverman to include in the letter only the salary for that faculty member, and this Suverman did.

Two days after announcement letters were issued, Professor Wick visited Dean Suverman's office. Suverman saw immediately that Wick was tense and upset.

"I would like to discuss my new salary—there must be a mistake in the announcement letter," Wick said. After a brief conversation concerning the contents of the letter, Suverman confirmed that the salary figure was indeed correct.

"But I thought my teaching and research performance this past year were excellent, and I am shocked that you awarded me only a 7% increase," Wick said.

Believing that Wick was an above average professor whom he wants to keep, Suverman explained that the legislature had not been very generous with faculty salary increases this year. He also said that no professor had received a great increase.

Wick wasn't satisfied. He asked whether his performance was lacking in the eyes of the University and what the average increase was for

---

*Reproduced with permission of Robert Knapp, College of Business, University of Colorado, Colorado Springs, CO.

the entire faculty so that he could determine how he did relative to his colleagues.

Suverman declined to release any more information than was in the announcement letter.

"I can't understand that," said Wick. "You have a well-deserved reputation as always being open and frank with the faculty."

The telephone rang, and Suverman picked it up.

After waiting impatiently for a few minutes, Wick hurriedly arose from his chair and started to leave the Dean's office. As he did so, Suverman, still on the phone, called out to Wick that he would finish his call shortly. The door was closing behind Wick, and Suverman wasn't sure his message was heard.

After finishing his phone conversation, Suverman pondered what to do. Wick was doing a good job, and Suverman didn't want to see such a valuable professor become dissatisfied and unmotivated. If Wick knew that the average increase was only 4% and that he had received the third highest increase among the 23 faculty members, Suverman felt that Wick was reasonable enough to gladly accept that situation. Perhaps, he thought, he should just tell Wick this privately and ask him not to reveal it.

Suverman also realized that Wick apparently did not know that, because the University was a public institution operating under an "open information" law, all faculty salaries were published in a roster available in the library to anyone who requested it. While the University did not hide this fact, it did not advertise it either. Consequently, many newer faculty members did not know of the existence of the roster.

Perhaps, Suverman mused, he should send a letter to all the faculty telling them about the roster. On the other hand, this might distress President Hadley and, anyway, the roster wouldn't be available for another month.

He thought it would be even more risky to announce in a memo or in a faculty meeting the average salary increase awarded by the college. Although he felt this was the fairest approach, Suverman was certain that if he asked for Hadley's permission in advance, it would be denied.

Better to just go ahead and do it, he concluded. Hadley might never find out. If he did, Suverman believed he could defend his action by arguing that the University secrecy policy was wrong and should be changed, and by explaining to the President his desire not to discourage a good faculty member. He could also point out that accounts in local newspapers and in-house newsletters had fairly accurate estimates of the average compensation allocated to the University. Some faculty members read these and some did not, and no one was really sure how accurate they were.

Instead of going that route, perhaps the safest approach would be to do nothing and hope that Wick would get over it.

Suverman finally decided to wait a few days, watch Wick carefully, and see if anyone else complained.

Discussion

1. How would you evaluate and possibly change the university's policies?
2. Which actions would you recommend for Dean Suverman? Why?
3. Would your answer to question 2 be any different if the average faculty salary increase was 10% instead of 4%?
4. What should Dean Suverman have done when Professor Wick walked out of his office?

Case Study 5–3

*INEQUITIES**

"Well, your company is certainly fair enough, Lars—$22,000 a year is right in the ballpark for new accountants."

Lars gulped. He had recommended Jeff himself, because they had been in school together for a while, but Lars had graduated two years ago. Jeff had dropped out for a while, fiddled around, and then gone back to finish. "Ah, $22,000?" Lars said weakly.

"Yeah, not a bad offer. The fringes are pretty good, too. What are they paying you, Lars?"

"Ah, $21,500."

"What? How come? You had better grades than I did."

"Well, two years ago the starting salary was $20,000. I've done quite well, really—gotten two good raises. I guess that the demand for accountants is picking up again."

"Believe me, it is. I had two other job offers. One was $21,500, and one was $22,500, but it was a lousy company. I think I'll go with yours."

"You know, Jeff, it just doesn't seem fair. I mean, here I've been working for two years, and I'm not getting as much as you'll get to start."

Jeff smiled. "Remember your economics, Lars. Supply and demand. Supply is up a bit, but demand is up more—and the market is talking. If a company wants a new accountant, they have to pay the price."

Discussion

1. How can the company handle this problem to avoid inequities? Can the problem be solved?
2. What should Lars do?

*From Donald P. Crane, PERSONNEL, p. 357. Copyright 1974 by Wadsworth, Inc. Reprinted by permission of Kent Publishing Company, 20 Park Plaza, Boston, MA.; a division of Wadsworth, Inc.

Case Study 5–4

ACE REPAIR COMPANY

The Ace Repair Company had developed its supervisory staff mainly by promoting line employees to first-line supervision positions. After a recent re-evaluation of jobs, accomplished through the job analysis procedure of interviewing the supervisors, the jobs in the departments supervised by employees who were promoted from within have all been evaluated higher than the comparable jobs in departments supervised by employees who did not work their way up. These positions would be paid a higher rate based on the higher evaluations.

Discussion

1. Why are these jobs evaluated higher?
2. Why are these jobs paid a higher rate?
3. How should the inequities, i.e., equal pay for comparable work, be resolved?

Case Study 5–5

WAGE RATES*

"I suppose that wage rates are related to the local economy," Samuel Miller, a British MBA candidate at Indiana University, commented. "But I still can't help but get annoyed at the situation."

"I will receive my MBA degree next June from one of the best American business schools," he continued. "I had hoped to return to England to work for either a British or American firm there. But I find that the pay offered there is ridiculous. My American friends in the MBA program are being offered $15,000 a year for their first job. They also get at least two or three offers each. But American firms offering me a position in England are talking about $7,000 or $8,000 a year if I return to England to work for them. At the same time, an American friend of mine who will go to England for his first job will be getting $15,500 a year. Only one British firm has offered me anything (the British are quite suspicious of American business education generally), and they offered me $5,000 and acted like they were doing me a favor. It just isn't fair!"

Mr. William Maxwell, a recruiter for a larger, multinational American firm, joined the conversation. "European students in American busi-

---

*From Donald P. Crane, PERSONNEL, pp. 354–355. Copyright 1974 by Wadsworth, Inc. Reprinted by permission of Kent Publishing Company, 20 Park Plaza, Boston, MA; a division of Wadsworth, Inc.

ness programs present a real problem for us," he commented. "Often they are very capable, intelligent young people with exactly the type of management training we would like to have them obtain. If they are from countries such as France and West Germany, where we have large operations, they are particularly desirable since they are bilingual as well. But the difficulty is that we can't really pay them according to American scales. To do so would wreck our pay scales abroad. How can we convince a young West German, who has a German university degree and speaks English, that he is worth only one half to one third of a countryman of his who happens to have studied in the United States? Actually, the pay differential may be justified, given the low development of business education in Europe, but you can't very well argue that in public."

Discussion

1. *Is it fair to base pay rates on local standards when the people in question have training which might make them more valuable to the firm hiring them?*
2. *Why does a European with a college education begin work at roughly one third to one half of the American pay scale?*
3. *Suppose your firm was expanding rapidly in Europe and needed large numbers of capable executives. Would you consider offering young Europeans in American business schools salaries as high as you were willing to pay young Americans?*

Case Study 5–6

BANK WAGES AT BEMUS BAY*

The Busti National Bank has just decided to open a branch in Bemus Bay, an exclusive resort located about 20 miles from Arkwright, a large city. There is no bank there at present.

Busti is anxious to determine the appropriate wage for the clerical staff it expects to hire. Clerks in the bank's offices in Arkwright receive a starting wage of $125 a week, but through promotions they can work up to $160. As a matter of company policy, these wage rates have been set at the midpoint of the range for other banks in Arkwright.

A survey of the local businesses at Bemus Bay, primarily realty and insurance offices and offices for local stores, indicates that the "going

---

*George Strauss, Leonard Sayles, PERSONNEL: THE HUMAN PROBLEMS OF MANAGEMENT, 3rd Ed., copyright 1972, p. 590. Reprinted by permission of Prentice-Hall, Inc., Englewood Cliffs, NJ.

rate" for qualified clerical personnel is $150–$175 a week. The higher rates in Bemus Bay may be attributed in part to the substantially higher cost of living in this resort town, the limited number of young women seeking employment, and the fact that there are no other banks in Bemus Bay. Banks in Arkwright have traditionally paid lower wages than other businesses, on the grounds that banks offer better working conditions and higher prestige.

Discussion

1. What should the Busti Bank establish as its hiring rate for clerical personnel? What factors should be considered in making the decision?
2. Could the bank justify to its Arkwright employees the fact that it was paying higher wages in Bemus Bay?

Case Study 5–7

JOB PRICING ASSIGNMENT (A)

Use the job evaluations prepared in the Point Rating Assignment (A) and your local area wage surveys to:

1. establish pay grades
2. develop a pay range for each job in the system.

Case Study 5–8

JOB PRICING ASSIGNMENT (B)

Use the job descriptions prepared in the job description exercise and the AAIM evaluations of these jobs performed in the Point Rating Assignment (B) to:

1. establish pay grades
2. develop a pay range for each job in the system (or each pay grade in the system).

Chapter Six

Performance Appraisal

INTRODUCTION

Closely tied to the job evaluation process at most organizations is the employee evaluation or performance appraisal system used by most organizations. According to a recent survey 89.4% of all organizations, both large and small, used some form of performance appraisal program. (Locher:246) For most organizations, performance evaluation is a management information system that provides input into all aspects of human resources management. For the individual, performance appraisal provides feedback about how well (or poorly) the individual's supervisor thinks the person is performing.

Obviously, employee evaluation can be a valuable management tool. Its use also has some critical legal ramifications, especially regarding fair employment practices. This chapter will examine performance appraisal, its many uses, and the conditions that make its use more effective. It will also survey some of the many different types of performance appraisal programs in use.

DEFINITION

In order to discuss performance appraisal a clear understanding of what is meant by the term is required. Many different organizations use the term as an umbrella to cover a variety of functions. As it will be used in the following pages, performance appraisal is defined as the subjective process of appraising the relative value of an employee to the company in terms of abilities, job performance, and potential. Usually the evaluation consists of a judgment made by one person of the way a subordinate employee has been fulfilling obligations to the organization since the last evaluation. It is an interpersonal process that occurs regularly between the supervisor and the people supervised. Appraisals should follow each job, task, or project as it is completed. Performance appraisal should be done on a regularly recurring basis. The results of performance appraisal would really be known before the formal appraisal is performed.

USES OF PERFORMANCE APPRAISAL

As was stated in the introduction, performance evaluation is a management information system. (Chruden and Sherman:231) Many very important personnel-related decisions are made based on the results of performance appraisal. A listing of the uses of performance appraisal would include:

- Determining compensation
- Improving employee performance
- Determining promotion
- Identifying training needs
- Justifying transfers
- Planning manpower requirements
- Justifying discipline
- Providing feedback on performance to employees
- Providing feedback on performance to managers
- Justifying discharge
- Determining work objectives

Far and away the most widely cited use of performance appraisal is for determining compensation, or increases in compensation. Running a strong second is its use as a base for identifying areas for employee performance improvement. Although certain pay ranges may be established for certain jobs, the placement of an individual in a particular pay grade depends to a large extent on that employee's individual performance evaluation. Appraisals are also used to guide the employee's development, especially in helping the organization achieve its objectives. The other uses, while important, are not found as frequently in business and industrial applications.

Four of the uses listed above, determining promotion, justifying transfers, justifying discipline, and justifying discharge, have potential legal ramifications. The Federal Government has numerous laws, rules, and regulations that govern the use and application of performance appraisal programs. These guidelines will be explored in the next section.

LEGAL IMPLICATIONS

Although the requirements of "good management" dictate that performance appraisal be performed on a regular basis—people do want to know where they stand in the eyes of their employers—there is an overriding reason, a legal reason, for the proper administration of the evaluation system. Two of the most important legal pronouncements on the issue are the *Uniform Federal Guidelines on Employee Selection Procedures*, a 1978 attempt to unify all Federal selection procedures, and the 1971 U.S. Supreme Court *Griggs vs. Duke Power* decision.

The Uniform Guidelines focus on two areas. First, there is concern when the bottom line does not reflect equity. Second, selection procedures, including performance appraisal, must be validated. The guidelines impact performance appraisal in that they provide detailed standards regarding minimum validation requirements. In the Griggs case, the Supreme Court ". . . defined the point at which employer practices such as performance appraisal results in illegal discrimination. At that point employer practices have an adverse impact on minorities and cannot be justified by business necessity." (Baroni:40)

There are other legal decisions that affect performance appraisal and its use in business. Also among the significant legal decisions regarding the appraisal of performance is the case of *Rowe vs. General Motors*. "In this case, the Fifth Circuit Court of Appeals concluded that the lack of Blacks who were promoted or transferred resulted from reliance on all-white supervisory recommendations which were based on subjective and vague standards." (Klasson, Thompson, and Luben:78) One other significant case, *Wade vs. Mississippi Cooperative Extension Service*, supported charges of discrimination in the areas of employee compensation and training. "Data must be provided that show a relationship between appraisal instruments and job analysis and show that the appraisal instrument is a valid predictor of job performance." (Henderson:220)

In order for organizations to comply with Federal Guidelines and Court decisions, the following guidelines for designing and using appraisal systems are suggested:

1. The overall appraisal process should be formalized, standardized, and as much as possible, be objective in nature.
2. The process should be as job related as possible.
3. A thorough job analysis for each position evaluated must be performed.

4. Subjective supervisory ratings should be just one component of the program.
5. Appraisers must be adequately trained in the use of the techniques.
6. Appraisers must have an adequate opportunity to observe employees.
7. When possible, multiple independent appraisals should be used.
8. The administration and scoring of performance appraisals should be standardized and controlled.
9. Opportunities for promotion and transfer must be posted and made available to all interested personnel.
10. An employee-initiated promotion/transfer procedure should exist which does not require the immediate supervisor's recommendation.

Following these guidelines will help to some of the legal questions that have been raised over the years regarding appraisal systems. These legal questions include:

- the use of ill-defined criteria
- affection by sexual and racial bias
- unstandardized conditions for scoring
- improper validation.

All of the legal requirements include mention of validity of the appraisal instrument. Validity is demonstration that the appraisal document actually tests what it purports to test. Validity can further be subdivided into the categories of concurrent, content criterion related, predictive, face, construct, convergent, and discriminant. Evaluation instruments also must show a reliability—the ability to achieve the same results every time they are used. Reliability can be demonstrated through a variety of techniques, including the test-retest method, the subdivided test method, and the parallel test method.*

CONDITIONS NECESSARY FOR APPRAISAL

In order to meet the requirements for a successful evaluation system, several conditions must be present in the organization. (Wallace and Fay:176–177) First is that employees must be able, to

---

*Most industrial psychology texts include a complete description of validity and reliability as they apply to measuring instruments. See for example McCormick and Ilger's, *Industrial Psychology* (Prentice-Hall, 1980, pages 52–55).

some extent, to control their own performance both in terms of quantity and quality. This can be either individually or as part of a group. A worker who can only respond to a machine cannot be fairly evaluated if she cannot influence the pace or speed of the machine.

Second, it must be important to the organization that employees produce above certain minimum expectation levels. There are some tasks where a single individual producing more than expected will disrupt the work and cause more problems than the better performance is worth. A third factor, and in light of the legal implications of performance appraisal, a very important condition, is that the individual or group's performance can be appraised in a valid and reliable way. Some useful criteria have been established for objective evaluation of employee performance. As long as these standards are included in the job descriptions they fall within the intent of the court decisions regarding the use of performance appraisal. These standards including the following:

- Number of Units Produced per Unit Time
- Number of Transactions Completed per Unit Time
- Worth of Transactions, in Dollars, Completed per Unit Time
- Earning or Commissions Earned per Unit Time
- Quantity of Suggestions submitted
- Quality of Suggestions submitted
- Percent increase in Profits
- Percent increase in Sales (dollars or units)
- Percent decrease in Cost
- Number of Inventory Turnovers per Unit Time
- Reject rate
- Number of absences
- Dollars Lost to Accidents
- Dollars Lost to Down Time
- Number of Complaints Received
- Number of Compliments Received

A fourth condition for the effective use of appraisal systems is that the evaluators be well trained. The following are the minimum requirements for appraisers.

1. The appraiser must have had an opportunity to observe the employee at work. Usually the supervisor is in the best position to do this.
2. The appraiser must understand the performance requirements and the conditions involved in the individual meeting these criteria.

3. The appraiser must have an appropriate point of view. The expectations of a first line supervisor of his employees are different than those of the plant manager. The supervisor is probably more attuned to the realities of the production floor.

Even when the preceding characteristics are present in evaluators, they still must be trained in the evaluation method used. A weakness of many performance evaluation programs is that managers and supervisors are not adequately trained for the task as evaluators and provide little meaningful feedback of their evaluations to subordinates. Evaluators must be carefully trained in order to do their job.

SELECTION/SPECIFICATION OF AN APPRAISAL METHOD

There are many types of appraisal instruments available for use by organizations. Some have been developed for specific organizations, others are more general in nature. The next section of this chapter will describe some of the different types of appraisal systems currently in use. Before examining these though, some selection criteria for choosing appraisal or evaluation systems are suggested.

First, the system employed must be relevant. The system and performance standards should relate to the objectives of the job.

Second, the system should be free from contamination by outside influences. Criteria beyond the control of the person being evaluated must not directly or indirectly influence the evaluation.

Third, the program used should have demonstrated reliability. No matter who performs the appraisal, the results should not differ significantly.

METHODS OF EVALUATION

There are many different methods available for evaluating performance. This section will summarize some of the most frequently used methods. The methods described are presented in no special order, although they are grouped by their general nature. [This text, while occasionally providing some editorial commentary about some of the appraisal systems, will not recommend a specific system.]

Rating Scales: These generally fit the format of a form containing one or more ranges of performance characteristics. The evaluator usually rates the level of employee performance in each category.

- *Global Ratings:* A global rating is the simplest of all the rating systems. A global rating simply asks, on perhaps a scale of from 1 to 10, a single evaluation of the employee's perform-ance. On such a scale, it is generally acknowledged that a rat-ing of 10 would be given to an employee who is outstanding in all aspects. The rating of 10 is reserved for those employees who are literally indispensible to the organization. A rating of 1 would be given to a thoroughly incompetent worker. (This rating of 1 would also probably indicate that the employee would soon be subject to disciplinary action by the organ-ization.)

- *Behaviorally Anchored Rating Scales (BARS):* The behavior-ally anchored rating scale, or BARS, provides the evaluator with more definition in the rating than does the Global Rating. A continuum scoring scheme is still used, but the worker's be-haviors are individually rated. Most BARS will use between 5 and 10 separate scales. Typical behaviors found on BARS in-clude knowledge of work, initiative, quality of work, quantity of work, and so on. These should correspond to the important aspects of the job, as identified in the job analysis, reflected in the job description, and used in the job evaluation. The rating scales developed would have individual adjectives developed for each of the behavioral traits. For example, if the trait to be rated is job knowledge, the top rating might correspond to the situation of "complete awareness of the latest techniques and their application to the operation." The bottom rating might be described as "no awareness of current practices and using outdated methods." Intermediate steps on the scale for this be-havior would have different, but vividly descriptive phrases that would guide the appraiser in identifying the proper rat-ing. Sometimes relatively simple adjectives, such as unsatis-factory, marginal, satisfactory, average, above average, supe-rior, excellent, and outstanding are used. This can lead to difficulty, though, regarding interpretation of the meanings of these words. Figure 6–1 shows an example of a portion of a typical BARS rating form.

Essay Methods: Essays are usually open-ended discussions regard-ing the employee's strengths and weaknesses. In the essay method, the appraiser must describe the employee within a number of

FIGURE 6–1. Behaviorally Anchored Rating Scale for Evaluating Judgment and Knowledge of Grocery Clerks

Extremely good performance	7	—
	—	—By knowing the price of items, this checker would be expected to look for mismarked and unmarked items.
Good performance	—	—
	—	—You can expect this checker to be aware of items that constantly fluctuate in price.
		—You can expect this checker to know the various sizes of cans—No. 303, No. 2½.
Slightly good performance	5	—When in doubt, this checker would ask the other clerk if the item is taxable.
	—	—This checker can be expected to verify with another checker a discrepancy between the shelf and the marked price before ringing up that item.
Neither poor nor good performance	4	—
	—	—When operating the quick check, the lights are flashing, this checker can be expected to check out a customer with 15 items.
Slightly poor performance	3	—
	—	—You could expect this checker to ask the customer the price of an item that he does not know.
	—	—In the daily course of personal relationships, may be expected to linger in long conversations with a customer or another checker.
Poor performance	2	—
	—	—In order to take a break, this checker can be expected to block off the checkstand with people in line.
Extremely poor performance	1	—

Source: L. Fogli, C. L. Hulin and M. R. Blood, "Development of First-Level Behavioral Job Criteria," *Journal of Applied Psychology*, vol. 55 (1971), pp. 3–8. Copyright 1971 by the American Psychological Association. Reprinted by permission.

broad categories, such as the appraiser's overall impression, the promotability of the employee, the jobs the employee is most qualified to perform, and the training and development assistance required by the employee. Obviously, the success of the essay method depends on the written communications skills of the appraiser.

- *Critical Incident Method:* In this method the supervisor or whoever is performing the evaluation should maintain a log or diary about each employee. In this diary the supervisor should record all critical behaviors, both positive and negative, that illustrate the employee's performance on the job. For example, if an employee was observed by the supervisor to be giving extra assistance to a customer, it might be noted:

  "5-8-84: went beyond normal expectations to help customer select best product for desired application."

  Similary, if there were a negative behavior shown, it could be noted:

  "6-14-84: extremely rude to a customer causing a loss of sale and undoubtedly a large amount of ill will to be generated."

  These critical incidents provide a detailed record of the employee's behaviors and give the required support or documentation necessary for an effective evaluation.

- *Field Review Method:* Closely related to the written method of performance evaluation is the field review method. Instead of the evaluator preparing a written report, the trained observer interviews the employee's supervisor. Based on the answers to various questions, an overall evaluation of the worker's performance is determined. This method's reliability depends on the skill of the interviewer in asking and interpreting answers to the questions.

Checklists: Checklists are usually relatively lengthy lists of potential employee behaviors. The appraiser checks those behaviors or characteristics that describe the employee being evaluated. Some of the commonly occurring behaviors on these checklists include statements such as these:

About attitude—

The worker is receptive to changes

About adaptability—

The worker learns new duties quickly

About dependability—

The worker comes to work on time

About quality—

The worker cares about his/her work

The listing could be extended to include many more categories, including effort, conduct, judgment, personality, initiative, and many statements about each. All should be traceable back to the job evaluation system. Several different types of checklists are described below. A number of examples are shown in the accompanying figures.

- *Simple Checklist:* A listing of between 15 and 50 characteristics which the evaluator checks as these characteristics apply to the employee being evaluated. Figure 6–2 shows an example of a typical simple checklist.
- *Weighted Checklist:* Each item on the checklist has a relative worth to the organization. When expressed as either all positive or all negative, the items checked provide a "score" or numerical evaluation of the employee. Usually the weights are assigned by people other than those doing the rating.
- *Forced Choice Checklist:* This method involves grouping the checklist items into subgroups, usually of from two to five items. From this subgroup listing the evaluator must select the item that "most" describes the employee and the item that "least" describes the employee. Often the choices are very close together in meaning, such as "energetic" and "trustworthy." The appraiser must honestly describe the employee when selecting between these characteristics. The rater, in effect, acts as a recorder and not as a judge. The judgment and analysis is left up to the experts in the personnel department. Figure 6–3 shows part of a typical forced choice checklist.

Ranking: Among the least sophisticated of the evaluation systems is that of ranking employees. This is a comparison of employees, with the net result being a subjective statement that Jones is best, Smith is the worst, Brown is the second best, and so on. Employees are evaluated on their overall usefulness to the organization. Here are some more sophisticated versions of this methodology:

- *Rank Order Method:* This method uses more characteristics than the simple "usefulness to organization" criteria. All employees are ranked and assigned a numerical score from 1 to n, depending on their "place" regarding that characteristic, for each of the selected behaviors. The overall ranking is a compilation of these individual rankings.

- *Forced Distribution:* The forced distribution method uses the characteristics of job performance and promotability as the characteristics to be ranked. The rater is required to assign each rated employee to a specific category, such as top 10% or bottom 10%. The slots are appropriated on the assumption that the work force is normally distributed; that there will be more people in the middle and as many above as below the middle range. Typically these rankings use five categories corresponding to the highest 10%, next 20%, middle 40%, lower 20%, and lowest 10%. Each employee must be placed in one of these classifications.

- *Person-to-Person Comparison:* This was the original ranking. It was based on five factors: physical qualities, intelligence, leadership, personal qualities, and general value. A number of key people are chosen as standard, their names placed on cards, and then rated one factor at a time. The highest-rated person is placed at the top and the one considered lowest at the bottom. One each is then selected from the middle and halfway on each side of the middle. All people to be rated are sorted in relation to the five "standard" key men in each of the basic factors.

Results Oriented: The last employee evaluation technique to be discussed is results oriented or management by objective (MBO). This philosophy was initially suggested by Peter F. Drucker. "It seeks to judge the performance . . . on the basis of their success in achieving the objectives they have established through consultation with their superiors." (Chruden and Sherman:243) Goals or targets are set by supervisors and employees on a regular basis. At the end of each set evaluation period both the employee and the supervisor assess progress towards meeting these goals. Generally the objectives are based on cost-related outcomes, such as profit, scrap rates, sales, cost of goods sold, and so forth. Figure 6–4 shows some examples of the types of objectives used in successful MBO programs. Management by objective requires that individual responsibilities be defined in terms of the objectives of the total organization. The expected results must be consistent with the controllable areas of responsibility.

The following conditions are absolutely essential for MBO to work:

1. MBO should be a system of management, not an addition to the manager's job.

Checklist for Clerical Personnel

	Poor	Fair	Average	Good	Excellent
Cooperation with Associates	☐ Will not cooperate with others. Does not fit in with associates.	☐ Cooperates well with certain individuals. Cannot work with all associates without bias.	☐ Presents an indifferent attitude. Works with others only as required.	☐ Works in harmony with others. Well liked by associates.	☐ Demonstrates an inspiring attitude of cooperation with associates.
Attendance	☐ Absences affect departmental work.	☐ Absent occasionally	☐ Frequently absent due to known health problem.	☐ Frequently absent for a variety of reasons.	☐ Regular attendance.
Punctuality	☐ Tardiness affects departmental work.	☐ Tardy occasionally.	☐ Frequently tardy due to same reason.	☐ Frequently tardy due to a variety of reasons.	☐ Always on time.
Grooming	☐ Exceptionally well-groomed. Always dresses appropriately.	☐ Grooming and/or dress could be improved.	☐ Grooming and dress generally good. Meets generally accepted standards.	☐ Grooming and dress always good. Meets generally accepted standards.	☐ Occasionally dresses inappropriately for this environment.

Supervisory Personnel Only

	Poor	Fair	Average	Good	Excellent
Ability to Plan and Schedule Work	☐ Unable to plan and schedule work to meet production standards.	☐ Occasionally must take corrective action because of poor planning/scheduling.	☐ Plans and schedules work in acceptable manner.	☐ Plans and schedules work well. Gets good results and meets deadlines.	☐ Excellent planning/scheduling. Gets maximum efficiency with labor/materials.
Leadership Ability	☐ Does not accept opportunity to lead when presented.	☐ Take leadership position but cannot achieve results.	☐ Assumes leadership most of the time with acceptable results.	☐ Does not seek opportunity to lead.	☐ Excellent, natural leader. Gets maximum results with subordinates.
Management Skills	☐ Does not understand basic principles of management.	☐ Plans well but cannot follow through with execution/control.	☐ Applies management principles with moderate success.	☐ Good Manager. Gets good results in area of responsibility.	☐ Excellent management skills. Has potential for more responsible position.

Overall Evaluation

Poor	Fair	Average	Good	Excellent
☐	☐	☐	☐	☐

FIGURE 6–2(a). Checklist for Clerical Personnel

Management Skills:	Excellent	Above Average	Average	Below Average	Poor	No Basis For Judgment
Ability to Plan	☐	☐	☐	☐	☐	☐
Involvement of Subordinates in Planning	☐	☐	☐	☐	☐	☐
Ability to Organize Work	☐	☐	☐	☐	☐	☐
Ability to Solve Problems	☐	☐	☐	☐	☐	☐
Soundness of Judgment	☐	☐	☐	☐	☐	☐
Accessibility to Those Being Served	☐	☐	☐	☐	☐	☐
Cooperation With Others	☐	☐	☐	☐	☐	☐
Fairness & Uniformity in Dealing With Others	☐	☐	☐	☐	☐	☐
Sets Realistic Goals and Timetables	☐	☐	☐	☐	☐	☐
Meets Internal Timetables	☐	☐	☐	☐	☐	☐
Meets External Timetables	☐	☐	☐	☐	☐	☐
Achieves Assigned Goals	☐	☐	☐	☐	☐	☐
Adherence to Established Policies	☐	☐	☐	☐	☐	☐
Execution of Position Responsibilities	☐	☐	☐	☐	☐	☐

Personal Characteristics:						
Use of Time	☐	☐	☐	☐	☐	☐
Attendance	☐	☐	☐	☐	☐	☐
Punctuality	☐	☐	☐	☐	☐	☐
Grooming	☐	☐	☐	☐	☐	☐
Credibility	☐	☐	☐	☐	☐	☐
Ability to Cope With Change	☐	☐	☐	☐	☐	☐
Ability to Accept Criticism	☐	☐	☐	☐	☐	☐

Overall Evaluation:

Poor	Fair	Average	Good	Excellent
☐	☐	☐	☐	☐

Additional Comments:

_____

_____

_____

FIGURE 6–2(b).   Checklist for Administrative Personnel

	Not Observed	Outstanding	Excellent	Average	Unsatisfactory
(a) Intelligence (With reference to the faculty of comprehension; mental acuteness)		Exceptionally quickwitted; keen in understanding	Grasps essentials of a situation quickly.	Understands normal situations and conditions.	
(b) Judgment (With reference to a discriminating perception by which the values and relations of things are mentally asserted.)		Unusually keen in estimating situations and reaching sound decisions.	Can generally be depended on to make proper decisions.	Fair judgment in normal and routine things.	
(c) Initiative (With reference to constructive thinking and resourcefulness; ability and intelligence to act on own responsibility.)		Exceptional in ability to think, plan, and do things without waiting to be told and instructed.	Able to plan and execute missions on his own responsibility.	Capable of performing routine duties on own responsibility.	
(d) Force (With reference to moral power possessed and exerted in producing results.)		Strong, dynamic.	Strong.	Effectual under normal and routine circumstances.	
(e) Leadership (With reference to the faculty of directing, controlling, and influencing others in definite lines of action and of maintaining discipline.)		Inspires others to a high degree by precept and example. Requires a high standard of discipline.	A very good leader.	Leads fairly well.	
(f) Moral courage (With reference to that mental quality which impels one to carry out the dictates of his conscience and convictions fearlessly.)		Exceptionally courageous.	Courageous to a high degree.	Fairly courageous.	
(g) Cooperation (With reference to the faculty of working harmoniously with others toward the accomplishment of common duties.)		Exceptionally successful in working with others to a common end.	Works in harmony with others.	Cooperates fairly well.	

170   **FIGURE 6–2(c).** Checklist for Navy Personnel

(h) Loyalty (Fidelity, faithfulness, allegiance, constancy—all with reference to a cause and to higher authority.)	Unswerving in allegiance; frank and honest in aiding and advising.	A high sense of loyalty.	Reasonably faithful in the execution of his duty.	
(i) Preserverance (With reference to maintenance of purpose or undertaking in spite of obstacles or discouragement.)	Determined, resolute.	Constant in purpose.	Fairly steady.	
(j) Reaction in emergencies (With reference to the faculty of acting instinctively in a logical manner in difficult and unforeseen situations.)	Exceptionally cool-headed and logical in his actions under all conditions.	Composed and logical in his actions in difficult situations.	Fairly logical in his actions in general.	
(k) Endurance (With reference to ability for carrying on under any and all conditions.)	Capable of standing an exceptional amount of physical hardship and strain.	Can perform well his duties under trying conditions.	Of normal endurance.	
(l) Industry (With reference to performance of duties in an energetic manner.)	Extremely energetic and industrious.	Thorough and energetic.	Reasonably energetic and industrious.	
(m) Military bearing and neatness of person and dress (With reference to dignity of demeanor, correctness of uniform, and smartness of appearance.)	Exceptional.	Very good.	Fair.	

A report containing adverse matter must be referred to the officer reported on for statement pursuant to article 1701 (8) USNR. His statement should be attached to this report. Statements of minor deficiencies either in character or performance of duties must be brought to the attention of the officer reported on either orally or in writing.

HAS THIS BEEN DONE? _____ WHAT IMPROVEMENT, IF ANY, HAS BEEN NOTED? _____

_____
(Signature of reporting senior)

FIGURE 6–2(c). Checklist for Navy Personnel *(continued)*

Indicate the response that best describes the person being evaluated:

1	Easy to talk to
2	Does not anticipate difficulties
3	Rarely wastes time
4	Understands explanations quickly
1	Punctual worker
2	Careful worker
3	Hard worker
4	Co-operative worker
1	Dishonest worker
2	Disloyal worker
3	Overbearing worker
4	Disinterested worker
1	Leader
2	Wastes time on unimportant items
3	Hard worker
4	Not easily rattled worker

Questions taken from a variety of different evaluation forms.

FIGURE 6–3.   Forced Choice Checklist

Objectives for a Salesperson:

Number of new customers
Number of sales closed
Dollar value of sales
Number of motivational courses completed
Number of customer complaints
Number of customer compliments
Number of sales calls

The numerical goals for each category should be established by mutual
agreement between the salesperson and the sales manager.

FIGURE 6–4.   Sample Objectives for a MBO Program

2. The managers who adopt MBO as a system of managing must plan to drop some of their more time-consuming vocational hobbies—they must learn to delegate.

3. The system of management by objective entails a behavioral change on the part of both the superior and the subordinate.

There are both advantages and disadvantages to using MBO. Among the advantages is the ability of managers to measure performance in terms of concrete objectives. It permits the individual being evaluated to help monitor progress toward the goals. Emphasis is placed on future performance, not past performance. MBO provides individuals with a greater sense of accomplishment.

Criticisms of MBO primarily lie in the nature of the way work is structured in our society. "There are simply too few jobs for which cost-related outcomes can be generated . . . . Most jobs in this society are not independent, but are tied in closely with many other jobs." (Wallace and Fay:181) Another criticism leveled at MBO is that the objectives are short term in nature. Quarterly or annual results may cause actions to be taken—or not taken—that will enhance the immediate profit picture at the expense of long-range growth. For example, delaying a modernization program will show a healthy profit, but in the long run the lack of modernization will undoubtedly affect the competitive position of the organization. Similarly, if a function is eliminated, such as maintenance, the immediate costs of running the organization will decrease. These will show up as a tremendous savings. But the long-term implications of not performing maintenance can be catastrophic.

Despite the criticisms, MBO has gained a widespread acceptance. When cost-related outcomes are available for a job and the effects of one individual on those outcomes can be isolated, they are an excellent basis for merit adjustments.

ERRORS

Because performance appraisal systems are administered by people, there are a number of errors that might enter the evaluation process. The most common of these rating errors are described below:

Halo Effect: In the halo effect, a rating of excellent in one quality influences the appraiser to give the appraisee a similar rating or higher in other qualities than actually observed.

Horns Effect: In the horns effect, a rating of unsatisfactory in one quality influences the appraiser to give the appraisee a similar rating or lower on other qualities than actually observed.

Central Tendency: Central tendency provides a rating of average or around the midpoint for all qualities.

Lenient Rating: The appraiser rates the appraisee higher than the normal or average appraiser.

Strict Rating: The appraiser rates the appraisee lower than would the normal or average appraiser. The appraiser is overly harsh in rating appraisee performance qualities.

Bias About Recent Behavior: The appraiser rates the employee by recent behavior and fails to recognize the most commonly demonstrated behavior during the entire appraisal period.

THE APPRAISAL PROCESS

Thus far this chapter has discussed the principles of performance appraisal. The methodology of performing a performance appraisal includes several steps: identifying the appraisers, identifying the people to be appraised, setting a time for appraisal, appraising, and conducting the appraisal interview.

Many people in the organization can perform employee evaluation. These include the immediate supervisor, who should have the ideal position from which to identify the strong and weak points of the employees; the supervisor's supervisor who is far enough removed from daily contact to avoid personality bias, yet close enough to be able to observe employee performance; peers or co-workers who have possibly the best insight into identifying who is and who is not doing the job. The immediate subordinates also are excellent sources of performance appraisal data, as is the employee him- or herself. This is especially effective when goals can be stated. Some organizations also use committees. Committee members usually come from management positions and have had ample opportunity to observe the employee perform the required tasks. In some organizations personnel specialists often assist in appraisal. These well-trained people can provide guidance to the individuals who have actually observed behaviors of the people to be evaluated.

The people to be appraised within an organization can theoretically include everyone in the organization. In the past few years, however, there has been a notable trend toward eliminating performance appraisal among non-exempt employees and focusing on performance appraisal at the executive, managerial, and professional levels of the organization.

Although tradition has been to perform an annual performance appraisal, the process should be a continuous one. According to a survey done at General Electric, the performance review and evaluations should be done on a day-to-day basis. (Henderson:405)

The evaluation interview is a key part of the appraisal process. This provides the superior with an opportunity to discuss the subordinate's performance record and to explore areas of possible improvement and growth. Interviews can be valuable tools or wretched affairs that must be endured. In order for an interview to be successful it must do the following:

1. Emphasize strengths
2. Suggest more acceptable behaviors
3. Concentrate on areas of growth
4. Identify growth areas to reasonably achieveable objectives

The conduct during an interview should be such that the appraiser listens more than talks. Some studies have shown that the appraiser should only talk during 10% of the appraisal interview. (Johnson:72) The questions asked during the interview should vary, but they should be structured to require a verbal response, not just a yes or no answer. What is known as the sandwich interview—good, bad, good—should be avoided. This method alerts the individual that after the initial compliment, the criticism will follow, followed in turn by another compliment. Many employees figure out the system and never achieve positive growth due to the appraisal.

Performance interviews generally take one of three formats. The first of these is the TELL AND SELL METHOD. In this interview the appraisee is sold on the evaluation and motivated to better performance by the appraiser. The TELL AND LISTEN METHOD requires the employee to listen to a well-stated evaluation and requires the appraiser to listen to the appraisee's reaction to the appraisal. It requires the supervisor to acknowledge that there will be differences of opinion. The last of the interview methods is the PROBLEM-SOLVING METHOD. This technique requires the appraiser and the appraisee to discuss strengths, weaknesses, and areas for growth. It attempts to stimulate growth in the subordinate.

Some organizations have very loosely defined appraisal processes. Others have explicitly defined ones. At the end of this chapter, instead of looking at the Mountain View College appraisal system, there is included the complete performance appraisal booklet and forms required at one large organization, the Georgia Power Company (Appendix 6–1).

EMPLOYEE REACTIONS

Employees are very sensitive to performance appraisal. The bottom line of performance appraisal ultimately affects the paycheck of the worker. Even when there is a well-administered job evaluation system, the pay structure at some time reflects the appraisal scheme. An appropriate appraisal system can be used for progression beyond the midpoint of the pay range to the maximum. Subordinates often have a poor idea of the standards by which they will be evaluated. Employees often only hear the part of the appraisal interview that relates to the bottom line. Care must be taken so that employees perceive performance appraisal as separate or distinct from a straight salary review. Objective information should be used to guide the employee to perform his or her job better, or at least more in line with organizational objectives.

ADVANTAGES AND DISADVANTAGES OF PERFORMANCE APPRAISAL

For the most part, this chapter has avoided taking sides regarding the use of performance appraisal. A number of advantages of using a formal employee evaluation system have been suggested. These include:

1. Furnishing reliable information for proper placement, counseling, and guidance of employees.
2. Providing confidence that supervisors will be neither prejudiced nor biased in dealing with subordinates.
3. Establishing a basis for discussion of the weak points that hinder an employee's progress.
4. Establishing records that justify the need for employee training.
5. Enhancing morale by letting the employee know his or her standing at any point.
6. Aiding employees in identifying candidates for advancement or promotion.
7. Providing the basis for wage increases based on increased productivity.
8. Identifying workers who might be candidates for transfer to tasks that would better utilize their talents.
9. Promoting the worker's faith in management's fairness.
10. Providing the basis to justify a wage or salary increase.
11. Helping to settle arbitration disputes.

A number of criticisms have also been leveled at evaluation over the years. Some of these objections, along with the source of the objection, are listed below.

1. Formal performance appraisal programs will not accomplish their objectives with poor supervisors. (Britten:28)
2. Appraisal forms are often distorted by supervisors in order to attempt to obtain maximum increases for their people.
3. No matter how well defined, judgments are usually subjective and impressionistic.
4. Ratings by different managers are usually incomplete.
5. Trying to base promotion and layoff decisions on appraisal data leaves the decisions open to acrimonious debate. There is often inadequate data to support decisions.
6. Although managers are urged to give feedback freely and often, there are no built-in mechanisms to ensure that they do. (Levinson:31)
7. Rating and evaluation are combined into one process that does not accomplish the differing goals of the two processes.
8. Too often performance reviews are written for the wrong audience.
9. Many performance reviews are based on vague generalities and are not specific.
10. There is the inability of the manager to select good measurements, especially in an MBO system.
11. Too many managers measure activity and not accomplishments. (Yager:132)

SUMMARY

Performance appraisal, despite its criticism, is still a useful management process. It can:

1. Provide adequate feedback to people on their work performance.
2. Serve as a basis for changing job behavior to more productive behaviors.
3. Provide data for judging the performance of employees.

In order to be successful the following guidelines should be remembered.

- Job performance characteristics must be based on a thorough and complete job analysis.
- Raters require complete training and instruction regarding the use of the rating instrument.

- The rating should be administered under controlled and standardized conditions.
- The rating instrument should always be the subject of validation studies.

Performance appraisal, when properly used, can be a useful tool for managing within any organization. Care must be taken not to abuse the appraisal process.

Review Questions

1. What is the major use of performance appraisal for the individual?
2. What is the major use of performance appraisal for the organization?
3. Define performance appraisal.
4. Discuss the uses of performance appraisal.
5. What is the most widely cited use of performance appraisal?
6. What are other uses of performance appraisal besides determining compensation?
7. What are the two most important legal pronouncements regarding performance appraisal?
8. What is the *Uniform Federal Guidelines on Employee Selection Procedure*?
9. What is the significance of the *Griggs vs. Duke Power Case*?
10. What is the significance of the *Rowe vs. General Motors Case*?
11. What is the significance of the *Wade vs. Mississippi Cooperative Extension Service Case*?
12. How can an organization comply with the Federal Guidelines on employee selection?
13. What is validity regarding appraisal instruments?
14. What is reliability regarding appraisal instruments?
15. What conditions are necessary for successful evaluation systems within an organization?
16. What are some typical performance standards used in performance appraisal?
17. What are the minimum requirements for qualified performance appraisers?
18. Describe how an appraisal method is specified.
19. What is a rating scale?
20. What is a global rating?
21. What is a BARS?
22. How does a BARS work?
23. How does the essay method of performance appraisal work?

24. Describe the critical incident method of performance appraisal.
25. Describe the field review method of performance appraisal.
26. How does a checklist work?
27. Describe how a simple checklist works regarding performance appraisal.
28. Describe how a weighted checklist works regarding performance appraisal.
29. Describe how a forced choice checklist works regarding performance appraisal.
30. Describe ranking as it relates to performance appraisal.
31. Describe the rank order method of performance appraisal.
32. Describe the forced choice method of performance appraisal.
33. Describe the person-to-person comparison method of job evaluation.
34. What is meant by results-oriented performance appraisal?
35. Describe the management by objective method of performance appraisal.
36. How are goals or targets set in MBO?
37. What conditions must be present for MBO to work?
38. What are the advantages of using MBO?
39. What are the disadvantages of using MBO?
40. What are the common rating errors made in performance appraisal?
41. What is the halo effect?
42. What is the horns effect?
43. What is central tendency?
44. What is lenient rating?
45. What is strict rating?
46. What is meant by bias about recent behavior?
47. Who is in the BEST position to appraise employee performance?
48. When should performance appraisal occur?
49. What are the characteristics of an effective performance review?
50. What are the three formats of the performance appraisal interview?
51. Why are employees sensitive to performance appraisal?
52. Why should performance appraisal be distinct from a salary review?
53. What are the advantages of performance appraisal?
54. What are the disadvantages of performance appraisal?
55. What are the four major requirements for a successful performance appraisal program?

References

Baroni, Barry J., "The Legal Ramifications of Appraisal Systems," *Supervisory Management*, January, 1982.

Britten, Donald E., "Common Practices in Wage and Salary Administration," *Personnel Administrator*, January–February, 1974.

Chruden, H.J. and Sherman, A.W., *Managing Human Resources*, Southwestern Publishing Company, Cincinnati, 1984.

Henderson, R., *Compensation Administration*, Reston Publishing Company, Inc., Reston, Virginia, 1985.

Henderson, R., *Performance Appraisal*, Reston Publishing Company, Inc., Reston, Virginia, 1980.

Johnson, R. G., *The Appraisal Interview Guide*, AMACOM, New York, 1979.

Kay, E., Meyer, H.H. and French, J.R.P., "Effects of Threat in a Performance Appraisal Interview," *Journal of Applied Psychology*, October, 1965.

Klasson, Charles R., Thompson, Duane E. and Luben, Gary L., "How Defensible is Your Performance Appraisal System?" *Personnel Administrator*, December, 1980.

Levinson, Harry, "Appraisal of What Performance?" *Harvard Business Review*, July–August, 1976.

Locher, Alan H. and Teel, Kenneth S., "Performance Appraisal—A Survey of Current Practices," *Personnel Journal*, May, 1977.

Machlowitz, Marilyn, "Reviewing the Troops," *Working Woman*, September, 1981.

Odiorne, George S., *Management by Objectives*, Pitman, New York, 1965.

Schneier, Dena B., "The Impact of EEO Legislation on Performance Appraisal," *Personnel*, July–August, 1979.

Varney, Glenn H., "Performance Appraisal—Inside and Out," *Personnel Administrator*, November–December, 1972.

Wallace, Marc J. and Fay, Charles H., *Compensation Theory and Practice*, Kent Publishing Company, Boston, 1983.

Winstanley, Nathan B., "The Use of Performance Appraisal in Compensation Administration," *Conference Board Record*, March, 1965.

Yager, Ed, "A Critique of Performance Appraisal Systems," *Personnel Journal*, February, 1981.

Zollitsch, H.G. and Langsner, A., *Wage and Salary Administration*, Southwestern Publishing Company, Cincinnati, 1970.

Case Study 6–1

VALIDITY OF SELECTION DEVICES*

Smythe Textiles, a large manufacturer of sheets and pillowcases, is located in the southeastern United States. Smythe has been considered a progressive employer in its area for many years. The personnel department has historically been able to take only half of the individuals who apply for production jobs at Smythe.

Recently there have been a number of sewing machine operators hired who did not meet minimum production and quality standards, even after extended training. As a result, Bob Browning, the Personnel

Table 6–1–1

Employee	Age	Education	Marital status	Ethnic origin	Perceptual speed test	Units produced
1	30	10	S	NW	31	40
2	39	9	M	NW	62	42
3	31	12	D	NW	79	58
4	19	12	M	W	60	60
5	27	12	M	NW	50	31
6	20	10	D	W	53	53
7	24	9	S	W	50	50
8	33	9	M	W	47	48
9	23	12	M	W	49	45
10	36	12	M	W	42	45
11	26	10	M	NW	46	31
12	34	9	D	NW	40	53
13	28	11	M	W	40	40
14	25	12	S	NW	39	55
15	33	12	M	W	36	42
16	36	11	S	NW	35	59
17	22	10	S	NW	78	50
18	24	9	D	NW	40	56
19	32	9	M	W	62	59
20	35	12	S	W	48	32

Age: years at time of employment

Education: grade completed

Marital status: S = Single, M = Married, D = Divorced

Ethnic origin: W = White, NW = Non-white

All of these employees were female.

---

*Reprinted with permission of William L. Tullar, School of Business and Economics, University of North Carolina, Greensboro, NC.

Director at Smythe, has decided to use a test to select sewing machine operators. After a job analysis and much deliberation, Browning decided to use (among other things) a perceptual speed test. He knows, however, that he must validate the test, so he hires twenty new sewing machine operators who have taken the test but for whom the test was not part of the selection decision. Three months after the sewing machine operators were trained, Browning received data on each operator's average daily production.

As a personnel man wise in the ways of EEOC, Bob Browning knows he must have data on more than twenty sewing machine operators before he can draw conclusions about the validity of the perceptual speed test. However, Bob wants a preliminary indication of validity. So he assembles all the data found in Table 6–1–1. Bob included the other biographical data to check on the possibility of differential validity— that is, to see if the test is more valid for one subgroup of his sample than it is for the whole sample.

Bob used the Spearman Rho correlation coefficient[1] to calculate his correlations.

Discussion

1. *Did Bob find a strong relationship between scores on the test and units produced?*
2. *Did Bob find any evidence of differential validity?*
3. *If you set up a selection program for sewing machine operators, would you be able to use this test? If so, how would you use it?*

Case Study 6–2

THE CASE OF THE OUT-MODED VICE-PRESIDENT*

The other officers of Weber Corporation found various ways of distracting their attention from Bob Reith's disjointed harangue at the weekly meeting of the executive committee. Some doodled, one or two looked out the window, several engaged in whispered conversations, and a few simply stared down at the conference table before them. "Before any of you start interrupting me," Reith rambled on, "let me remind you that I was here

---

[1]*Students unfamiliar with this method should read Sidney Siegel, Non-parametric Statistics (New York: McGraw-Hill, 1956), pp. 202–213.*

From MANAGEMENT: FUNCTIONS AND MODERN CONCEPTS by Clayton Reeser. Copyright 1973 by Scott, Foresman and Company. Reprinted by permission.

when the old man was running the show, and I know what he would have said about acquiring a company that is losing money. All this talk about its tax loss carryover and its leverage position doesn't make any sense to me."

As he had done many times in the past, Verne Weber, son of the founder of Weber Construction Company, and president of Weber Corporation, the successor company, patiently let Reith have his say before directing the committee's discussion into productive channels.

Bob Reith had started to work for the senior Mr. Weber when he was eighteen years old. His drive soon became apparent to Weber, and by the time he was in his early twenties he was successfully managing construction projects. The military building boom caused by World War II resulted in the tremendous growth of Weber Construction Company, and Reith's ability to force a project to completion gained him a vice-presidency and the designation of Weber's "right-hand man" when he was just thirty. When the war ended and young Verne Weber joined his father's company, he was assigned to work for two years under Reith's tutelage.

Upon his father's death in 1954, Verne Weber succeeded to the presidency of the company. After several years of making certain that the company was firmly established in a growth position in the construction industry, Weber began to consummate his plans for diversifying the company's operations. He had hoped that Reith, who was the only remaining top manager from the old company, would be able to run the construction division part of the new company that he envisioned, but came to the reluctant realization that Reith's ability level was to boss an individual construction project, and that the managing of an international construction organization was completely over his head. Weber's expansion plans were delayed for two years until he finally attracted Tom Hoslett, a highly experienced manager in the largest construction company in the country, to accept the challenge of building Weber's construction division.

In 1960 the company's name was changed to Weber Corporation, and the firm branched out into equipment distributorships, auto leasing, resort hotels, and insurance. Weber was very careful not to enter a new field until he was able to entice the most competent managers that he could find to align their interests with the corporation in heading the diversified operations. As a result, Weber Corporation grew on a foundation of highly qualified top managers. The only exception was Bob Reith, who still held the title of vice-president, and whose role was formally defined as advisor to Mr. Weber. In a practical sense, the scope of the company's operations had gone beyond his ability to contribute anything of value, but he lacked the perception to recognize his inadequacies. His persistent meddling in all of the firm's affairs was a source of increasing resentment to the other senior managers.

Many times during the prosperous 1960s, Verne Weber's thoughts dwelt on the problem of what to do with Reith. He regularly suggested early retirement, but Reith's predictive reply was always, "I'm too healthy to think of retirement yet. And besides, I promised your father that I would always be around to give you a hand when you needed it." Once in 1967 he talked Reith into taking over the managing of the construction of a huge shopping center, thinking that would get him back into the area where he had shown ability as a young man. However, construction technology had passed Reith by, and when Hoslett finally demanded that he be replaced as head of the project, Reith's bungling had caused such delays that the shopping center resulted in the largest loss that the corporation had ever suffered.

Weber's success in putting together an industrial empire earned him the respect of all of the managers he had reporting to him. The only time there was serious disagreement was when they periodically, either individually or collectively, asked him to get rid of Reith. On an objective basis, Weber knew they were right. He realized that he should have discharged Reith years before. Had he done so, the man might have been able to build a new career at a job level compatible with his abilities. Thus, as Weber reasoned, his own weakness had caused the situation to get beyond the point where a discharge was an equitable solution.

One day in 1972, shortly after Reith's emotional stand against the acquisition that all of the other company officers strongly favored, Weber asked the advice of Lane Smith, a management consultant who was doing some work for the company. "Actually, Mr. Weber," said Smith, "many companies have drones in their management ranks. You might even be surprised to learn that some of them are much worse than Mr. Reith. For example, he apparently is neither an alcoholic, a compulsive gambler, or a woman chaser—and that is more than can be said for the problem of personnel of other firms. What trouble is he really causing?"

"Actually, it is just his talking at the meetings," Weber answered. "I can keep him away from the other managers except for those occasions. He has no decisions to make that could cause problems for the company. The dollar cost of his salary and office expense to this company is meaningless. I can put up with his well-meant counsel to me without any personal difficulty. It is just that the other managers can't stand him, and my conscience won't let me fire him."

"How about removing him from the executive committee, and all other committees that he might be on," Smith suggested. "You could think of plausible reasons to explain the action to him, and it would at least be a lot less damaging to him personally than a discharge.

Discussion

1. Discuss a factor other than merit or seniority that may result in some individuals receiving promotions.
2. In the Case of the Out-Moded Vice-President, what would be wrong with demoting Bob Reith to the level where he could perform competently?

3. *What do you think of the consultant's advice to simply re-move Reith from any contact with the other senior managers?*
4. *If you think the best decision would have been to discharge Reith, when was the most appropriate time to have done it?*
5. *What effect do you think Verne Weber's reluctance to dis-charge Reith would have on the attitudes of the senior man-agers toward Weber himself?*

Case Study 6–3

*ROBERT JACKSON**

Robert Jackson, 25, has been an advertising copywriter in your depart-ment for three years. He designs advertisements to be placed in newspapers and magazines. He must work closely with girls in the art department, with the sales department, and with the vice-president in charge of the whole division.

Bob is an extremely enthusiastic worker with good ideas. When you, the manager of the department, hired him, you hoped that he would advance rapidly. He still can, but he has considerable trouble in dealing with people. He is too impatient with the girls in the art depart-ment, seems to fidget whenever he notices one of them taking a break, and is constantly pushing them to finish his work. In dealing with the people in the sales department, he makes it perfectly clear that his ideas are always best. During a recent conference, when the Vice President was thinking out loud, Bob shouted out his own answer, and cut the VP off. It was a good answer, and the VP didn't mind, but some of the other people thought Bob had behaved badly. You are quite concerned about the animosity he is creating in your department.

A new company policy requires that each employee have an evalu-ation interview every six months. There are no performance-rating forms. This is Jackson's first evaluation under the new policy.

Discussion

1. *What should your strategy be in handling the evaluation in-terview with Jackson?*
2. *Role-play this interview. Jackson is quite sure that his ideas are good and will press for a substantial pay increase.*

---

*George Strauss, Leonard R. Sayles, PERSONNEL: THE HUMAN PROBLEMS OF MANAGEMENT, 3rd Ed., copyright 1972, p. 526. Reprinted by permission of Prentice-Hall, Inc., Englewood Cliffs, N.J.

Case Study 6—4

DETERMINATION OF PAY RATES OF INDIVIDUALS*

In a small manufacturing company, new employees are paid the minimum wage to start. After a period of from two to four weeks, if he is still around, the employer calls the new worker in and tells him his performance has merited a pay increase. Within two months the employer again commends the employee on his performance, pats him on the back, and gives him another raise. This employer claims that he hates seniority pay plans and insists that his is a merit system. Do you agree? Why or why not?

Case Study 6—5

SMITH's DEPARTMENT STORE

Smith's Department Store is a growing Sunbelt merchandiser which currently operates 22 stores in three mid- to large-size Southwestern cities. The total employment is currently about 6,000 employees, but expansion plans indicate that this will rise significantly as Smith's expands by opening new stores and distribution centers in current markets and new markets.

To help with the proper staffing of the new operations, Smith's has adopted a policy in which half of the new management personnel are hired from outside and half are promoted from a variety of departments within the organization.

Discussion

1. Does this seem like a good policy? Why?
2. What are the advantages and disadvantages of this policy?
3. Are there any other policies that might be more effective in this area?
4. How might this conflict with the various EEO laws and rules discussed earlier?

---

*David W. Belcher, WAGE AND SALARY ADMINISTRATION, 2nd Ed., Copyright 1962, p. 375. Reprinted by permission of Prentice-Hall, Inc., Englewood Cliffs, N.J.

Corporate Human Resource Objectives

It is the responsibility of all managers to recognize the importance of the human resources—people—through whom they are able to accomplish their jobs. Georgia Power Company recognizes this fact in the following corporate objective:

It is the objective of Georgia Power Company that each manager recognizes the dignity of human endeavor in one's work, be responsive to the values, rights, and needs of each employee, and provide an environment in which all employees may achieve their potential to the maximum degree possible.

In addition, employees have a performance responsibility to the company which they accept as a condition of employment. Georgia Power Company managers wish to help employees achieve their performance responsibility through accomplishing the following corporategoal:

It is the goal of the Georgia Power Company that each manager provide an environment in which all employees know what is expected of them and how well they are doing and provide an opportunity for employees to accomplish the requirements of their immediate jobs and to grow with the company.

Our employees are our most important asset, and managers are obligated to work diligently in getting the maximum contribution from their employees. Managers are continuously responsible and obligated to encourage improved job performance from all employees.

Developmental Performance Appraisal Process—General

A. Definition of Developmental Performance Appraisal

A developmental performance appraisal is a formal discussion between a superior and a subordinate for the purpose of discovering how and why the subordinate is presently performing on the job, and how the subordinate can perform more effectively in the future so that the subordinate, the superior and the organization all benefit. It is not done just to find out what a person's performance is worth, but it is done to make people worth more—to themselves and the organization.

B. Developmental Performance Appraisal Policy

It is the policy of Georgia Power Company that each manager or supervisor will conduct an annual developmental perform-

APPENDIX 6–1   Georgia Power Company Employee Performance Appraisal System ance appraisal interview with all employees (except those covered by a union contract) under their direct supervision. This appraisal interview will include a discussion of any salary adjustments based on merit.

C. Purposes of the Developmental Performance Appraisal

A developmental performance appraisal has several purposes. The most significant ones are:

(1) To let the subordinates know where they stand in regard to their overall job performance as viewed by their superiors. The appraisal ensures a clear understanding as to the scope of the job, provides for an identification of major accountabilities and makes an assessment as to how the employee is currently doing.

(2) To advise subordinates as to what is expected of them in the future. The appraisal identifies where future performance can be improved and outlines growth possibilities and strategies for the subordinate.

(3) To encourage subordinates to be goal oriented and performance conscious.

(4) To assist the company in manpower planning, development, placement, and compensation decisions.

(5) To provide subordinates an opportunity to give their superiors feedback regarding performance and other job related matters.

D. Performance Appraisal—A Continuous and Positive Process

Performance appraisal is a management function and should be a *continuous process* between superior and subordinate. Appraisal should be a daily responsibility of management. The formal, annual review provides an opportunity for a discussion of overall performance between superior and subordinate and a written record of that discussion.

The developmental performance appraisal should be a positive experience for all—the superior, the subordinate and the company. This does not happen in every case, but it should be the goal—and has to be the goal—if a truly developmental experience is to occur for the subordinate.

APPENDIX 6–1.   Georgia Power Company Employee Performance Appraisal System

Performance Appraisal — Individual Development

Employee Name	Employee No.	Current Job No./Title
Division/Department	Annual Merit Review Date	Location

I. Job Content (To be completed at beginning of review year) List the accountabilities of the employee's position. Use additional paper if needed.

Accountability Number [ ]

Accountability Number [ ]

Accountability Number [ ]

Accountability Number [ ]

Accountability Number [ ]

Accountability Number [ ]

Accountability Number [ ] Work Habits (Optional)

APPENDIX 6–1. Georgia Power Company Employee Performance Appraisal System

II. Goals with Measurable Performance Standards (To be completed at the beginning of review year.) Describe how the employee is expected to fulfill each accountability. State the behavior or standard which would exhibit competent performance.

Accountability Number	
Accountability Number	
Accountability Number	
Accountability Number	
Accountability Number	
Accountability Number	
Accountability Number	
Accountability Number	

APPENDIX 6–1. Georgia Power Company Employee Performance Appraisal System

III. Performance Evaluation

First describe how the employee is fulfilling or failing to fulfill each accountability in comparison with the Performance Standards outlined in Section II. Then rate the employee on each accountability using the definitions below.

Marginal	Fair	Competent	Commendable	Distinguished
Rating for employees whose performance clearly falls short of established goals.	Rating for employees whose performance has approached but not met established goals.	Rating for employees whose performance consistently meets established goals.	Rating for employees whose performance clearly and consistently exceeds established goals.	Rating for employees whose performance far exceeds established goals on a consistent basis.

Accountability Number ☐

☐ Distinguished
☐ Commendable
☐ Competent
☐ Fair
☐ Marginal

Accountability Number ☐

☐ Distinguished
☐ Commendable
☐ Competent
☐ Fair
☐ Marginal

Accountability Number ☐

☐ Distinguished
☐ Commendable
☐ Competent
☐ Fair
☐ Marginal

Accountability Number ☐

☐ Distinguished
☐ Commendable
☐ Competent
☐ Fair
☐ Marginal

Accountability Number ☐

☐ Distinguished
☐ Commendable
☐ Competent
☐ Fair
☐ Marginal

Accountability Number ☐

☐ Distinguished
☐ Commendable
☐ Competent
☐ Fair
☐ Marginal

APPENDIX 6–1. Georgia Power Company Employee Performance Appraisal System

IV. Describe the employee's strengths as demonstrated in the last 12 months.

V. List areas in which the employee needs to improve.

VI. At the present time what are the employee's future growth possibilities?

VII. Development Action Plan: List Activities which will help the employee improve present peformance and grow with the company.

VIII. Overall Performance Rating. (See Appendix A of the instruction manual for definitions of terms used in overall rating.)

☐ Marginal ☐ Fair ☐ Competent ☐ Commendable ☐ Distinguished

IX. Employee Comments

Employee Signature	Date	
Rater (Immediate Supervisor)	Date	Title
Endorser (Second Level Supervisor)	Date	Title

APPENDIX 6–1. Georgia Power Company Employee Performance Appraisal System

How the Developmental Performance Appraisal Works

A. Contents of the Review

1. Evaluation of the past review record period—Sections III through VIII

   (a) Discussion of the employee's performance, strenghts, developmental needs, future growth possibilities, and a developmental action plan.

   (b) Discussion of any merit salary increase being given.

   (c) Employee's opportunity to add comments and employees signature.

2. Planning for the Next Review Period—Sections I and II

   (a) Identifying next year's accountabilities.

   (b) Developing measurable goals for each accountability.

B. The Performance Appraisal Form

The performance appraisal form is used to ensure that essential elements are covered verbally (face to face by superior and subordinate) and that a written report is kept.

(1) *Page One—Job Content.* The subordinate's major accountabilities are listed on page one. Accountabilities are the major activities in a job for which performance is required. In determining the employee's accountabilities, begin by:

   (a) Reviewing the job description; corporate/departmental goals & objectives; and the activities and programs, etc. that are accounted for in the budget.

   (b) Developing the overall mission statement for the job. (i.e. What is the purpose of the job?)

   (c) Listing the major activities which must be accomplished in order to achieve the mission.

   In most jobs, these major accountabilities will range from 4 to 6 in number and they will cover 90% of the subordinate's total work activity.

An example of an accountability for a Plant Manager is as follows:

APPENDIX 6–1.   Georgia Power Company Employee Performance Appraisal System

"To operate the generating facility with the highest rate of plant availability consistent with proper maintenance and operating procedures.

For further clarification of "What is and What is not an Accountability" see Appendix C. See Appendix D for Worksheet on How to Determine Accountabilities and Appendix G for additional examples of accountabilities.

(2) *Page Two—Goals with Measurable Performance Standards.* The performance results required to fulfill each major accountability are to be stated on page two. These goals will illustrate what is required for competent performance. Competent performance, as defined in Appendix A, describes "significant accomplishment and achievement and represents the performance level expected" of all employees.

The development and writing of measurable goals is a skill which must be learned. However, once this skill is mastered, the manager becomes more results oriented and more performance conscious.

A distinction should be made here between an objective and a goal. An objective is a broad aim, purpose or mission, such as the generation of electrical energy. A goal is a time-dated, quantifiable, measurable work activity to be accomplished, such as—will reduce meter reading errors by .05% during the first six months of 19XX as comapred to the same period last year. Obviously, a superior can be more objective in evaluating the accomplishment of this goal when it is stated in time-dated and measurable terms. In addition to being time-dated and measurable there are other factors which must be considered when developing competent level goals. See Appendix E for further explanation of these factors.

In determining the employee's goals and performance standards, follow the steps listed below:

Step 1: Take one accountability at a time.

Step 2: Determine the result areas.

i.e., What are you going to look at to determine the kind of job the employee does? (Timeliness, Quality, Quantity, Cost)

Step 3: Determine the method of measurement.

i.e., What means will be used to measure this performance?

APPENDIX 6–1. Georgia Power Company Employee Performance Appraisal System

Step 4: Determine the level of performance expected—the goal.

It is important to consider the employee's available resources, their authority and control, and ensure the level is a challenge, but attainable.

A measurable goal for the above Plant Manager is as follows:
"Competent performance is evident with plant availability being between 75–80% in 1979 for each unit."
See Appendix F for Worksheet on How to Determine Goals and Appendix G for additional examples.

Without measurable performance goals, employees are likely to be substantially evaluated on subjective factors such as work habits which may not have a direct relationship to the person's output or results. These qualities may be used and rated in the performance appraisal process if it can be demonstrated and mutually understood that they are "job related" and a requirement of the position. If they are to be used, they must be listed on page one, at the beginning of the review period, in the block marked Work Habits, and specific goals must be established on page two.

For employees hired, transferred, promoted, or demoted during the year, their new accountabilities and goals should be discussed with them at the time they enter their new job. The accountabilities and goals should be defined with the job's learning curve. An employee entering a new job may be facing the challenge of completely learning all facets of the job or only learning a small segment of the job. The employee's expectations should be set based upon their knowledge of the new position; one employee's goal may be similar to that of an employee already in the job.

PAGES ONE AND TWO SHOULD BE COMPLETED AND DISCUSSED WITH THE SUBORDINATE AT THE BEGINNING OF THE REVIEW YEAR.

(3) *Page Three—Performance Evaluation.* In this section, the superior *describes* how the employee performed; that is, was the goal fulfilled as stated or was performance over or under the stated goal. Each accountability is then rated, based on the employee's accomplishments as described. If performance was other than competent, either higher or lower than the stated goal, the superior uses judgment in rating the subordinate above or below competent. Ratings of marginal, fair, competent, commendable and distinguished are to be used.

APPENDIX 6–1.   Georgia Power Company Employee Performance Appraisal System

For example, the Plant Manager mentioned above fulfilled the goal in the following manner and thus received a competent rating on this particular goal.

"During 1979, a normal operating year with no unusual circumstances, plant availability for each unit averaged 77%."

This narrative description of the performance of the goal is indicated on page three of the form (Performance of Evaluation) and serves as the basis for discussion of how the employee has accomplished the goals.

NOTE: When describing and evaluating an employee's performance relative to a particular goal, it is important to consider all of the factors listed in Appendix E even though they may not be stated specifically in the goal. For example, the goal may state that a particular program will be developed by a certain date and not directly address the quality of the program and the resources required. However, when describing and evaluating the employee's performance against this goal, these factors must be considered.

Those employees who changed jobs during the year are to be rated only on their present job's accountabilities and goals. The employees who are still in a learning stage should be evaluated as to their progress thus far. Employees learning & producing at a reasonable performance level are seen as competent. Those learning & producing above or below a reasonable level are rated appropriately.

    (4) Page Four—Personal Development Planning. On Page Four the subordinate's strengths, needs, and future growth possibilities are discussed by the superior. In discussing strengths, the superior has the opportunity to compliment the employee in areas of excellence. In talking about needs, the superior identifies areas in which the employee should make some changes in skills, knowledge, behavior, or performance. Future growth possibilities should be discussed with the subordinate. These possibilities may be in the form of (1) a possible expansion of present accountabilities, (2) a possible lateral move to gain more experience, (3) a possible promotion to a higher position or (4) or combination of these activities.

From this discussion of performance, strengths, needs, and growth possibilities, the superior and subordinate should jointly

APPENDIX 6–1.   Georgia Power Company Employee Performance Appraisal System

agree on a Developmental Action Plan for the subordinate. This Developmental Action Plan is specific in that it tells the subordinate what should be done in order to improve present performance and/or what the employee needs to do in order to grow and develolp in the future. This plan is tailored to the particular needs of the individual and normally includes both job and personal improvement activities. These activities may be in the form of formal educational programs, Company training programs, on-the-job training or self-study programs. The subordinate may also add to the Developmental Action Plan with suggestions of what should be done to improve present job performance and growth with the Company. The Action Plan should be viewed as a very important element in the Developmental Appraisal process.

Finally, an overall rating of the employee's performane is indicated and explained to the subordinate by the superior. The ratings to be used in evaluating the overall performance are defined in Appendix A. In most work units, a small number of employees exceed competent performance and an even smaller number of employees do not meet the expectations for competent performance. However, the majority of employees achieve the overall performance level of competent. The overall performance rating is used in determining merit salary adjustments (see supplementary instructions to the Salary Administration Manual). The rating indicated here should be the same rating used on the Salary Recommendation Form.

Supervisory Accountabilities

Positions which are managerial or supervisory in nature will generally have two common accountabilities; one for "budgets" and one for "people." These accountabilities may be stated in a variety of ways; specific emphasis may vary from position to position depending upon circumstances and environment, but in most cases, management views both of these accountabilities as critical and major responsibilities for a supervisor.

1. The budgeting accountability relates to the responsibility of a manager for dollars expended. Every manager is evaluated on how well the financial efficiency of the department/division is monitored and controlled.
2. The people accountability refers to a manager's responsibility for, and to, subordinates. The Company's corporate objectives emphasize the importance of fairness and objectivity in managing employees, and every supervisory employee will be ex-

APPENDIX 6–1.   Georgia Power Company Employee Performance Appraisal System

pected to support these objectives fully. In that regard, one of the more important objectives within the people accountabilities for all Supervisory employees should address results of the equitable application of Company policies and procedures to all employees, especially in the area of equal opportunity and affirmative action.

In addition, employees at the manager level and above are to be expected to assist in meeting Company EEO goals. As such, they should be held accountable for their efforts to meet the goals for their department/division as well as for the Company overall.

Responsibility for Performance Appraisal

It is the managerial responsibility of each superior to continuously appraise the performance of subordinates. The superior has to take the initiative in the annual appraisal process by telling the subordinate what is to be accomplished, how it is to be accomplished and when it is to be accomplished. Though the superior initiates the process, better results are obtained when the *subordinate participates* in defining accountabilities, in establishing measurable goals and in stipulating the content of the developmental action plan. Through this participation, the subordinate will have a greater commitment to the goals and action plans.

Performance Appraisal and Equal Opportunity

In order to achieve the Company's Equal Opportunity and Affirmative Action goals and to comply with the Federal laws and Company policy:

> " . . . . . *that all employees will be treated*
> *equally during their employment in matters*
> *of promotion, upgrading, selection for*
> *training, layoff and termination, transfer,*
> *benefits, and rates of pay.*"

we must ensure that the performance evaluation process is free of discrimination. This is necessary because many of the above personnel decisions are based on the employees' performance evaluation. It is the superior's responsibility to ensure that the performance evaluation is conducted in a non-discriminatory manner.

APPENDIX 6–1. Georgia Power Company Employee Performance Appraisal System

Administration of the Developmental Performance Appraisal System

A. Frequency and Timing of the Formal Review

Each employee covered by the program must be viewed once each year. The annual review date will be the same for all employees with the effective date approximately January 1, each year.

Due to a large number of Performance Appraisals required, the completion of the documents should begin by October 1. The yearly supplementary instructions to the Salary Administration Procedures should be mailed by the beginning of November to enable supervision to complete the performance appraisal and merit review interviews.

The Performance Appraisal document should be submitted with the approved PCA Form as soon as possible after the Supplementary Salary Instructions are received. This is necessary to ensure that the PCA's are processed by the effective annual review date.

B. Signatures

The rater and endorser (immediate and second level supervisor) should sign the performance appraisal form after it has been tentatively completed by the rater for discussion with the employee, *but before the actual employee interview.* Any differences of opinion between immediate and second level supervision must be resolved before discussion with the employee. Any significant changes that develop out of the performance appraisal interview with the employee should be brought to the endorser's attention.

The employees signature *is* desired and it should be explained that by signing the appraisal form, employees are only indicating that they have seen the form and have had the opportunity to discuss it with their supervisor. They are *not* indicating agreement with the evaluation. If after explaining the above, the employee does not wish to sign the appraisal form, indicate such by writing—"Employee has seen and discussed this form with supervisor but refuses to sign the form," across the signature line.

APPENDIX 6–1. Georgia Power Company Employee Performance Appraisal System

C. Recording the Review

Reviews are recorded on Performance Appraisal-Individual Development Form 700603A. Completed original forms are attached to the PCA Form when these forms are submitted for annual merit increases (See Supplementary Instructions to the Salary Administration manual). Copies of the completed Performance Appraisal forms are kept by the employee and supervisor.

D. Employees Covered by the Procedure

This procedure is applicable for all exempt and non-exempt employees, (except those covered by a union contract).

DEFINITION OF TERMS

Accountabilities: The major activities in a job for which performance is required.

Developmental Action Plan: A listing of things the subordinate and/or superior is going to do to improve the subordinate's skills, knowledge, or abilities.

Goal: A time dated, quantifiable work activity which is to be accomplished.

Objective: A broad aim, purpose or mission to be accomplished.

Performance Appraisal: The assessment of a subordinate's performance by the immediate superior along with guidance for future improvement.

Promotion: A change in an employee's position, responsibility, title and or compensation of a magnitude specified by salary administration.

Superior and Subordinate: The roles and position of authority of two people engaged in the appraisal process. The terms do not mean that one person is "superior" or is "inferior" to another person.

Rating: A five level rating guide for marginal, fair, competent, commendable and distinguished used to evaluate the degree of accomplishment of each accountability and to describe overall performance.

APPENDIX 6–1.   Georgia Power Company Employee Performance Appraisal System

Below are the ratings to be used to evaluate accomplishment of *individual accountabilities.*

Marginal—Rating for employees whose performance clearly falls short of established goals.

Fair—Rating for employees whose performance has approached but not met established goals.

Competent—Rating for employees whose performance consistently meets established goals.

Commendable—Rating for employees whose performance clearly and consistently exceeds established goals.

Distinguished—Rating for employees whose performance clearly exceeds established goals on a consistent basis.

Below are the ratings to be used to evaluate *overall* performance.

Marginal—Rating for employees whose performance clearly falls short of established performance standards or expectations in the majority of principal job accountabilities. Improved performance is expected and required as a condition of continued employment in the position.

Fair—Rating for employees whose performance has approached, but not met established performance standards or expectations in the majority of principal job accountabilities. The need for further development is definitely recognizable.

Competent—Rating for employees whose performance consistently meets established performance standards or expectations in the majority of principal job accountabilities. This rating recognizes significant accomplishment and achievement and represents the performance level expected.

Commendable—Rating for employees whose performance clearly and consistently exceeds established performance standards or expectations in the majority of principal job accountabilities.

Distinguished—Rating for employees whose performance far exceeds established performance standards or expectations in all principal job accountabilities on a consistent ba-

APPENDIX 6–1. Georgia Power Company Employee Performance Appraisal System

sis. Normally reserved for those few individuals whose outstanding performance is obvious to all.

What Is An Accountability

1. Accountabilities are the major activities in a job for which performance is required.
2. The four to six major things you are held accountable for in your job are your accountabilities. These four to six accountabilities usually occupy ninety percent or more of your time on the job.
3. Accountabilities are the fewest separate and distinct work activities necessary to be done in order for you to achieve the mission of your job.

What Is Not An Accountability

1. Accountabilities are not the knowledge one has of the job.
2. They are not minor, or detailed work activities.
3. Accountabilities are not personal skills one possesses.
4. They are not the means to do a job, but they are the end product.
5. Supervising is not an accountability.
6. Planning, organizing, motivating, and controlling people are not accountabilities.
7. Accountabilities are not personal characteristics such as dependability, attitude, initiative, ingenuity and the like.
8. Technical qualifications one possesses are not accountabilities.
9. Ability to do a job is not an accountability.
10. Appearance, dress, grooming is not (in most cases) an accountability.

How To Determine Accountabilities

| MISSION | What is the overall purpose of your job? |

| ACCOUNT-ABILITIES (Objectives) | What are the major activities which must be accomplished in order to achieve your mission? List below. |

1. _____
2. _____

APPENDIX 6–1.   Georgia Power Company Employee Performance Appraisal System

3. _____
4. _____
5. _____
6. _____

CRITERIA TO EVALUATE GOALS

The establishment and performance of goals should be measured by superior and subordinate relative to the following criteria:

1. The goal should be *time-dated* indicating when results are to be achieved.
2. The goal should be *measurable* in some quantifiable manner.
3. Appropriate consideration should be given to the *quality* of performance—how well the task is done is important.
4. Financial considerations must be considered—what is the *cost* to do this particular task?
5. What *resources* are needed to accomplish the task?
6. Is the goal consistent with company goals, policies, procedures and good business ethics?
7. Will the results sought *justify* the expenditure of time, resources and effort?
8. Is the goal in an area in which the employee has *authority* to ensure execution?
9. Is the goal realistic and *attainable*, does it represent a real *challenge* to the employee and is it what is expected for *competent* peformance?
10. In what way does this goal help the organization achieve its basic *mission* of providing goods and services to our customers?

APPENDIX 6–1. Georgia Power Company Employee Performance Appraisal System

How To Determine Goals Worksheet

JOB _____

STEP 1 ACCOUNTABILITY	STEP 2 RESULTS AREAS	STEP 3 METHOD OF MEASUREMENT	STEP 4 RESULTS
START WITH THE RIGHT ACCOUNTABILITIES USE ONLY ONE ACCOUNTABILITY AT A TIME	WHAT ARE YOU GOING TO LOOK AT TO DETERMINE THE KIND OF JOB THE EMPLOYEE DOES (TIMELINESS, QUALITY, QUANTITY, COST)	WHAT MEANS WILL BE USED TO MEASURE THIS PERFORMANCE?	WHAT IS THE LEVEL OF PERFORMANCE EXPECTED? CONSIDER RESOURCES AVAILABLE, AUTHORITY AND CONTROL. IS THE LEVEL A CHALLENGE BUT ATTAINABLE?

APPENDIX 6–1. Georgia Power Company Employee Performance Appraisal System

205

Step Increase Waiting Periods

	(1)	(2)	(3)	(4)	(5)	(6)	(7)	(8)	(9)	(10)
Gr-1	8980	9279	9578	9876	10175	10350	10646	10942	10955	11232
Bi-Wk	344.00	356.00	367.20	378.40	390.40	396.80	408.00	419.20	420.00	430.4
Hourly	4.30	4.45	4.59	4.73	4.88	4.96	5.10	5.24	5.25	5.3
O/T	6.45	6.68	6.89	7.10	7.32	7.44	7.65	7.86	7.88	8.0
GS-2	10097	10337	10671	10955	11078	11404	11730	12056	12382	12708
Bi-Wk	387.20	396.00	408.80	420.00	424.80	436.80	449.60	462.40	474.40	487.2
Hourly	4.84	4.95	5.11	5.25	5.31	5.46	5.62	5.78	5.93	6.0
O/T	7.26	7.43	7.67	7.88	7.97	8.19	8.43	8.67	8.90	9.1
GS-3	11017	11384	11751	12118	12485	12852	13219	13586	13953	14320
B-Wk	422.40	436.00	450.40	464.80	478.40	492.80	506.40	520.80	535.20	548.8
Hourly	5.28	5.45	5.63	5.81	5.98	6.16	6.33	6.51	6.69	6.8
O/T	7.92	8.18	8.45	8.72	8.97	9.24	9.50	9.77	10.04	10.2
GS-4	12367	12779	13191	13603	14015	14427	14839	15251	15663	16075
Bi-Wk	474.40	489.60	505.60	521.60	537.60	552.80	568.80	584.80	600.80	616.0
Hourly	5.93	6.12	6.32	6.52	6.67	6.91	7.11	7.31	7.51	7.7
O/T	8.90	9.18	9.48	9.78	10.08	10.37	10.67	10.97	11.27	11.5
GS-5	13837	14298	14759	15220	15681	16142	16603	17064	17525	17986
Bi-Wk	530.40	548.00	565.60	583.20	600.80	618.40	636.80	654.40	672.00	689.6
Hourly	6.63	6.85	7.07	7.29	7.51	7.73	7.96	8.18	8.40	8.6
O/T	9.95	10.28	10.61	10.94	11.27	11.60	11.94	12.27	12.60	12.9
GS-6	15423	15937	16451	16965	17479	17993	18507	19021	19535	20049
Bi-Wk	591.20	611.20	630.40	650.40	670.40	689.60	709.60	728.80	748.80	768.8
Hourly	7.39	7.64	7.88	8.13	8.38	8.62	8.87	9.11	9.36	9.6
O/T	11.09	11.46	11.82	12.20	12.57	12.93	13.31	13.67	14.04	14.4
GS-7	17138	17709	18280	18851	19422	19993	20564	21135	21706	22277
Bi-Wk	656.80	679.20	700.80	722.40	744.80	766.40	788.00	810.40	832.00	853.6
Hourly	8.21	8.49	8.76	9.03	9.31	9.58	9.85	10.13	10.40	10.6
O/T	12.32	12.74	13.14	13.55	13.97	14.37	14.78	15.20	15.60	16.0
GS-8	18981	19614	20247	20880	21513	22146	22779	23412	24045	24678
Bi-Wk	727.20	752.00	776.00	800.00	824.80	848.80	872.80	897.20	921.60	945.6
Hourly	9.09	9.40	9.70	10.00	10.31	10.61	10.91	11.22	11.52	11.8
O/T	13.64	14.10	14.55	15.00	15.47	15.92	16.37	16.59	16.59	16.5

APPENDIX 6–1. Georgia Power Company Employee Performance Appraisal System

	1	2	3	4	5	6	7	8	9	10
GS-9	20965	21664	22363	23062	23761	24460	25159	25858	26557	27256
Bi-Wk	804.00	830.40	857.60	884.00	911.20	937.60	964.80	991.20	1017.60	1044.8
Hourly	10.05	10.38	10.72	11.05	11.39	11.72	12.06	12.39	12.72	13.0
O/T	15.08	15.57	16.08	16.58	16.59	16.59	16.59	16.59	16.59	16.5
GS-10	23088	23858	24628	25398	26168	26938	27708	28478	29248	30018
Bi-Wk	884.80	914.40	944.00	973.60	1003.20	1032.80	1062.40	1092.00	1120.80	1150.4
Hourly	11.06	11.43	11.80	12.17	12.54	12.91	13.28	13.65	14.01	14.3
O/T	16.59	16.59	16.59	16.59	16.59	16.59	16.59	16.59	16.59	16.5
GS-11	25366	26212	27058	27904	28750	29596	30442	31288	32134	32980
Bi-Wk	972.00	1004.80	1037.60	1069.60	1102.40	1134.40	1167.20	1199.20	1232.00	1264.0
Hourly	12.15	12.56	12.97	13.37	13.78	14.18	14.59	14.99	15.40	15.8
O/T	16.59	16.59	16.59	16.59	16.59	16.59	16.59	16.59	16.59	16.5
GS-12	30402	31415	32428	33441	34454	35467	36480	37493	38506	39519
Bi-Wk	1165.60	1204.00	1243.20	1281.60	1320.80	1359.20	1398.40	1437.60	1476.00	1515.2
Hourly	14.57	15.05	15.54	16.02	16.51	16.99	17.48	17.97	18.45	18.9
O/T	16.59	16.59	16.59	16.59	16.59	16.59	16.59	16.59	16.59	16.5
GS-13	36152	37357	38562	39767	40972	42177	43382	44587	45792	46997
Bi-Wk	1385.60	1432.00	1478.40	1524.00	1570.40	1616.80	1663.20	1708.80	1755.20	1801.6
Hourly	17.32	17.90	18.48	19.05	19.63	20.21	20.79	21.36	21.94	22.5
O/T	16.59	16.59	16.59	16.59	16.59	16.59	16.59	16.59	16.59	16.5
GS-14	42722	44146	45570	46994	48418	49842	51266	52690	54114	55538
Bi-Wk	1637.60	1692.00	1747.20	1801.60	1856.00	1910.40	1964.80	2020.00	2074.40	2128.8
Hourly	20.47	21.15	21.84	22.52	23.20	23.88	24.56	25.25	25.93	26.6
O/T	16.59	16.59	16.59	16.59	16.59	16.59	16.59	16.59	16.59	16.5
GS-15	50252	51927	53602	55277	56952	58627	60302	61977	63652	65327
Bi-Wk	1926.40	1990.40	2054.40	2119.20	2183.20	2247.20	2311.20	2376.00	2440.00	2504.0
Hourly	24.08	24.88	25.68	26.49	27.29	28.09	28.89	29.70	30.50	31.3
O/T	16.59	16.59	16.59	16.59	16.59	16.59	16.59	16.59	16.59	—
GS-16	58938	60903	62868	64833	66000	—				—
Bi-Wk	2259.20	2334.40	2409.60	2485.60	2529.60					
Hourly	28.24	29.18	30.12	31.07	31.62					
O/T	16.59	16.59	16.59	16.59						

APPENDIX 6–1.   Georgia Power Company Employee Performance Appraisal System

Employee Name	Employee No.	Current Job No./Title
George J. Jones	*0000*	*Plant Manager*

Division/Department	Annual Merit Review Date	Location
Power Supply	*1-15-82*	*Any Location*

1. Job Content (To be completed at beginning of review year) List the accountabilities of the employee's position. Use additional paper if needed.

Accountability Number [1]

To operate the generating facility with the highest rate of plant availability consistent with proper maintenance and operating procedures.

Accountability Number [2]

Heat rate will be maintained as low as practical for each unit.

Accountability Number [3]

Will operate the plant as safe as possible during the year.

Accountability Number [4]

The quality of our maintenance efforts will be maintained coupled with a reduction in maintenance expenses.

Accountability Number [5]

Will operate the plant as close to the capital and operating budget as possible in 1981.

Accountability Number [ ]

THIS IS AN EXAMPLE ONLY, IT SHOULD NOT BE CONSIDERED COMPLETE OR NECESSARILY REALISTIC FOR THE REFERENCED POSITION.

Accountability Number [ ] Work Habits (Optional)

APPENDIX 6–1. Georgia Power Company Employee Performance Appraisal System

II. Goals with Measurable Performance Standards (To be completed at the beginning of review year.)
Describe how the employee is expected to fulfill each accountability. State the behavior or standard which would exhibit competent performance.

Accountability Number | 1

Competent performance is evidenced with plant availability being between 75-80% in 1981 for each unit.

Accountability Number | 2

Competent performance will be evidenced when heat rate for each unit, measured when units are operating at full load, will be as follows for 1981:

Unit No. 1 – 9300   Unit No. 3 – 9200
Unit No. 2 – 9300   Unit No. 4 – 9200

Accountability Number | 3

The accident frequency rate will be maintained at 1.25 or lower for 1981 thus indicating competent performance.

Accountability Number | 4

(1) Competent performance is evidenced in that forced outages will be reduced to not more than four in 1981.
(2) The overall maintenance budget will not exceed $17.2 million which is 106% of the 1981 actual expense.

Accountability Number | 5

Competent performance will be evidenced in that we will not exceed the capital and operating budget over 7% for 1981. Also the base payroll will not exceed the budget in 1981 and overtime cost will not exceed 10% of base payroll in 1981.

Accountability Number

Accountability Number

Accountability Number

APPENDIX 6–1.   Georgia Power Company Employee Performance Appraisal System

III. Performance Evaluation

First describe how the employee is fulfilling or failing to fulfill each accountability in comparison with the Performance Standards outlined in Section II. Then rate the employee on each accountability using the definitions below.

MARGINAL	FAIR	COMPETENT	COMMENDABLE	DISTINGUISHED
Rating for employees whose performance clearly falls short of established goals.	Rating for employees whose performance has approached but not met established goals.	Rating for employees whose performance consistently meets established goals.	Rating for employees whose performance clearly and consistently exceeds established goals.	Rating for employees whose performance far exceeds established goals on a consistent basis.

Accountability Number ☐ 1

During 1981, a normal operating year with no unusual circumstances, plant availability for each unit averaged 77%.

☐ Distinguished
☐ Commendable
☒ Competent
☐ Fair
☐ Marginal

Accountability Number ☐ 2

During the past 12 months, the average heat rate for each unit while at full load measured as follows:
Unit No. 1 – 9250   Unit No. 3 – 9100
Unit No. 2 – 9300   Unit No. 4 – 9150

☐ Distinguished
☒ Commendable
☐ Competent
☐ Fair
☐ Marginal

Accountability Number ☐ 3

Accident frequency rate for the year was 1.03, which was the lowest among all generating plants.

☐ Distinguished
☐ Commendable
☒ Competent
☐ Fair
☐ Marginal

Accountability Number ☐ 4

There were five forced outages during 1981, but one was attributed to faulty equipment beyond supervisory control. Maintenance expenditures fell within budget for the year.

☐ Distinguished
☐ Commendable
☒ Competent
☐ Fair
☐ Marginal

Accountability Number ☐ 5

The capital and operating budget for 1981 was exceeded by 12% and the year was a normal operating year with no unusual circumstances. Base payroll fell within 1981 budget, but overtime costs were 15% of base payroll, 5% above the set goal.

☐ Distinguished
☐ Commendable
☐ Competent
☒ Fair
☐ Marginal

Accountability Number ☐

☐ Distinguished
☐ Commendable
☐ Competent
☐ Fair
☐ Marginal

APPENDIX 6–1.   Georgia Power Company Employee Performance Appraisal System

IV. Describe the employee's strengths as demonstrated in the last 12 months.

(1) Technical knowledge of generating plant operations — has met plant's major production and efficiency measurements.
(2) Communication and motivational skills — plant morale is high and safety record indicates strong leadership.

V. List areas in which the employee needs to improve.

(1) Long range planning, particularly in the budgeting process.
(2) Manpower and material cost awareness.

VI. At the present time what are the employee's future growth possibilities.

Shows potential for greater responsibilities, but more time in current job should serve to further develop current strengths while allowing him to show improvement in certain areas.

VII. Development Action Plan: List Activities which will help the employee improve present performance and grow with the company.

(1) As supervisor, I will consult with budget staff to develop an annual meeting for all Plant Managers on budget preparation and review. Additionally, I plan to meet monthly with George to discuss budget performance.
(2) George needs to spend more time developing and/or reviewing reports on overtime costs and provide management with explanations when costs exceed 10% in any given month.

VIII. Overall Performance Rating. (See Appendix A of the instruction manual for definitions of terms used in overall rating.)

☐ Marginal   ☐ Fair   ☒ Competent   ☐ Commendable   ☐ Distinguished

Employee Comments

Employee Signature	Date	
Rater (Immediate Supervisor)	Date	Title
Endorser (Second Level Supervisor)	Date	Title

APPENDIX 6–1.   Georgia Power Company Employee Performance Appraisal System

SALARIED PERFORMANCE APPRAISAL

Employee Name	Employee Number	Date	Dept. No.

Job Classification Title	Years in Classification	Appraisal Period From To

Salaried Performance Appraisal Purposes: To recognize and reinforce good performance. To improve job performance through an objective appraisal of past performance. To maximize the capability of salaried employees in the positions they hold. As an aid in this process, the employee has the option of preparing a self appraisal and of submitting comments after the appraisal interview (see below).

SUMMARY STATEMENT OF RESPONSIBILITIES, ASSIGNMENTS, AND WORK PERFORMED BY THIS PARTICULAR EMPLOYEE (Related performance evaluated on reverse of this form.):

_____

_____

_____

_____

_____

_____

_____

Overall Job Performance Rating

☐ Unsurpassed   ☐ Usually Exceeds Requirements   ☐ Fully Meets Requirements

☐ Usually Meets Requirements   ☐ Unsatisfactory

Did employee complete a self appraisal? ☐ Yes (please attach) ☐ No	Any employee comments following the interview? ☐ Yes (please attach) ☐ No

Employee Signature:	Date

Prepared by:	Classification

Reviewed by:	Classification

APPENDIX 6–1.   Georgia Power Company Employee Performance Appraisal System

212

DEGREE OF PERFORMANCE						JOB SPECIFICS
Check (√) the appropriate box _____						Give examples of job behavior for each performance factor to justify the performance rating. Include negative and/or positive job behavior as needed to support your rating.
PERFORMANCE FACTORS						
Quantity of Work The volume of work produced, projects completed.						
Quality of Work The neatness, accuracy and dependability of results.						
Job Knowledge The extent of familiarity with established operations/procedures.						
Problem Solving Considering all phases of a problem in order to arrive at a decision.						
Innovation The creation and implementation of new ideas, concepts, applications.						
Communications The effectiveness in transmitting and receiving all relevant information.						
Cooperation The willingness to work with and for others.						
Safety Consciousness Activities and attitudes toward the spirit and rules of company ss safety.						
Cost Consciousness Effective activity toward reducing costs in and outside own area of responsibilities.						
Leadership (Supervision Only) How well subordinates are motivated, their productivity, efficiency, promotability, development and ability to work as a team.						
Optional Factor						
Optional Factor						
Optional Factor						

APPENDIX 6–1. Georgia Power Company Employee Performance Appraisal System

"Yeah, I've got my own incentive program."

Chapter Seven

INCENTIVE PAY (PERFORMANCE RELATED PAY)

INTRODUCTION

Included in many wage and salary administration programs is the development, implementation, and administration of incentive systems. When wage incentive plans are properly designed, implemented, and administered, they can provide a significant boost to an organization's productivity. In fact, properly designed and effectively administered, the wage incentive principle could well be one of the few concepts in our entire economic structure under which everybody wins and nobody loses.

" . . . The main goal of an incentive plan is to raise productivity through a system of payment, which fully compensates the worker for the extra effort put in. The worker will regard a system fair, if the compensation is in direct proportion to the output." (Lokiec:95–96) This rewards increased production outputs, without requiring a comparable increase in fixed costs. Incentives are also based on the assumption that workers are motivated, to a significant extent, by an opportunity to increase earnings.

There are two major distinctions to be made in describing different types of incentive programs. One type of incentive plan bases compensation on the productivity of the individual at the assigned task. This reward, based on a production count, is immediate. The second general type is a group incentive plan, or a productivity sharing approach. This rewards a group of employees, perhaps all the employees of a company, for the overall gains their unit or the entire company experiences. These usually are long-term rewards and are paid as bonus payments, generally on a quarterly, semiannual, or annual basis.

Several surveys have been conducted during recent years which illustrate the widespread use of incentives. Robert Rice reported in *Industrial Engineering* magazine that 59% of the manufacturing companies in this country have wage incentive plans. (Rice:19) In a survey conducted by Mitchell Fein, he stated, "Incentives have major application where workers exercise control over their output." (Maynard:6–17) Fein also reported that organizations which adopted individual wage incentive systems showed an average increase in productivity of 51.5%. (Fein:49) John Patton, of Patton Consultants, Inc., said, " . . . our experiences over the past 30 years substantiates this [Fein's] finding." (Patton:20) Commenting on group incentive plans, Clifford N. Sellie, of Standards International, stated, "Group incentives are particularly attractive in group plans that are based on simple overall calculations." (Sellie:62)

Despite their widespread use, incentive plans can be and have been the subject of criticism. Poorly designed, implemented, or maintained plans can quickly lead to opposition not only by workers, but by management as well. E. B. Watmough, in a critical look at incentive plans, stated, "Most reasons [incentive plans fail] stem not from a physical disagreement with the basic incentive idea, but from endlessly recurring mistakes in the installation, administration, and maintenance of the many systems in operation." (Watmough:356) The literature has an abundant sampling of failures. Care must be taken to properly design and maintain incentive plans.

This chapter will describe the requirements for an effective incentive system. "Wage incentive plans that work help a company's productivity and profit picture. Management is happy because the workers are producing more product in less time, which reduces the cost per piece. Workers are satisfied because they are now earning higher wages and know exactly what is expected of them." (Ferrell:53)

WAGE INCENTIVE PLANS—TECHNICAL DEVELOPMENT (INDIVIDUAL PLANS)

In order to develop a successful individual wage incentive program a number of conditions must be met. These prerequisites include the following.

First, there must be a sound, well-run and well-maintained work measurement system. The work measurement system provides the basic information for the incentive system, the time standard. Time standards must be set using accepted industrial engineering practice. Although a variety of procedures, such as stopwatch time study, predetermined time analysis, or standard data systems may be used, the objective is the same: All of the work measurement procedures strive to develop, for a given job, the standard time required to complete the job.

The standard time has traditionally been defined as the time required by a typical worker, working at a normal pace, to complete a specific task, using a defined method, with adequate allowance for personal, fatigue, and delay times. This definition though, has several points which require additional explanation.

First is what, or who, is a "typical" worker? A typical worker is generally considered to be one who is neither too fast nor too slow. A typical worker is neither the best nor the worst. A typical worker is not the best or most experienced, nor is the typical worker brand new on the job. The typical worker is a competent worker who is representative of the workers who normally would perform the task being studied. Typical or average workers are generally known and agreed upon by supervisors as well as by fellow employees.

A second point needs clarification in the standard time definition. This is the concept of normal pace. Normal pace is the rate of work designated by the company as being normal. Although this may sound like a non-definition, what it means is that the normal pace is an arbitrary definition of speed at which a worker is expected to work. There is nothing scientific or magical about the normal pace. The rate of work selected as normal is ordinarily one which may be maintained by most workers without overexertion. Some companies establish it as walking at three miles per hour, some others define it as shoveling 56 tons of sand a day. Regardless of how it is defined, a uniform normal pace *should* apply to all comparable jobs as defined by the job evaluation system. Industrial engineers must have this concept of normal fixed in their minds and, upon observing the job under study, compare the worker's performance on that job with this concept of normal pace. This is a skill that is referred to as performance rating. Since it is a skill, constant practice is necessary to maintain it. The practice of performance rating has been the subject of criticism over the years. Improper rating can destroy the work measurement process.

A third portion of the standard time definition that needs further clarification is the phrase, "defined method." Traditionally this has been stated as the "best" method, but best is a relative term. Instead, it is much more correct to refer to the defined method or standard practice. This implies that the worker is performing the job as instructed, using a procedure that has been approved by the industrial engineering department. Failure to standardize work methods will lead to inaccurate standards.

Most commonly a poorly defined method will develop into what is known as a "loose rate." This means more time is allowed for the job in the time standard than is actually required by a typical worker working at a normal pace. A corresponding problem that might develop is a "tight rate." When a job has a tight rate less time is allowed by the standard than is really required by the operator to complete the task. Neither situation, loose rates or tight rates, is healthy. Both lead to different amounts of money being paid for the same amount of work performed. Both are symptoms of an incentive system that is not technically sound.

The final part of the definition of time standard that needs explanation is the allowance for personal, fatigue, and delay time. This is an acknowledgment that the worker cannot work all day long without some respite. The worker will need an opportunity to pause periodically to physiologically recover from fatigue as well as to attend to personal needs. There is also a chance that there will be an unavoidable delay. Something may occasionally happen, such as a machine breaking down, that will delay the worker. The time standard has to make allowance for this. This allowance, often called a PFD allowance, for personal, fatigue, and delay, is generally a constant percentage of time added to the measured time standard. The amount varies, depending upon the type of work done or through the results of collective bargaining with a labor union. Certain jobs, performed under adverse environmental conditions, would naturally require a larger allowance. For example, a steel worker who must work adjacent to a blast furnace would need more of an allowance than someone involved in electronic assembly operations in an air-conditioned factory. The fatigue caused by the warm or hot steel mill would require more recovery than working in a pleasant atmosphere. It is suggested that the PFD allowance be set based on a study of the job, but it usually is a constant that is company policy or the result of negotiations.

When properly set, the time standard is a measure of the work the company expects the worker to produce during a day. It has sometimes been referred to as "A Fair Day's Work." A more realistic description of this concept comes from the AFL-CIO's Bertram Gottlieb, who called it, " . . . an acceptable level of work." (Gottlieb:596) This definition of a standard, developed and set by a sound and well-run work measurement system is the **first** and most important prerequisite to a successful incentive program. An incentive system is technically sound when it is based on valid work measurement standards. Although it is easy to criticize the work measurement techniques as being less than 100% accurate, Mitchell Lokiec, the International Ladies Garment Worker's Union

Director of Management Engineering, summarized it best when he said, "Unfortunately, the scientific tools available to the engineering profession may never be perfect. In spite of this, we are in a position to arrive at solutions that are socially and economically more acceptable than in any other way. They are also more accurate. . . ." (Lokiec:122)

A **second** condition necessary for the wage incentive system deals with the standard practice or work method described above. The standard practice must be well documented. Equipment and tools used have to be specified, as does the workplace layout. The procedures to be used have to be explicitly defined. At times it may seem to be a lot of trouble, maybe even too much trouble, to document with this much detail, but it should be done to avoid future difficulties. If complaints arise about rates being tight or loose, comparison of the current work method with a complete standard practice can identify the sources of the variances.

A **third** prerequisite for the wage incentive system is the establishment of a job evaluation system. As described earlier in this text, the job evaluation system will determine the relative worth of every job in the company. This information, coupled with the sound technical development of time standards, establishes a base rate or "Fair Day's Pay" for every job. A fair day's pay, again in the words of Gottlieb, is " . . . an adequate day's pay. . . ." (Gottlieb:596) Once this is developed, the statement, "A fair day's pay for a fair day's work" or "An adequate day's pay for an adequate day's work," will have meaning. The pay level for each job is set, or negotiated, based on the relative worth of the job and the requirements of the job, as measured by the time standard.

The **fourth** condition is the willingness of the company to communicate or explain the incentive system completely to the employees, supervisors, and if applicable, to the union. Management must be completely open with all parties involved. Everybody must understand the system if it is to be successful. Not only must everybody concerned understand the mechanics, but they must also understand the reasons for installing the incentive program. The people will make or break the system. The one common denominator in successful companies is that they are aware that their product is only the end result of the people in their employ.

Once established, the program must be maintained. Management must provide the resources to make sure that the following happen.

1. Make certain that the standard practices for each job are maintained. It is, as stated earlier, important to have the standard practice and the jobs performed agree. The standard practice

must reflect the working conditions the job is performed under.

2. Maintain the validity or technical soundness of the time standards. This is often done through the process of auditing the rates. Regular comparison of the jobs as performed with the published standards will ensure that the system does not get out of control. Periodic production counts are another way of making sure that incentives accurately reflect the amount of work being performed.

3. Prepare and maintain a complete wage incentive manual. This should be a simple, straightforward, up-to-date document that explains the principles, practices, and procedures used in the system, as well as listing the incentive standards in use.

4. Make certain that actual changes in the method are rapidly reflected in the standard. The quicker the system reacts, the better. As methods change, the rates may become loose or tight and thereby affect the earnings of the workers. When earnings are inconsistent, it is easy to lose the confidence of the individuals who must live with the plans on a daily basis.

5. Maintain a record of quality requirements as they pertain to the specific operations. Quality cannot be neglected in order to increase productivity.

The five conditions described—sound work standards, complete documentation, open communication, proper administration, and quality control—are all necessary conditions or pre-conditions for a successful wage incentive program. In addition to these prerequisites, there are other conditions that are necessary for the success of the individual wage incentive system.

First, the incentive system should guarantee every employee the opportunity to earn an incentive. Extra effort by the worker would result in extra pay for the worker. Each job should have an equal likelihood of having employees earn incentive pay. Second, no upper limits should be placed on earnings. With a valid technical foundation, an incentive plan should accommodate any super performance. Although it might be unexpected, a worker should be able to earn twice the "fair day's pay" if twice the expected daily production is attained.

Third, a daily minimum wage should be guaranteed. This minimum may be the minimum wage mandated by law, or it may be a higher minimum, expressed as a percentage of standard. The proper application of guaranteed minimum rates is the foundation upon which the whole system rests. The guaranteed minimum rate should provide a floor below which earnings can never fall. It also must offer the worker reasonable protection from factors beyond his control which tend to reduce earnings.

Fourth, and perhaps most importantly, the incentive system must be simple enough so that the worker can calculate his or her own wages. Everybody wants to know what or how much they are earning now, and most individuals want to be able to double check their paycheck with the amount they expected to earn.

A fifth condition for a successful plan is that the job must have some degree of manual or operator control. Jobs that are entirely machine paced do not fit the conventional incentive pay system. A worker in that case must wait for the machine and can work no faster than the machine. Incentive pay based on production would be virtually impossible to achieve.

INDIVIDUAL WAGE INCENTIVE PLANS— MECHANICS

Before the mechanics of wage incentive plans can be discussed, some background is necessary. There are many types of individual incentive plans, many of which have been individually tailored to fit particular organizations. Regardless of the specifics of a plan, the following are descriptive terms for most incentive plans. *Daywork* is the straight hourly wage paid to workers regardless of the productivity of the workers. The amount paid, or the rate, is either arbitrarily established or negotiated with a union. *Measured Daywork* is also a straight hourly wage paid to workers, but the rate paid reflects the expected productivity of the worker. Measured daywork rates are based on a sound work measurement system and reflect what might be called a "fair day's pay." To avoid confusion, this book will mean measured daywork whenever it references daywork. Daywork is *always* paid on jobs where the process controls the workpace.

In many incentive plans the additional wages, or bonus, the worker earns for production over standard is paid entirely to the worker. The more productive the worker, the greater the earnings. The organization benefits from increased productivity by having increased output produced with the same fixed costs. However, many plans insist on a sharing of the gains brought about by increased worker productivity. Workers who exceed the standard are rewarded with extra pay, but not entirely in proportion to their additional output. The company, in return for providing the resources, shares the gains. Some plans pay higher rates for production over standard, and some plans even pay variable rates for production over standard. These latter plans usually pay higher rates as the production exceeds standard by increasing amounts.

The payment schemes tend to become confusing and their use is not encouraged.

Regarding wage payment, some incentive plans guarantee daywork for all production up to standard, and an incentive, whatever its relative worth, for work over standard. Others start paying the bonus when production exceeds a certain level, such as 80% of standard, while yet others will guarantee no minimum pay except for the legally mandated minimum wage. When a plan does guarantee a full day's pay it is referred to as a plan that has a "guaranteed minimum."

Finally, some tasks, while not entirely operator paced, have some portions where it may be desirable to have an incentive in place. When part of a job is machine paced, that portion of the job is paid on a daywork basis. Incentive payments only apply to that portion of the job that is operator controlled.

It would be impossible for this, or any other book, to describe all, or even a large percentage, of the wage incentive plans in use today. The following sections will describe some representative wage incentive systems illustrative of the conditions described above. These plans will be described and then illustrated through the use of a fully explained example.

DAYWORK

Daywork compensates the worker for the time spent on the job. The rate of pay is based on the expected production, as set by a technically sound work measurement system. The rate of pay reflects the expected earnings of a typical operator, working at a normal pace, using the specified method. An adequate allowance is made for personal, fatigue, and delay factors. This is based on the relative worth of the job as established by a job evaluation system.

Example—Daywork: A "fair" payrate for a particular job is determined to be $5.16 per hour. The before tax compensation* of a worker who worked an eight-hour day, would be

$$\text{Pay} = (\text{Number of Hours Worked}) (\text{Hourly Rate})$$
$$= (8 \text{ hours}) (\$5.16 \text{ per hour})$$
$$= \$41.28$$

---

*All earnings mentioned in this chapter will be concerned with before-tax compensation.

PIECEWORK

The piecework individual incentive plan is a straightforward incentive plan in which the worker is compensated for each unit completed. The standard time indicates the number of units that should be completed during a given time period. This expected production is combined with the fair day's wage for that type of work based, of course, on the relative worth of the job. The result is a piece rate for each unit produced. Earnings depend directly on the number of units produced. The following examples will show applications of piecework under several variations. Figure 7–1 shows earnings as a function of production for a straight piecerate plan.

Example-piecework (100% operator controlled, no minimum rate guaranteed)

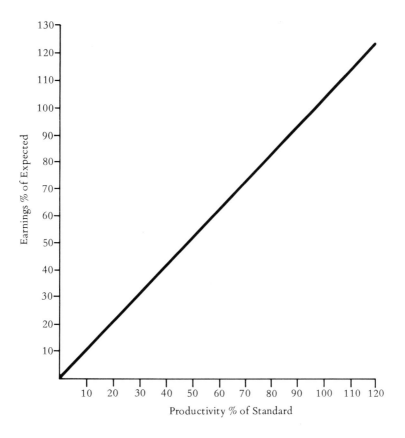

FIGURE 7–1. Earnings as a Function of Production/Piecework

A task has had a time standard of .0121 hours set for its completion by the industrial engineering department. In order to calculate the number of pieces that would be expected to be produced in one hour, the following calculation converts the standard, expressed as hours per piece, to pieces per hour,

$$
\begin{aligned}
\text{pieces/hour} &= 1/(\text{hours/piece}) \\
&= 1/(.0121 \text{ hours/piece}) \\
&= 82.64 \text{ pieces/hour}
\end{aligned}
$$

The hourly wage that has been determined to be acceptable for this type of job, or that has been negotiated between a labor union and the company, is $4.50 per hour. The piecerate for each unit produced is calculated with the following relationship:

$$
\begin{aligned}
\text{dollars/piece} &= (\text{dollars/hour})/(\text{pieces/hour}) \\
&= (\$4.50/\text{hour})/(82.64 \text{ pieces/hour}) \\
&= \$.0545 \text{ per piece}
\end{aligned}
$$

Income is calculated using the equation:

$$
\text{earnings} = (\text{piecerate})(\text{number of pieces produced})
$$

If the worker on this job produced 500 pieces in an 8-hour day, the income would be:

$$
\begin{aligned}
\text{earnings} &= (\$.0545/\text{piece})(500 \text{ pieces}) \\
&= \$27.25
\end{aligned}
$$

This would have to be compared with the legally mandated minimum wage. If this amount exceeded the minimum wage then the piecerate earnings would be paid, otherwise the actual minimum wage would be the day's earnings.

In a piecerate incentive plan income is directly related to production. The more the worker produces, the more the worker earns. There is a direct financial incentive for the worker to be more productive. It must be pointed out that most incentive plans that are designed like this one pay the piece rate only on "good" or acceptable products. The worker does not benefit from fast but careless work.

Example—Piecework (100% operator controlled, 100% daywork guaranteed)

A task has a standard time of .045 hours and is paid on a piecework incentive plan with a 100% daywork guarantee, for an eight-hour day. The daywork guarantee is $46.00.

(a) If an employee produces 182 units in a given day, what will the earnings be for that day?

First, the hourly pay rate is calculated. This is:

$$(\$46/hour)/(8\ hours/day) = \$5.75/hour$$

Next, the hourly production rate, based on the standard, is calculated:

$$.045\ hours/unit = 22.22\ units/hour$$

The piece rate is determined:

$$(\$5.75/hour)/(22.22\ pieces/hour) = \$.259/piece$$

For a daily production of 182 units, the pay would be:

$$(\$.259/piece)(182\ pieces) = \$47.14$$

This reflects a slight bonus payment for production over the standard.

(b) If an employee completes 150 units in a day, what will the pay be for that day?

Using the piece rate calculated in part (a) above, or $.259 per unit, the daily pay would be:

$$(\$.259/piece)(150\ pieces) = \$38.85$$

Since this is below the guaranteed daywork rate of $46.00, the pay for the day would be the guaranteed rate of $46.00. This difference between the incentive earnings and the guaranteed earnings is sometimes called "make-up pay."

Example—Piecework (100% operator controlled, 80% daywork guaranteed)

A task has a standard time of .008 hours and is paid on a piecework incentive plan with an 80% daywork guarantee for an eight-hour day of $32.00.

(a) If an employee produces 1,200 units on a given day, what will the earnings be for that day?

The hourly pay rate is calculated:

$$(\$32.00/hour)/(8\ hours/day) = \$4.00/hour$$

This $4.00 figure represents only the guarantee, which is 80% of expected earnings, or 80% of the fair day's pay. In order to calculate the piece rate, the full 100% daywork equivalent must be determined. Since $4.00 represents 80% of this unknown rate, the following equation can be solved for the rate:

$$\$4.00 = (.8)(rate)$$
$$\$4.00/.8 = rate$$
$$\$5.00 = rate$$

Now the piece rate can be calculated using the standard time and the known dayrate. The hourly production rate, in terms of pieces per hour, is calculated:

$$.008 \text{ hours/piece} = 125 \text{ pieces/hour}$$

The piece rate is:

$$(\$5.00/\text{hour})/(125 \text{ pieces/hour}) = \$.04/\text{piece}$$

A production of 1,200 units would provide earnings for the worker in the amount of:

$$(\$.04/\text{piece})(1200 \text{ pieces}) = \$48.00$$

This exceeds the 80% guarantee and the worker would be paid the incentive earnings.

(b) If the worker produced 800 units what would the day's earnings be?

Using the piece rate of $.04 per piece that was calculated in the first part of this example, the worker's earnings would be:

$$(\$.04/\text{piece})(800 \text{ pieces}) = \$32.00$$

This happens to be the 80% rate of pay that is guaranteed by this plan. Thus, 800 units must represent 80% of the expected daily production. Production below 800 units on a given day would be paid at the guaranteed rate of $32.00, while any and all production over this level would be paid at the piece rate.

This plan, as described in the preceeding example, is also known as the Gantt Plan. When incentive plans are called Gantt Plans it means that they will guarantee to pay 80% of the expected day's production, regardless of how the worker actually performs. Continual performance below the 80% level will lead to some form of corrective action being taken with the employee. This may either be disciplinary measures or additional training. Figure 7–2 shows earnings as a function of production for a typical Gantt Plan.

Example—Piecework (70% operator controlled, 30% machine paced, 100% daywork guaranteed)

A job is known to be machine paced 30% of the time. This means that for 30% of the day the individual efforts of the operator have no direct influence upon production. The operator must wait on the machine. During this portion of the job the operator must be compensated at the day rate. If, for the operator-paced part of the task, the standard time is .068 hours, and if the day rate is $6.50 per hour, the earnings for a daily production count of 131 would be calculated as follows.

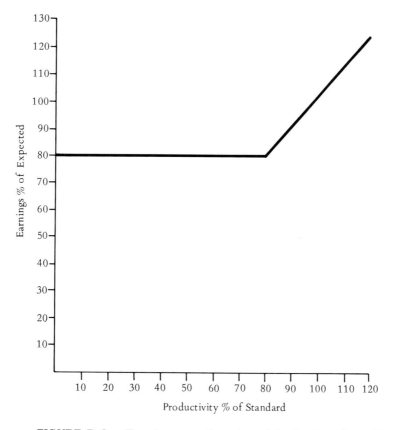

FIGURE 7–2. Earnings as a Functon of Production/Gantt Plans

First, the guaranteed time must be determined. This is the machine-paced time, which for this example is 30% of the eight-hour working day. This 30% must be compensated at the daywork rate of $6.50 per hour. During an eight-hour day, this 30% of the day represents:

$$(30\%)(8 \text{ hours}) = 2.4 \text{ hours}$$

The earnings for these 2.4 hours are

$$(\$6.50/\text{hour}) (2.4 \text{ hours}) = \$15.60$$

For the remainder of the job, the piece rate must be calculated. Using the standard of .068 hours, this means:

$$.068 \text{ hours/piece} = 14.7 \text{ pieces/hour}$$

Based on the pay rate of $6.50 per hour, the piece rate for the operator-controlled portion of the job is determined:

$$(\$6.50/\text{hour})/(14.7 \text{ pieces/hour}) = \$.44/\text{piece}$$

For the indicated daily production of 131 units, the piecerate pay would be:

$$(\$.44/\text{piece})(131 \text{ pieces}) = \$57.64$$

In order to determine the daily earnings, the $15.60 for the machine-paced portion of the job must be added to the piecerate earnings. This gives a daily earnings of $73.24. This compares favorably with a straight eight-hour daywork pay of:

$$(\$6.50/\text{hour})(8 \text{ hours}) = \$52.00$$

This method of calculating incentive earnings is acceptable for a partially machine-paced task, but does not work for an entirely process controlled job. In that case the general procedure is to pay daywork for the task. However, Charles F. James, Jr. suggests that an incentive system for machine- or line-paced operations is developed by establishing a standard based on downtime . . . a motivational system can be designed for machine- or line-paced operations with the principal objective of reducing downtime. James' incentive system differs from the ones we have been discussing in that it rewards the worker who appears to be doing minimum work, as reflected in the incentive for keeping the machine running (James:52). This may mean that an employee would be paid a relatively high premium if he would be alert for potential downtime causes and correct them before downtime occurs; however it may also mean that this extra alertness that we have motivated is not characterized by a faster, more industrious pace, but actually results in a situation where an operator appears to be physically working less than anyone else. The operator, by keeping the machine running, is actually working less but accomplishing more.

STANDARD HOURS

Some incentive plans determine the earnings based on the hours earned rather than directly on the pieces produced. Some organizations perform other managerial functions, such as cost accounting and using hours as a common denominator for measurement. It is far more convenient for those organizations to use incentive plans that are based on earned hours rather than a direct production count. The use of a standard hours plan, while giving the same results as piecerate incentives, involve a conversion of the production count, using the time standard, to the equivalent number of hours. Those hours are paid at the hourly rate established for the job.

Example—Standard Hours Incentive (100% daywork guaranteed, 100% operator controlled)

A job is paid at an hourly rate of $5.75. The standard for the job is .072 hours. In order to determine the earnings for an operator on this job, the daily production count must be known. If a worker produced 141 units, the time required, or expected, for this production rate, is calculated using the relationship:

$$\text{Earned Hours} = (\text{Standard Hours})(\text{Number of Units})$$

For this example, the earned hours, or EH, are:

$$\begin{aligned} EH &= (.072 \text{ hours/unit})(141 \text{ units}) \\ &= 10.15 \text{ hours} \end{aligned}$$

The wage payment, or earnings for the day, is the product of the earned hours and the hourly rate:

$$\begin{aligned} \text{Earnings} &= (10.15 \text{ earned hours})(\$5.75/\text{hour}) \\ &= \$58.36 \end{aligned}$$

Because 100% daywork is guaranteed, in this example if the earned hours drop below eight, wage payments would still be made for eight hours. For example, if the worker on this job produced 79 units on another day, the earned hours would be:

$$\begin{aligned} EH &= (.072 \text{ hours/unit})(79 \text{ units}) \\ &= 5.69 \text{ hours} \end{aligned}$$

Payment would be based on eight hours of work, or:

$$\begin{aligned} \text{Earnings} &= (8 \text{ hours})(\$5.75/\text{hour}) \\ &= \$46.00 \end{aligned}$$

Example—Standard Hours (75% daywork guaranteed, 100% operator paced)

A job that is entirely operator paced has a time standard of .038 hours and an hourly pay rate of $4.68.

(a) Determine the standard hours earnings for a worker who produced 143 units in a day.

The first step is to calculate the earned hours:

$$\begin{aligned} EH &= (.038 \text{hours/unit})(143 \text{ units}) \\ &= 5.43 \text{ hours} \end{aligned}$$

Since the worker is guaranteed 75% of daywork, or six hours of pay every day, the worker would be paid:

$$Earnings = (6 \text{ hours})(\$4.68/\text{hour})$$
$$= \$28.08$$

This naturally must be checked with the prevailing minimum wage legislation.

(b) On the same job another worker produced 242 pieces on the same day. That worker's earned hours would be greater. How much would the daily pay be?

The earned hours for this day for this worker are first calculated:

$$EH = (.038 \text{ hours/piece})(242 \text{ pieces})$$
$$= 9.2 \text{ hours}$$

The daily earnings for this job are calculated based on the earned hours, since they exceed the guaranteed hours.

$$Earnings = (9.2 \text{ earned hours})(\$4.68/\text{hour})$$
$$= \$43.06$$

Example—Standard Hours   (100% guaranteed, 60% operator paced)

A job pays an hourly wage of $8.30, is 40% machine paced, and has a standard time of .0058 hours for the operator-controlled portion of the job. The job guarantees full daywork payment regardless of production. Calculate standard hours earnings for a worker who produced 1,038 units in a day.

For the 40% of the job that is machine paced, the worker would earn at the daywork rate of $8.30 per hour. This portion of the earnings would be paid for 40% of the work day, or 3.2 hours. The Machine Paced Earnings, or MPE, are:

$$MPE = (3.2 \text{ hours})(\$8.30/\text{hour})$$
$$= \$26.56$$

The production of 1,038 units converts to standard hours:

$$EH = (1038 \text{ units})(.0058 \text{ hours/unit})$$
$$= 6.02 \text{ hours}$$

These earned hours are also paid at the $8.30 hourly pay rate:

$$Incentive \ Earnings = (6.02 \text{ hours})(\$8.30/\text{hour})$$
$$= \$49.97$$

The total daily earnings is the sum of the incentive earnings and the MPE, or:

$$Earnings = \$49.97 + \$26.56$$
$$= \$76.53$$

This compares favorably with the guaranteed day rate of $66.40, paid for eight hours at $8.30 per hour.

Example—Standard Hours (85% daywork guaranteed, 20% machine paced)

This final standard hours example looks at a 20% machine-paced job in which there is only an 85% daywork guarantee. The hourly rate, as established via the job evaluation system, is $6.15. The industrial engineering department has established a standard of .025 hours for the task.

(a) Calculate the standard hours earnings for an employee who produces 145 parts during a day.

The portion of the job that is machine paced is paid at the straight hourly rate. Twenty percent of the eight-hour day is 1.6 hours, so this part of the earnings is calculated:

$$MPE = (1.6 \text{ hours})(\$6.15/\text{hour})$$
$$= \$9.84$$

Next, the production is converted to earned hours:

$$EH = (145 \text{ parts})(.025 \text{ hours/part})$$
$$= 3.63 \text{ hours}$$

The earned hours, when combined with the allowed machine-paced hours, totals 5.23 hours. Since this plan guarantees 85% of daywork, or 6.8 hours, the day's earnings in this instance are the earnings paid for the guaranteed hours, or:

$$\text{Earnings} = (6.8 \text{ hours})(\$6.15/\text{hour})$$
$$= \$41.82$$

(b) Calculate standard hours earnings for an employee who produces 220 parts.

Once again the machine-paced portion of the job is paid at the hourly rate and is allowed 1.6 hours which are equivalent to earnings of $9.84. The 220 parts are responsible for earning the worker:

$$EH = (220 \text{ parts})(.025 \text{ hours/part})$$
$$= 5.5 \text{ hours}$$

When these earned hours are combined with the 1.6 machine-paced hours, they total 7.1 hours. Because this exceeds the 6.8 hours that are guaranteed, an incentive payment is called for. The earned hours are paid as follows:

$$EH = (5.5 \text{ hours})(\$6.15/\text{hour})$$
$$= \$33.83$$

This is combined with the $9.84 earnings for the machine-paced portion of the job, for a total earnings of $43.67. This amount exceeds, slightly, the $41.82 guaranteed daily earnings.

VARIABLE RATE INCENTIVE PLANS

Some incentive plans, such as the Taylor Plan, pay a different piece rate for production above the expected, or standard. The rate differential is often a higher piece rate for production over standard, although it can be a lower rate. At times the higher rate applies only to production over standard; other times it applies to all production once the standard is exceeded.

Example—Variable Rate Piecerate Incentive (100% daywork guaranteed, 100% operator controlled, bonus paid only on the production over standard)

A job is subject to a variable rate incentive plan with a base rate of $5.22 an hour, as established by the job evaluation plan. Production over standard is paid at the rate of $5.98 per hour. The standard for the job is .06 hours. If a worker produced 157 pieces in a day, the pay would be determined as follows. Using the standard time of .06 hours per unit, the worker would be expected to produce at the following hourly production rate:

$$.06 \text{ hours/unit} = 16.67 \text{ units/hour}$$

In an eight-hour day the expected production would be:

$$(8 \text{ hours/day})(16.67 \text{ units/hour}) = 133 \text{ units}$$

Production up to this rate would be paid at the guaranteed rate of $5.22 per hour, or:

$$(\$5.22/\text{hour})/(16.67 \text{ units/hour}) = \$.313/\text{piece}$$

Each unit above the 133 would be paid at the higher rate of $5.98 per hour, or:

$$(\$5.98/\text{hour})/(16.67 \text{ pieces/hour}) = \$.359/\text{piece}$$

In this example, since the daily production of 157 units exceeded the expected 133, all parts in excess of standard are paid at the bonus rate. First, the guaranteed or base rate earnings are calculated:

$$(133 \text{ pieces})(\$.313/\text{piece}) = \$41.63$$

Then the incentive rate earnings are calculated:

$$(157 - 133 \text{ pieces})(\$.359/\text{piece}) = \$8.62$$

The total earnings for the day are calculated:

$$\$41.63 + \$8.62 = \$50.25$$

Figure 7–3 shows the earnings for this type of plan as a function of production.

Example—Variable Rate Piecerate Incentive (100% day rate guaranteed, 100% operator controlled, bonus paid for all production once incentive is exceeded)

A task is reimbursed via a Taylor Plan variable rate incentive. This means that all production is paid at the incentive rate once

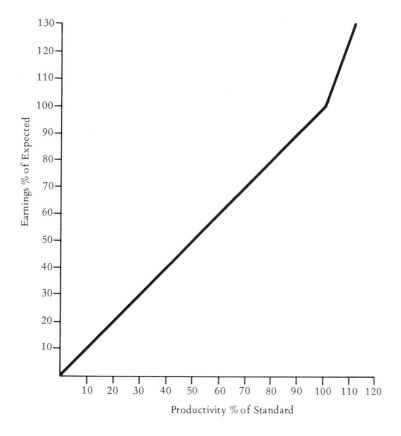

FIGURE 7–3.   Earnings as a Function of the Production/Variable Rate Incentive Plan

the standard is exceeded. Figure 7–4 shows the earnings for this type of plan as a function of production.

The base rate for this job, for production up to standard, is $4.95 per hour. The bonus rate is $5.45 per hour. The standard time established for this task is .0043 hours.

(a) A worker produces 1,860 units a day. What would the before-tax earnings be?

Based on the production standard of .0043 hours per unit, the expected daily production is determined:

$$.0043 \text{ hours/piece} = 232.5 \text{ pieces/hour}$$
$$(232.5 \text{ pieces/hour})(8 \text{ hours/day}) = 1860 \text{ pieces/day}$$

Because the expected production is equal to the actual production, the base rate is paid and the daily payment is based on

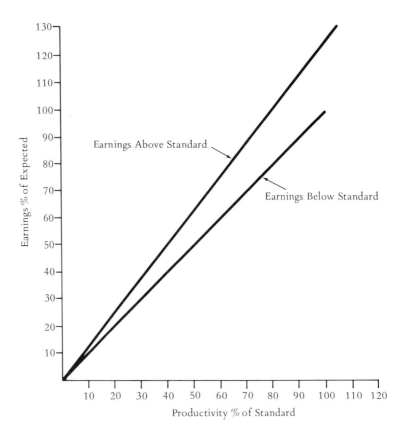

FIGURE 7–4.   Earnings as a Function of Production/Taylor Plan

the piece rate established. Using the standard of .0043 hours/piece, this becomes:

$$(\$4.95/\text{hour})/(232.5 \text{ pieces/hour}) = \$.0213/\text{piece}$$

The 1,860 pieces produced would earn:

$$(1860 \text{ pieces})(\$.0213/\text{piece}) = \$39.62$$

(b) If the production for a given day is 1,865, what would the daily earnings be?

Because production on this day exceeds the expected production of 1,860, the higher, or bonus rate, of \$5.45 is used to determine the piece rate for the wage payment.

$$(\$5.45/\text{hour})/(232.5 \text{ pieces/hour}) = \$.023/\text{piece}$$

The entire day's production in this example is paid at this higher rate, and the day's earnings become:

$$(\$.023/\text{piece})(1865 \text{ pieces}) = \$42.90$$

By exceeding the standard, even if just by one piece, the worker earns the bonus for the entire day's production. Use of this type of incentive plan encourages the worker to meet the standard. The standard hours format could just as easily have been used in a variable rate incentive program.

(c) Use the standard hours method of payment to determine the earnings for an individual who produced 1,865 units in a day. The 1865 units would have earned the following hours:

$$EH = (1865 \text{ units})(.0043 \text{ hours/unit})$$
$$= 8.02 \text{ hours}$$

Whenever the earned hours exceed eight, the higher hourly rate is paid:

$$\text{Earnings} = (8.02 \text{ hours})(\$5.45/\text{hour})$$
$$= \$43.71$$

(Note: The difference in earnings between the piece rate and the standard hours calculation methods is due only to arithmetic rounding.)

RESTRUCTURING INCENTIVE PLANS

Unfortunately, it is not unusual for incentive plans to become outdate and inaccurate. The resulting inconsistency in wage payments can be a virtual nightmare for both the management and workers in an organization.

In order to prevent this undesirable situation, the standards must be regularly audited to ensure that they reflect the work actually being performed. As jobs change, the standards and corresponding piece rates should change to reflect this. The result will be a successful wage incentive plan.

Sometimes however, due to a variety of reasons, plans do become outdated. In order to rectify this situation the following steps should be taken.

1. The complete support of management and agreement of the labor union to the restructuring must be secured. In some instances this may result in a significant cost- and re-engineering of all of the organization's standards.
2. The entire process of restructuring the system must be thoroughly communicated to the employees and their supervisors. This has to be done frequently and on a regular schedule.
3. The jobs that are out of line must be identified.
4. A schedule for the restructuring must be established and then adhered to. Everyone must know when the "new" rates will be used.
5. New rates must be established for appropriate jobs according to the schedule.
6. New piece rates must be established from the new standards.
7. The restructured system should be installed per the schedule.
8. Regular audits should commence.

The following case history* illustrates a typical restructuring.

Case History*

An actual description of the restructuring of an incentive pay system following the model guidelines aforementioned follows.

The company involved operates a manufacturing plant with 300 employees belonging to a union having AFL-CIO affiliation. This plant has operated continuously at the same location for 60 years. Employees were working on a standard hour incentive plan which replaced an aggregate plantwide group incentive. The standard hour plan was de-

---

*Reprinted from Brady, Thomas F., "The Restructuring of an Incentive Pay System: A Successful Case History," 1984 Annual International Industrial Engineering Conference *Proceedings*, © 1984, Institute of Industrial Engineers, 25 Technology Park/ Atlanta, Norcross, Georgia 30092.

signed and installed in 1952. Two industrial engineers have been employed since 1952. Most of their duties have consisted of establishing new incentive rates, some methods improvement, cost analysis, working with product engineering, "filling-in" for absent production supervisors, and other special projects for the plant manager.

During the early part of 1982 the company, with agreement by the union, decided their incentive system was not yielding satisfactory results. I was contacted to survey the situation and make recommendations.

My analysis of payroll and production data, several "walk-through" observations, and management personnel interviews revealed the following:

1. Seventy-one different job titles
2. Average incentive performance = 174%
3. Hours on incentive by directs = 81%
4. Incentive performance range = 60–400%
5. Average hourly earnings = $8.74
6. Base Rates: 52 different multiplying rates with an accumulation of negotiated "add-ons" plus cost of living allowances
7. Methods: In many cases actual work procedures could not be correlated with operation card descriptions.
8. Direct/Indirect Ratio: 6:1
9. Average pace rating during "walk-throughs" = 100–110%. In some departments not much real work was being performed during the last 1½ hours of the shift.
10. Little correlation of employment levels with changes in production volume, particularly regarding indirects.
11. Ineffective contract language regarding incentives.

Based upon the information obtained and status of the situation the following recommendations were made:

1. Replace the base rate "multiplying rate" system with a job evaluation point plan.
2. Perform a methods improvement program.
3. Make time studies to establish rates consistent with operating practices.
4. Analyze indirect labor operations.
5. Establish direct and indirect staffing guidelines for various levels of production volume.
6. Conduct incentive plant training sessions for management and union personnel.
7. Develop a wage administration program policy manual intended to become an appendix to the collective bargaining agreement.
8. Negotiate the new plan with the union.
9. Assist in establishing standard data.

The proposed program was scheduled for a 49-week time period and was accepted by management.

Initial informational meetings with management and union personnel were conducted and followed-up with training programs for both *groups in wage incentives and job evaluation. As a result of these meetings a representative of each department was selected as a liaison between department employees, the consultant, and management. In some cases this representative was the formal department steward. The purpose of these representatives was to provide a one person contact regarding any items of the program.*

As usual in programs of this type, resistance was given by some first line foremen. In one particular case the resistance did not cease until top management personally communicated with the foreman. This is one reason why top management support for programs of this type is essential.

Progress was made on the program through the Job Analysis, Job Description, Job Evaluation phases and into the methods improvement and work measurement parts of the program.

Frequent meetings with the union committee and the employee representatives were held. Purpose of these meetings was to explain technical details and to help the members allay any fears or misconceptions on the part of the employees they represented.

One week prior to the implementation date a meeting was held with the full union committee, the program representatives, the international union staff representative, and the international union industrial engineer. The format of this meeting was one of a normal contract negotiation session. A 60-page report including the job evaluation plan with the new job class rates, and a policy manual regarding how the revised incentive plan was to operate was the guide for negotiations. The session lasted all day and after some concessions and a modified economic buy-out the committee accepted the proposal. A special union meeting was held and the new plan was approved by the members.

Implementation of the new program provided fewer problems than expected and resulted in an annual savings to the company of $256,000. The concensus of management, union, and the majority of employees is that they should have implemented a program of this type many years ago.

In reflecting on why this program was so successful, the following points surfaced:

1. *Frequent communication with all parties*
2. *Training in wage incentives for all parties*
3. *Develop a schedule and maintain progress*
4. *Conduct the program in a professional industrial engineering manner*
5. *Existence of a policy manual*
6. *Effective negotiation*

A postscript to this happy scenario is that the company is now conducting a robotic application survey in which it appears they will be introducing as many as five robots in their operations in the near future. Because they are following the same general format as they did in revising their traditional wage incentive plan I predict equal success in their first "high technology" introduction venture.

INDIVIDUAL WAGE INCENTIVES—A SUMMARY

The individual wage incentive plans described above have the following characteristics. The rewards of incentives are based solely on individual performance. This performance is mainly under the control of the operator. The standards of performance have been set by a qualified industrial engineering analyst, using technically sound work measurement procedures. In an individual wage incentive plan, the rewards are almost always immediate, that is, paid daily or weekly. In all of the preceding examples, the incentive was computed on a daily basis. This is a common industrial practice, although the actual payment may be made on a weekly basis to reflect the minimum wage laws.

The advantages of individual wage incentive plans are relatively obvious and straightforward. First and foremost, the individual incentive plan rewards the individual for his or her production. The more the worker produces, the more the worker earns.

Second, the individual incentives appeal to the basic need for money found in most people. Almost everyone will work harder, up to a point, when there is a justifiable reason to believe the increased productivity will bring about a personal gain.

Although individual wage incentives have advantages, there are also limitations. Individual wage incentives work best with jobs that are primarily operator controlled. Machine-paced tasks eliminate the ability of the worker to earn an incentive wage. Individual wage incentives can also lead to labor problems. Loose rates and tight rates, whether real or perceived, can cause grievances to be filled or even worse problems, such as wildcat strikes.

Incentives, because they reward production levels, can lead to quality problems. Safeguards must be taken to ensure that quality is not sacrificed for quantity. Unions, often because of a basic distrust of management, will not agree that standards are fair. A well-designed incentive system will take into account the existing degree of work continuity in a shop. If the actual work performed, such as in a garment-style shop, changes frequently, the incentive system must reflect the relearning the operators are subject to.

Finally, incentives are difficult and costly to maintain. Jobs change over time. Unless a concerted effort is made to keep standards compatible with the work performed, inequities and inconsistencies will develop which will lead to loose and tight rates. An organization must be committed to maintaining accurate standards for all jobs.

GROUP INCENTIVES

Besides individual incentives, there is another general type of incentive system known as group incentives. These group incentive plans are worker involvement programs which offer financial rewards by sharing productivity improvement with employees through plans which create high levels of involvement, produce results very quickly, and raise productivity to much higher levels than are attained by non-financial reward programs only.

The following are the basic characteristics of group incentive plans. Rewards, whether from increased sales or dollars saved, are based on the performance of the entire group. Because the savings are not always completely controlled by the efforts of the employees—for example savings may result from the purchase of new capital equipment, or increased sales may result from a new pricing policy set by management—the rewards are sometimes shared between the employees and the company.

The standards used in productivity sharing plans are not generally as technically sound as those used in individual plans. Often they are historical measures already in existence when the plan was initiated.

The group incentive plan bonuses are paid less frequently than the individual incentives. Quarterly, semiannual, and even annual bonuses are the normal method of rewarding employees under a group plan. These bonuses, while not paid as frequently, are often much larger than individual wage incentives.

Finally, because group incentives involve many employees, the results are often dramatic. The famous Hawthrone experiment at Western Electric in the 1930s verified that any plan that involves new and intensive attention to a group of workers will tend to create a surge of results.

There are advantages to group incentive systems. A prime objective of productivity sharing is to create conditions under which workers and management benefit by money in parallel paths to this common financial goal. Group incentive plans, since they evaluate overall performance, are applicable to a wide variety of tasks. They are not limited to operator-controlled jobs.

Group incentive plans can include all employees in the organization. Everybody, from the chief executive all the way to the floor sweepers, can share in the organization's increased productivity. Because everybody has a stake in what happens, everybody is willing to help solve the problems that arise. A feeling of employee/company loyalty can result. One survey showed decided improvements in employee/company relations.

Despite the advantages of group incentive plans there are some liabilities. Employees are rewarded based on how well the group performs. Individual performance can be ignored. Traditional managers sometimes have difficulty with this concept since the outstanding worker receives the same reward as any other. In practice it has been found that employees do not object to this if everybody is doing their best. Short-term gains are often much more attractive than long-term growth. Human nature is such that most people want their rewards now, not at some indeterminate time in the future.

One additional drawback to group incentive plans is the fact that they appear to penalize the competent worker. "Good foremen and good employees have less opportunity to reap smaller rewards under a share in the savings plan than the worst supervisors and employees. The worst . . . often earn more at the start in view of their past poor productivity . . . ." (Sellie:64)

It is important that the supervisors and the workers be convinced that the management is trying to be fair in the setting of standards. In this line of communication between management and the workers, the supervisory staff forms the strongest link and should not be disregarded. This advice is shared by union and management officials alike.

Regardless of these pro and con discussions about productivity sharing, managers generally believe that pay tied to productivity will motivate to higher performance, and, by any measure, pay tied to productivity is the most powerful motivator to improve work performance.

SCANLON PLAN

The Scanlon Plan, developed by Joseph Scanlon of the United Steelworkers of America, is the original productivity sharing plan. The basic concept underlying the Scanlon Plan is that efficiency depends upon plantwide cooperation. The purpose of the incentive pay is to produce teamwork.

Incentives in the Scanlon Plan are based on productivity improvement. This is generally computed as a ratio of total payroll to the sales value of production. On a regular basis, for example monthly, this historical ratio is compared with actual payroll and sales figures. If the actual payroll is less than the payroll projected by the ratio, then a percentage of the savings, usually 75%, is placed in a fund for payment to all of the covered employees. The other 25% would remain in a contingency fund and, if there were shortfalls, be returned to the company for its participation in the program. This base ratio must be periodically adjusted to reflect the dynamic environment. Other plan details relating to how and when sharing gains are paid, the highly structured suggestion plans, and labor management committees do not significantly differentiate the plan from others.

Example—Scanlon Plan: During the year preceding the adoption of a Scanlon Plan for productivity sharing, the payroll for a company was $4,642,000. During the same year, the sales for this company was $6,283,000. The basic ratio of payroll to sales value of production, or to sales, that will be used for computation of future incentive payments is:

$$(\$4,642,000)/(\$6,283,000) = .74$$

In the first month the plan was in operation, the payroll was $289,600 and sales were $526,100. The ratio for this month was:

$$(\$289,600)/(\$526,100) = .55$$

Because this ratio is *lower* than the basic ratio, the employees and the company will share in the gains. The total amount to be shared is the difference between the actual payroll and the payroll that the basic ratio indicated would have been paid to generate the sales volume. The calculations are shown here:

$$
\begin{aligned}
\text{Expected Monthly Payroll} &= (\text{Ratio})(\text{Monthly Sales})\\
&= (.74)(\$526,100)\\
&= \$389,314\\
\text{Actual Monthly Payroll} &= \$289,600\\
\text{Difference (Savings)} &= \$389,314 - 289,600\\
&= \$99,714
\end{aligned}
$$

A percentage of this savings, usually 75%, goes into a fund to be distributed to employees, with the balance to the company. At the end of the year, the semiannual period, or the quarter, all employees in the covered group would be paid a bonus.

Case studies of the Scanlon Plan installations have shown the following results:

1. Employee willingness to provide large numbers of useful, cost-saving ideas.
2. Employee willingness to accept technological change.
3. Development of a better work pace and work climate—an environment hostile to loafing.

4. Greater employee interest in quality.
5. Greater employee cooperation.
6. More flexible seniority programs that aid rather than impede productivity regarding such items as promotions and transfers.
7. Less overtime.
8. Employee insistence on efficient management.
9. Greater employee awareness on their impact on the company's ability to compete.
10. More realistic contract negotiations.
11. Fewer grievances.

Although there have been remarkable successes with the Scanlon Plan, not all applications have worked. Most of the successful applications have been in relatively small plants, 1,000 employees or less. In larger companies it may have been more difficult for workers to see that their contribution made a difference.

Another area of difficulty is in adjusting the ratio for changing conditions. If the ratio is lowered, for whatever reasons, the change may affect employee performance. A reaction that, "once I meet my quota, my quota is raised."

Aspects of the Scanlon Plan other than the pay matters—the suggestion system, the employee management committees, and so forth—change the nature of management's role. As employees assume more of management's traditional functions, managers may have trouble adapting.

When Scanlon Plans replace individual wage incentive plans the productive worker may suffer. It is likely that the day rate paid all employees in a particular job classification will be lower than the prior earnings of the employee on incentive. These are all potential difficulties that must be considered before the Scanlon Plan, or any group incentive plan, is installed.

THE RUCKER PLAN

The philosophy of the Rucker Plan is similar to the Scanlon Plan, but the bonus is computed based on a more sophisticated analysis. There are two major differences between the plans, though. The standard under the Rucker Plan is based upon a careful study of accounting records and is not considered bargainable. While the Scanlon Plan rewards only savings in labor costs, the Rucker Plan offers incentives for savings in other areas as well.

The ratio used in the Rucker Plan reflects productivity changes in the ratio of payroll dollars to dollar value added. When changes in products or processes occur, the ratio is revised.

Example—Rucker Plan

A company puts $.90 worth of resources, exclusive of labor, into a product to bring its worth to $2.00. The production value of this product is the $1.10 value that is added by the production process. Accounting and production records show that 25% of this value added is attributable to labor. This means for every dollar spent on labor, the value added to the production is $4.00. (Labor contributed one fourth of value added.) The productivity ratio is 4. If the monthly payroll for this firm is $250,000, the expected production value added would be four times this, or $1,000,000. If this company actually sold $1,250,000 of product, there would have been a productivity gain. The amount to be shared on a percentage basis comparable to labor's participation would be calculated as follows:

$$
\begin{aligned}
\text{Expected Value Added} &= (\text{Ratio})(\text{Actual Payroll}) \\
&= (\$250,000)(4) \\
&= \$1,000,000 \\
\text{Actual Value Added} &= \$1,250,000 \\
\text{Available for Bonus} &= \$1,250,000 - \$1,000,000 \\
&= \$250,000 \\
\text{Labor's Share} &= \text{Available/Ratio} \\
&= \$250,000/4 \\
&= \$62,500
\end{aligned}
$$

Some of labor's share might be set aside in a contingency fund in case there is a loss in a given month. Otherwise the balance will be paid in an annual bonus to the groups participating.

Although the plan is most frequently applied to production workers, it can be expanded to cover all employees in a company. The same analysis would determine each group's contribution.

IMPROSHARE®

Improshare was developed by Mitchell Fein and was first used in 1974. Improshare productivity measurements are based on traditional industrial engineering work measurement procedures modified to a selected base period. Productivity measurement with Improshare is considerably different from Scanlon or Rucker.

Productivity gains are shared 50/50 between employees and company. Improvements may come from any source—from increased effort, from better work methods, from increased coordination in scheduling, and so forth. The basic philosophy of Improshare is that workers and management "are all in this together" and should share the productivity gains equally.

Improshare believes that employees should be fairly compensated based on the job evaluation system. The bonus payments are made to workers based on the time actually worked. The bonus is expressed as a percentage and added to the base hourly rate.

The following example, based on Musgrave's work, shows how Improshare works. (Musgrave:293)

Example—Improshare

A company produces a product with a work force of 22, including both line and staff employees. In a given week each employee spends 40 hours at work, for a total of $(22)(40) = 880$ hours on the job for all the employees. During a particular week, to be used as the base period, the company produced 44 units. Based on industrial engineering standards and analysis of standard costs, each unit required eight hours of direct labor under normal conditions. The total direct labor requirement for 44 units would be $(44)(8) = 352$ hours. In the language of Improshare this 352 hours is called the "produced hours."

Since 880 hours were worked during the base period week, a factor called the Base Productivity Factor, or BPF, is defined:

$$BPF = \text{(Total Hours Worked)/(Produced Hours)}$$
$$= 880/352$$
$$= 2.50$$

This factor is used to adjust the time standard to reflect the overall required time. The adjusted time is called the Improshare standard.

$$\text{Improshare Standard} = \text{(BPF)(Direct Labor Standard)}$$
$$= (2.5)(8 \text{ hours})$$
$$= 20 \text{ hours}$$

The Improshare standard is then used as the base for future bonus calculations. If, in a future week, the same workforce produced 53 units, the bonus would be calculated as follows.

The Improshare earned hours for producing 53 units are first determined:

$$\begin{aligned} \text{Improshare Earned Hours} &= (\text{Units Produced})(\text{Improshare Standard}) \\ &= (53)(20) \\ &= 1{,}060 \text{ hours} \end{aligned}$$

Second, the actual hours earned during this week were the 880 computed earlier. The difference between these, or hours gained, is calculated:

$$\begin{aligned} \text{Hours Gained} &= (\text{Improshare Earned Hours}) - (\text{Actual Earned Hours}) \\ &= 1{,}060 - 880 \\ &= 180 \text{ hours} \end{aligned}$$

Because Improshare splits these gained hours 50/50 between labor and management, the bonus hours gained are determined:

$$\begin{aligned} \text{Bonus Hours Gained} &= (.5)(\text{Hours Gained}) \\ &= (.5)(180) \\ &= 90 \text{ hours} \end{aligned}$$

The bonus is expressed as a percentage of total hours:

$$\begin{aligned} \text{Bonus} &= (\text{Bonus Hours Gained})/(\text{Actual Earned Hours}) \times 100\% \\ &= (90/880) \times 100\% \\ &= 10.23 \text{ percent} \end{aligned}$$

The bonus would be added to everybody's base wage.

Improshare only counts finished goods. This discourages any attempt to rush work or short change quality. It can also encourage workers to cooperate.

Although Improshare sounds good, it does have some potential drawbacks. One of these is the use of historical production data to establish the Base Productivity Factor. Workers often make the quantity of work available fit the time available. A second potential problem area is the concept that everybody shares equally in productivity gains. Management sometimes has difficulty accepting the fact that the best worker earns the same as the worst. Although it is unusual, employees will accept this. Too many people are looking for simple solutions to our problems. Most of our problems have become more complicated and don't lend themselves to simple solutions. The everyday worker often tends to be much more accepting than does the supervisor or management.

GROUP INCENTIVES—A SUMMARY

"In many instances a group incentive plan is selected based on the belief that it will contribute to harmony and group effort. . . . Group pressure spurs slackers and influences conscientious workers. Furthermore, management benefits from smaller administrative costs because less inspection, clerical work, supervision, and daily checking up are required under group incentive plans." (Sellie:62) Incentives can be effective for groups, especially when used over a long period of time. According to a General Accounting Office (GAO) report of a survey it conducted, those firms that had a long-term use of productivity sharing programs showed an average 29% savings in work force cost.

The GAO also reported some non-financial benefits experienced by the companies responding to its survey. Over 80% claimed improved labor relations, more than 47% reported fewer grievances, while about 36% of the firms said absenteeism and turnover were reduced. The vast majority of firms expressed satisfaction with their productivity sharing plans and believed that the current benefits to the firm would continue to come from their continuation.

Despite the success of the plans, there are some complaints that apply across the board to all of the productivity sharing plans. These include complaints about individuals not doing their full share. In large groups it is often inevitable that there will be slackers. These slackers can disrupt the functioning of the entire group. A second common complaint is that, very frequently, individual incentives are done away with, and the very talented people will leave the company for greener pastures. Yet another reason given for difficulty with given incentives is the fact that some groups resent the employment of new workers. These new workers, lacking the experience of the "old hands," may drag down the entire group's productivity.

UNIONS AND INCENTIVES

There is no official union policy regarding wage incentives. Philosophically most unions are opposed to individual wage incentive programs, yet once having been exposed to properly administered plans, fight any attempt a company makes to drop incentive systems. Management and workers are not motivated in the same direction and they have different goals, aspirations, and needs. When workers excel and raise productivity, the company benefits and management is pleased, but the workers perceive they may not benefit.

The main objections that unions seem to have regarding wage incentives is with incentive abuses such as speed-ups, employee job security, earnings, and the like. Some of these objections deserve closer examination. First of these is the unions' concern about tight rates, or really the concern about the entire measurement process.

Work measurement usually means time study. According to Bertram Gottlieb of the AFL-CIO, time study, ". . . is an imprecise tool and lends itself to easy abuse . . . of the whole field of so-called 'scientific management.' Time study is the area in which most of labor's distrust and suspicions are centered. Ever since its introduction in the 1880s, most unions have opposed the use of stop-watch time study." (Gottlieb:15)

Reasons for this opposition include lack of information on how time study data is to be used by the company. This is often fostered by the refusal of the company to provide the results and procedures used. Despite the fact that the National Labor Relations Board has ruled that this information must be provided, some managements refuse to provide this data, claiming the information is confidential.

Unions also object to the accuracy of standards set by stop-watch study. While calling the standards only approximations, they list nine specific objections to time study procedures. (Gottlieb:17) Most controversial on this list is the rating of the worker's performance. Rating is the step of the time study procedure where the most judgment or guesswork is involved. Normal pace is supposed to represent a fair day's work or an acceptable day's work. To quote the late Dr. T. M. Glen, formerly of the University of Toledo, "obviously a fair day's work is anything you want it to be." (Gottlieb:598) Mitchell Lokiec of the ILGWU, when describing normal pace, called it, ". . . a result of the interplay of factors such as social environment, motivation, level of culture, social incentives, training, and so forth." (Lokiec:314)

Another objection unions have to time study is the fallibility of the time study analyst. They reject the claim that qualified analysts can measure the performance with an average error of 2%. This objection comes back to the complaint about performance rating.

Speed ups and tight rates are other objections raised about incentive plans. The unions fear that a company may set a rate or standard to reflect the desired production rate rather than the realistic rate. Again, performance rating is blamed as the mechanism for making this a problem. Observed times can always be adjusted through performance rating.

Yet another of the principal objections unions have to wage incentive systems relates to job security. Unions have a fear that a reduction in personnel will be brought about by high effort, given only a fixed production of goods and services, and that incentive installations will de-emphasize the necessity of unions, since the unions' major role is to achieve higher wages, which the incentive plan will automatically do.

One final reason cited by organized labor for objecting to incentive programs is the effect they have on work groups. Wage incentives tend to make workers compete with each other and that competition is reflected in earnings differential. The united feeling the workers have is ruined, so to speak, and the union loses. The function of the union is to improve the wages and working conditions of its members. Higher production and lower costs are managerial functions and prerogatives, and union leaders would not like to encrouch against them.

In summary, many of the objections unions have expressed about the individual wage incentive plans boils down to one issue—the trust, or lack of trust, between workers and management. Unions exist when workers feel management is out to get them. The late Philip Murray, one of the past leaders of organized labor in this country, ". . . expressed his belief that practically any sound system of wage payment can be made to work when a harmonious relationship prevails between labor and management." (Neibel:633)

While many labor leaders continue to be opposed to incentive wages, many local unions still negotiate contracts that have wage incentive provisions within them. When this has been done it is generally the result of the union clearly understanding what is being negotiated. This often includes training in standards setting and education for all the employees of a company. Successful application, though, requires a tremendous amount of dedication and cooperation between labor and management. Unfortunately, this level of cooperation is not found too frequently. According to a 1976 Bureau of Labor Statistics survey of 1,711 collective bargaining agreements covering 7.6 million workers, only 467 contracts allowed for some form of incentive pay.

Although unions may object to the use of individual wage incentives, they do support the use of group wage incentives. Joseph Scanlon was an officer in the United Steelworkers Union of America when he developed his Scanlon Plan. The economic recession of the 1980s saw many of the major labor agreements that were negotiated during this period include productivity sharing and profit sharing provisions. The increasing impact of foreign competition has prompted the leaders of labor and management to recognize the folly of their traditional adversary roles, and has led in recent years to a reduction in labor's hostility toward pay-for-performance programs. Many of the recent "give back" contracts are evidence of this new attitude.

ADMINISTERING AN INCENTIVE PROGRAM

Throughout this chapter it has been stated that, for an incentive plan to be successful, it may be properly designed, technically sound, and well run. Considerable attention has been focused on the design and engineering of the incentive plan. The administration of the incentive program has four major components.

First of these is management's commitment to the program. Management of the company must fully understand and support the incentive program. This includes providing overall leadership and acceptance. It also involves the willingness to invest in the program both by supporting the development and maintenance of the technical parts of the program and by providing the workers the means with which to increase their productivity. Finally, management must also be willing to share the gains of increased output or sales with the workers.

Management's responsibilities include the following specific requirements.

1. Each task or job must be well defined.
2. Workers must know the piece rate before the job begins.
3. Standards, once set, must remain constant unless the job content changes.
4. Any mistakes must be immediately corrected.
5. Departures from standard procedures must be justified.

The second part of a successfully operated incentive plan lies with the supervisors. The supervisors provide knowledge of methods, standards, and operating practices to new and old employees; understand and assist in the application of company practices and policies; cooperate on improving methods and time study standards to improve the productivity of the employees they supervise; and measure their own performance, as supervisors, by cost. Frontline supervision is responsible for continuing to administer the improvements brought about by the program. The first line supervisor is the leader of the employees.

Thirdly, the industrial engineer (IE) has a vested interest in seeing the program prosper. The IEs must focus on finding better processes, equipment, and methods. The IE must continually make sure that the technical portion of the incentive system, the time standards, provide a fair and consistent yardstick for all employees. (Sellie:66) The industrial engineer must not develop standards, issue the standards to the floor, and walk away. The industrial engineer must sell the system to the foreman and convince the supervisor that they are indeed on the "same team."

Finally, the employees, whether they are union members or not, have a responsibility to perform a fair day's or an acceptable day's work. Employees have a vested interest in the success of a company. Without the company, the employees don't have jobs. Generally, wages are more equitable when a union represents the employees. Alert union officials are aware, but on occasion need to be reminded that the company can exist without the union, but the union cannot exist without the company. Employees certainly have a vested interest in seeing that incentive systems are properly administered.

Specifically, several responsibilities for a union regarding the proper administration of a wage incentive plan are recommended. First, the union must insist on understanding how standards are established. Second, unions must accept the fact that the work done must comply with the established standard practices. Third, the union should insist on and comply with no cheating clauses regarding incentive payments. Fourth, unions should accept the fact that incentive pay for work above standard is fair. However, acceptance of incentives by both sides is no guarantee of success. It cannot be overemphasized that incentive systems are imperfect tools that require constant attention for improvement.

SUMMARY

For incentives to be successful as a motivational or reward tool for increasing productivity the plan used must be properly designed, effectively administered, and carefully controlled. Perhaps one of the best ways to make sure that the incentive program will work is to follow these three points for successfully increasing productivity.

1. Information breeds understanding.
2. We all want to be told in advance.
3. We will all cooperate in a program in the same proportion that we are part of that program.

One of the most successful incentive programs ever installed is the Lincoln Electric Plan. This plan has virtually doubled the earnings of the employees of the company. "Lincoln's greatest emphasis was on the establishment and maintenance of credibility and integrity with their employees . . . .the employees' confidence in management is borne out by their continuing efforts to improve productivity." (Fein:23)

Mitchell Lokiec of the ILGWU, when asked about the use of incentives, summarized it best. "It is my opinion that wage incentives have contributed toward the improvement of productivity in the garment industry, as well as to the potential earnings of workers." (Lokiec:128)

Review Questions

1. What is the major principle underlying incentive plans?
2. What are the two major types of incentive plans in use? How are they different?
3. What three conditions are required for a successful incentive system?
4. What is meant by the technical development of a wage incentive system?
5. Define standard time.
6. What is a typical worker?
7. What is meant by normal pace?
8. What is the standard practice?
9. What is a PFD allowance?
10. What is meant by "A Fair Day's Work?"
11. What is meant by "A Fair Day's Pay?"
12. What are the prerequisites for a successful wage incentive system?
13. What resources should management provide for a wage incentive system?
14. What conditions must be present for the success of an individual wage incentive system?
15. What is daywork?
16. What is a piece rate incentive system?
17. What is a standard hours incentive system?
18. What is meant by machine or process control?
19. What is meant by operator control?
20. What is meant by a guaranteed minimum?
21. Describe the effect of machine or process control on incentive earnings.

22. Describe the Scanlon Plan.
23. Describe the Rucker Plan.
24. Describe Improshare.
25. Summarize union objections to incentive plans. What is the major union objection to individual wage incentives?
26. Describe the responsibilities of management regarding the successful operation of incentive plans.
27. Describe the responsibilities of supervision regarding the successful operation of incentive plans.
28. Describe the responsibilities of employees regarding the successful operation of incentive plans.
29. Describe the responsibilities of industrial engineers regarding the successful operation of incentive plans.

Practice Problems

1. Determine the piece rate for a job that has a standard of .058 hours and a wage rate of $6.25 per hour.
2. A job, which is 100% operator controlled, is paid via a straight piece rate incentive based on a standard of .007 hours and an hourly rate of $5.00. Calculate daily earnings for an employee who produced:
   (a) 1,200 units
   (b) 1,000 units
3. A job is 100% operator controlled, with a 100% guarantee based on a standard of .092 hours and an hourly rate of $5.71. Calculate daily earnings for an employee who produced:
   (a) 75 units
   (b) 95 units
4. A job which is 85% operator controlled is paid via a straight piece rate incentive based on a standard of .062 hours and an hourly rate of $6.20. Calculate daily earnings for an employee who produced:
   (a) 85 units
   (b) 135 units
5. A job is 20% machine paced and paid via a straight piece rate incentive with a 75% guarantee based on a standard of .008 hours, and an hourly rate of $4.25. Calculate daily earnings for an employee who produced:
   (a) 650 units
   (b) 950 units
   (c) 1,250 units

6. A job, which is 100% operator controlled, is paid on a standard hours plan with a 100% guarantee. The standard is .2 hour and the hourly rate is $7.00. Calculate daily earnings for an employee who produced:
   (a) 50 units
   (b) 35 units

7. A job, which is 50% operator controlled, is paid on a standard hours plan with a 100% guarantee. The standard is .044 hours and the hourly rate is $5.16. Calculate daily earnings for an employee who produced:
   (a) 100 units
   (b) 150 units
   (c) 200 units

8. A job, which is 100% machine paced, is paid on a standard hours plan with a 100% guarantee. The standard is .05 hours with an hourly rate of $3.75. Calculate daily earnings for an employee who produced:
   (a) 160 units
   (b) 175 units

9. A job, which is 100% operator controlled, is paid on a standard hours plan. The standard is .006 hours, with an hourly rate of $5.55. Calculate daily earnings for an employee who produced:
   (a) 1,000 units
   (b) 1,250 units
   (c) 1,500 units

10. A job, which is 100% operator paced, is paid a variable incentive. Production up to standard is paid $5.00 per hour, production over standard earns $6.00 per hour. The standard is .025 hours. Calculate daily earnings for an employee who produced:
    (a) 300 units
    (b) 350 units

11. A job, which is 65% operator paced, is paid a variable incentive. Production up to standard is paid $6.25 an hour. If production exceeds standard, all work produced is paid at the hourly rate of $7.00. The standard is .045 hours. Calculate daily earnings for an employee who produced:
    (a) 180 units
    (b) 170 units
    (c) 100 units
    (d) 50 units

12. During a base period a company had a payroll of $5,525,000 and sales of $18,750,000. In the first month that a Scanlon Plan was in operation, the payroll was $620,000 and sales were

$2,850,000. Calculate the Scanlon Bonus payment for that month.

13. In a given organization labor contributes 20% of the production value added. In a given period, this organization's payroll for direct labor was $850,000. Sales during this same period were $5,000,000. Calculate the Rucker Plan Bonus for this period.

14. In a particular company employing 92 people, each unit produced required 25 hours of direct labor. During a base period 36,800 total hours were worked, while 1,000 units were produced. If, in a future 40-hour week, 120 units were produced, what percentage bonus would the workers earn under an Improshare Plan?

References

Aft, Lawrence S., *Productivity Measurement and Improvement*, Reston Publishing Company, Inc., Reston, Virginia, 1983.

Belcher, David W., *Compensation Administration*, Prentice-Hall, Englewood Cliffs, New Jersey, 1974.

Cooling, W. Colebrook, "Production Roundtable—How to Increase Production," *Proceedings*, AIIE 1980 Spring Annual Conference, AIIE, Norcross, Georgia, 1980.

Fein, Mitchell, "Work Measurement and Wage Incentives," *IE*, September, 1973.

Fein, Mitchell, *Rational Approaches to Raising Productivity*, AIIE, Norcross, Georgia, 1974.

Fein, Mitchell, "Improved Productivity Through Worker Involvement," *Proceedings*, IIE 1982 Annual Conference, AIIE, Norcross, Georgia, 1982.

Ferrell, Michael D., "A Plan of Action for Rehabilitating An Ailing Wage Incentive Program," *IE*, November, 1982.

General Accounting Office, *Productivity Sharing Programs: Can They Contribute to Productivity Improvement?* U.S. General Accounting Office, Gaithersburg, Maryland, March 3, 1981.

Gomberg, William, *A Trade Union Analysis of Time Study*, Prentice-Hall, Englewood Cliffs, New Jersey, 1955.

Gottlieb, Bertram, "Time Study and Union Safeguards," *AFL-CIO American Federationist,* November, 1965.

Gottlieb, Bertram, "A Fair Day's Work is Anything You Want It to Be," *Journal of Industrial Engineering,* December, 1968.

Henderson, Richard I., *Compensation Management,* Reston Publishing Company, Inc., Reston, Virginia, 1979.

James, Charles F., "Incentives for Machine Paced Operations," *IE,* September, 1975.

Lokiec, Mitchell, "Union Engineer's Views on Wage Incentives," *Femme-Lines,* August–September, 1963.

Lokiec, Mitchell, "Incentives and the Garment Industry," *Journal of Industrial Engineering,* June, 1966.

Lokiec, Mitchell, "A Statement on Incentives," *Bobbin,* April, 1968.

Lokiec, Mitchell, "Wage Incentive Shortcuts," *Bobbin,* March, 1969.

Lokiec, Mitchell, "Incentives Under Attack," *Bobbin,* September, 1971.

Lokiec, Mitchell, "What's Wrong With Wage Incentives," *Bobbin,* May, 1982.

Maynard, H.B., (editor), *Industrial Engineering Handbook,* McGraw-Hill, New York, 1971.

Musgrave, Ken, "Some Experiences with Improshare," *Proceedings,* IIE 1982 Annual Conference, AIIE, Norcross, Georgia, 1982.

Neibel, B., *Motion and Timestudy,* Richard D. Irwin, Homewood, Illinois, 1976.

Nelson, Roger D., "Making Wage Incentives Work in a Union Shop," *Proceedings,* AIIE 1978 Spring Annual Conference, AIIE, Norcross, Georgia, 1978.

Patten, Thomas H., *Pay,* Free Press (Macmillan), New York, 1977.

Patton, J.A., "Wage Incentives: From Failure to Success," *IE,* June, 1974.

Rice, Robert S., "Survey of Work Measurement and Wage Incentives," *IE,* July, 1977.

Russon, Charles N., "A Suggested Method of Auditing Incentive Plans and Related Industrial Engineering Practices," *Proceedings*, AIIE 1974 Spring Conference, AIIE, Norcross, Georgia, 1974.

Scheuch, R., *Labor in the American Economy*, Harper and Row, New York, 1981.

Sellie, Clifford, "Group and Individual Incentive Plans: A Comparison of Their Benefits, Drawbacks," *IE*, November, 1982.

Watmough, E.B., "The Case Against Incentives," *Journal of Industrial Engineering*, November–December, 1965.

Zollitsch, H.G. and Langsner, A., *Wage and Salary Administration*, Southwestern Publishing Company, Cincinnati, Ohio, 1970.

Case Study 7—1

WHEN CAN INCENTIVES BE IGNORED?*

A group of production employees is refusing to work any faster than "base rate" in protest against the elimination of a soft-drink machine near their work area. Top management is pressuring supervision "to do something" quickly, for scheduling throughout the plant is being affected by the decreased output here. The foreman is reluctant to succumb to employee pressure, both because of the bad precedent that would be set and because the machine itself was a nuisance—cups, bottle caps, and bottles were strewn about the area, and the dispenser encouraged loitering. Disciplinary measures are being considered against the ringleaders for organizing a "slowdown." Some members of management are urging caution, claiming, as the men themselves do, that the employees do not have to work at an incentive pace. The company provides the opportunity for workers to earn a bonus if they wish to work more intensively than a daywork pace, but this decision is up to the employees. Other members of management take the opposite point of view: in accepting work on a job with an incentive rate attached, the worker obligates himself to try for such additional earnings, and this is a concerted effort to hold back production.

Discussion

1. Comment on the merits of the divergent opinions within management on the employees' obligation to seek incentive earnings.
2. Discuss what management's approach should be to the workers' protest action. (There is no union in the organization.)

Case Study 7—2

THE PUZZLED MANAGER**

Tom Hoffman, department manager of the packaging department for the High-Grade Pharmaceutical Company, sat in his office and stared out of

---

*George Strauss, Leonard Sayles, PERSONNEL: THE HUMAN PROBLEMS OF MANAGEMENT, 3rd Ed., Copyright 1972, p. 634. Reprinted with permission of Prentice-Hall, Inc., Englewood Cliffs, NJ.

**French/Dittrich/Zawack: THE PERSONNEL MANAGEMENT PROCESS: CASES IN HUMAN RESOURCES ADMINISTRATION, Second Edition, Copyright 1982 by Houghton Mifflin Company. Used with permission.

the window. He had just come back from having lunch with Arnold Clark, the personnel director, and was thinking over their conversation about incentive systems. His thoughts ran as follows:

I think our employees could package a lot more materials each day if we had the proper incentives. We have this constant pressure for getting things out faster, and I'm not sure it's economical to keep adding employees. Of course, we are gradually adding better equipment which helps a lot. Maybe if we really got our packaging automated we could cut costs a good deal.

Arnold argues against incentives because incentive plans are always such a headache to administer and because the union is always on your back if you try to change standards. He also says we'll really have problems if we install an incentive system and then bring in new equipment.

I think what Arnold wants is a merit-rating system instead of a single rate for each job, but he's naive if he thinks that won't produce just as many hassles with the union. I sure wish I could figure out what to do. We've got to do something.

Discussion

1. *If you were called in as a consultant, what considerations would enter your recommendations?*
2. *List the advantages and disadvantages of various compensation plans.*

INDEX

69340